PATRICK ALLEN
CREA   £4.99
              23/120

Making Sense of Self-harm

Making Sense of Self-harm

The Cultural Meaning and Social Context of Nonsuicidal Self-injury

Peter Steggals
Visiting Researcher, Newcastle University, UK

© Peter Steggals 2015

All rights reserved. No reproduction, copy or transmission of this publication may be made without written permission.

No portion of this publication may be reproduced, copied or transmitted save with written permission or in accordance with the provisions of the Copyright, Designs and Patents Act 1988, or under the terms of any licence permitting limited copying issued by the Copyright Licensing Agency, Saffron House, 6–10 Kirby Street, London EC1N 8TS.

Any person who does any unauthorized act in relation to this publication may be liable to criminal prosecution and civil claims for damages.

The author has asserted his right to be identified as the author of this work in accordance with the Copyright, Designs and Patents Act 1988.

First published 2015 by
PALGRAVE MACMILLAN

Palgrave Macmillan in the UK is an imprint of Macmillan Publishers Limited, registered in England, company number 785998, of Houndmills, Basingstoke, Hampshire RG21 6XS.

Palgrave Macmillan in the US is a division of St Martin's Press LLC, 175 Fifth Avenue, New York, NY 10010.

Palgrave Macmillan is the global academic imprint of the above companies and has companies and representatives throughout the world.

Palgrave® and Macmillan® are registered trademarks in the United States, the United Kingdom, Europe and other countries.

ISBN 978–1–137–47058–4

This book is printed on paper suitable for recycling and made from fully managed and sustained forest sources. Logging, pulping and manufacturing processes are expected to conform to the environmental regulations of the country of origin.

A catalogue record for this book is available from the British Library.

Library of Congress Cataloging-in-Publication Data
Steggals, Peter, 1975–
    Making sense of self-harm : the cultural meaning and social context of non-suicidal self-injury / Peter Steggals.
        pages cm
    Summary: *Making Sense of Self-Harm* provides a much needed alternative examination of a potent and increasingly prevalent pattern of distress and estrangement that has come to haunt contemporary society. By exploring nonsuicidal self-injury through the lens of cultural sociology and the insights of thinkers like Michel Foucault, Norbert Elias and Susan Bordo, the book describes it more as a kind of idiomatic practice in need of understanding than as a medical illness in need of biological explanation. Grounding analysis in compelling interviews with people who self-harm and in multiple cultural representations of the practice from books and magazines to music and movies, Steggals uncovers the history of self-harm, maps its hidden meanings and traces its peculiar resonance with the symbolic life of late-modern society, eventually coming to make sense of a phenomenon that so many find profoundly disturbed and disturbing. — Provided by publisher.
    ISBN 978–1–137–47058–4 (hardback)
    1. Self-injurious behavior.   2. Cultural psychiatry.   3. Social psychiatry.
    I. Title.
RC569.5.S48S74 2015
616.85'84450651—dc23   2015021823

*For my mother, Doreen, who was the very first person
to ask me 'why do people do it?'*

Contents

Acknowledgements ix

Introduction: The Signifying Wound 1
1 What is Self-harm? 17
2 The Problem of Good Understanding 52
3 The Ontological Axis 85
4 The Aetiological Axis 122
5 The Pathological Axis 158
6 The Belaboured Economy of Desire 193
Conclusion: Making Sense of Self-harm 214

Notes 219
References 223
Index 237

Acknowledgements

This book originates from research that was funded by the Economic and Social Research Council (CL09/10/104) and conducted at the School of Geography Politics and Sociology, Newcastle University, and I am deeply indebted to both institutions for the opportunity they afforded me. I thank Dr Stephanie Lawler and Professor Elaine Campbell for their guidance, patience and humour throughout the research process, and Professor Roland Littlewood and Dr Ruth Graham for their critical input and encouragement to write and publish this book. Thanks also to Eleanor Christie and Nicola Jones at Palgrave Macmillan, and to my copyeditor Jayne MacArthur. Thanks to my wife Serena for her tireless support. And, finally, thanks also to those people who participated in this research and without whose generous contribution it would not have been possible.

Introduction
The Signifying Wound

For many people in the 1990s self-harm seemed to come from nowhere. It appeared abruptly in the cultural consciousness, as inexplicable as it was disturbing, and escalated rapidly through the decade from a little known and little discussed act of deviance that had been mostly associated with punks, goths and the mentally troubled to a potent social symbol of distress and estrangement, not to mention a significant object of public anxiety. Suddenly, Princess Diana was on television talking about how she had cut herself with razor blades, a penknife and a lemon slicer because she needed to express, to get out of herself, the emotional pain that she felt was trapped inside.[1] And then there was a controversial photograph, considered brilliantly cool by some and deeply troubling by others, of a thin young man from a rock band with the words '4REAL' carved into his forearm, his wounds fresh and bloody. By the end of the decade self-harm had become what the journalist Marilee Strong (1998) described as 'the addiction of the 90s'; a highly recognisable if somewhat haunting presence in our lives, which regularly appeared in the social imaginary of newspapers and magazines, songs, television shows and movies (Sutton, 2005; Adler and Adler, 2011; McShane, 2012). Celebrities confessed to it, journalists and social commentators expressed concern over it and the experts warned of a still largely hidden facet of modern life affecting schools, universities, prisons and homes (Babiker and Arnold, 1997). In the words of the psychiatrist Armando Favazza (1998), self-harm had 'come of age'.

But if self-harm entered the consciousness of contemporary culture and society during the 90s then it has only continued to escalate and spread in the years that have followed. Prevalence rates have increased since the beginning of the new century (Nada-Raja *et al.*, 2003; Brophy, 2006), and a recent 'Health Behaviour in School-aged Children' report co-produced with the World Health Organization found that levels of self-harm among English teenagers have tripled over the last decade, with nearly 20 per cent of 15 year olds stating that they had self-injured in the past year.[2] And such statistics, it should be noted, are not restricted to teenagers. Contrary to popular opinion, many adults self-harm and many, although not the majority, only began this habit of self-injury after their teenage years were well behind them (Tantam and Huband, 2009; Adler and Alder, 2011). Having come of age in the 90s, self-harm is now well established in a symbiotic relationship with the zeitgeist. Whatever else it may be, and whatever function it may provide or desire it may fulfil, it is clear that it represents a powerful and evocative crystallisation of a whole way of thinking about, experiencing and expressing feelings of personal distress, social estrangement and emotional pain that bears a peculiar resonance with late-modern 'Western' society.[3]

But despite its familiarity self-harm has retained the capacity to shock and disturb us, and has proven strangely resistant to clinical exploration and scientific analysis which, when confronted with it, have all too often and all too easily fallen into a well-attested state of exasperation and bafflement. The psychiatrist Allen Frances notes that when faced with self-harm the 'typical clinician (myself included) is often left feeling a combination of helpless, horrified, guilty, furious, betrayed, disgusted, and sad' (1987, quoted in Favazza, 1996: 289). While psychotherapist Fiona Gardner describes this kind of professional reaction as 'generally one of shock, fear, anger, disgust and revulsion, which may lead to hostility and anxiety... such patients are seen as difficult, frustrating, and demanding of enormous amounts of professional attention' (2001: 8). It may be a familiar presence in our lives and culture but it is also one wrapped in an enigmatic, dark and troubling aura, a kind of haunting otherness that intrigues and disturbs us at the same time and which, unusually, holds the capacity to upset both professionals and public alike. The diagnosis of the psychiatrist D.W. Pierce, that self-harm is a 'confused and confusing' practice, seems in some ways as apt now as it did when he first formed it in the 1970s (1977: 377). Certainly, there is something inherently and characteristically liminal about self-harm, something that crosses and unsettles boundaries, confuses common assumptions and refuses to be hemmed in or pinned down. It is something physical yet psychological; a symptom of disorder, impulsiveness and addiction yet also a coping mechanism and therefore an agent of self-control; a symptom of self-destruction strongly associated with suicide yet also a form of 'self-help' (Favazza, 1996), and a triumph of the life instinct over the death instinct (Menninger, 1938); part curse and part cure then, it is something that helps yet torments; something that belongs to the person who practises it, indeed often their sole possession, yet also something alien and invasive, a formidable enemy.

Perhaps an insight into this confusion can be found in the writer Susan Sontag's enigmatic statement that while '[m]any things in the world have not been named... many things that have been named, have never been described' (2009: 275). Self-harm has clearly been named, although its naming has not been without controversy and contestation. The explosion of awareness about self-harm that characterised the 90s was, to some extent, the expansion into common, everyday language of a new word, a new name, while its recent inclusion in the *Diagnostic and Statistical Manual of Mental Disorders, 5th Edition* (DSM-5) has renewed this naming process (American Psychiatric Association, 2013), providing a more technical sounding name for it, 'nonsuicidal self-injury', and testing the limits of the old adage that there is power in naming things. If we can be sure of anything it is that self-harm's otherness, its uncanny capacity to upset and confuse us, does not lie in its lack of a name. Rather, we have not matched knowledge to naming, we have not found a way to understand it properly and make it make sense; in other words, we have not described it well enough or fully enough. And what I mean here is not a description of what causes it or why specific people might practise it—books like Helen Spandler's *Who's Hurting Who?* (1996), Tantam and Huband's *Understanding Repeated Self-injury* (2009) and Adler and Adler's *The Tender Cut* (2011) have already done an excellent job of accounting for this. Rather, the kind of description I have in mind here is what the anthropologist Clifford Geertz calls 'thick description' (1973); a description of self-harm as a distinct and recognisable form in our contemporary cultural language, a kind of 'idiom' (Nichter, 1981), or prepackaged pattern of meanings and actions that helps lend shape, structure and significance to people's experiences and expressions of personal distress and social estrangement. Otherwise put: if self-harm speaks to us, if it somehow codifies and articulates something important about the symbolic world of contemporary life, then the point behind this book is to try to make sense of what it is saying.

Beginning a Conversation

My own first encounter with self-harm was a perfect reflection of its enigmatic capacity to disrupt, disturb and yet fascinate. I was working in the forensic psychology department of a female prison in the north of England where part of my duties included interviewing prisoners who had either engaged in self-harm or who had attempted suicide, the idea being to identify problem areas and make risk assessments. The first time I had to perform this duty I was called to talk to a woman in her mid-20s, who I shall call 'Fiona'. The wing Fiona was located in was mostly empty when I arrived, the majority of prisoners having left to attend work or education placements in other buildings within the prison grounds. Just one figure was left, standing at the far end of the corridor in a white t-shirt and jogging bottoms, her blond hair pulled back into a ponytail, exposing a thin face, which was scarred red and painfully raw. From where I was standing I couldn't really see what she had done to herself but even from that distance it seemed brutal and shocking. For just a moment we stood and looked at each other down the corridor and I felt a flare of anxiety in my stomach. 'Don't let it be her' I thought 'please don't let it be her'. But of course it was and just a few minutes later, whether I liked it or not, we were sitting down together in a small side office and preparing to begin the interview.

After her breakfast that morning Fiona had managed to smuggle a plastic knife from the prison canteen back to her cell and had used it to cut and scrape off nearly all the skin from her face leaving everything but her eyes and mouth scarred and sore. Behind the damaged skin it was almost impossible to discern any kind of facial expression, which made conversation daunting and difficult, and while she sat looking at me with a steady and impassive gaze I struggled and stuttered my way through introducing myself and explaining why I was there. Her gaze and her self-injury were of a piece. Both were a kind of protest as if she was saying that the prison made her feel faceless, an object rather than a person, and her ordinary face now nothing more than a mask that she was trapped behind. Of course, she had now removed that mask, but more than this, in removing hers she had also removed my own. Back on my desk, safely nestled in an office that now felt impossibly distant, there was a small stack of booklets that I had been given on the three-day training course that was supposed to have prepared me for this moment, and on a shelf nearby there were a number of reassuringly thick psychiatric and clinical psychology textbooks. Just half an hour before, I had been looking at these as if preparing for an exam; at the time they had seemed to radiate a comforting sense of professionalism, a kind of mask of expertise and authority, but now all that had been pulled away and as I sat opposite Fiona I felt bewildered, exposed and embarrassingly out of my depth. Under that steady gaze sitting in a broken and wounded face I could no longer wear the mask, no longer believe in it, and with that loss the standard sense of control that was usually and effortlessly guaranteed by the prison keys attached to my belt was also suddenly and simply gone.

And so we sat and faced each other and there was silence. The clipboard sitting in my lap and the standard interview schedule that was attached to it offered one possible response to this silence and indeed an escape from it; a bureaucratic shield that I could hide behind and an automatic process that hardly required my presence any more than the mechanical administration of a questionnaire. But somehow, faced with Fiona, I felt that I couldn't run or hide. She was challenging me to *get it*, not just to process her through the prison's 'safer custody' system or explain away her behaviour, but to understand the point behind her injuries and the meaning of her actions. In the face of this challenge the clipboard felt shamefully inadequate and even horribly inappropriate. The only other option was to drop the fantasy of authority and expertise and simply to ask her what was wrong; to begin, and to work at keeping up, a conversation as opposed to the formal structured interview I had anticipated, and although it began awkwardly, this conversation began nonetheless.

Of course, moments like these take on grander dimensions when they are recalled to make a point, and in one sense this was just another morning at work, challenging mornings in the prison service being far from unusual. But still, looking back now it seems pivotal to me. I can trace back to this moment the movement that carried me away from the materialist and biologically based psychology that I had been so interested in before and sending me instead toward a more meaning-based approach to understanding people and their actions. I can trace back to this moment the broadening of my interpretive horizons to survey beyond the localised feature that is individual consciousness and cognition, and out across the wider, more expansive and richer landscape of the semiotic, the cultural and the social. And I can also trace back to this moment the beginning of a broader effort, at times difficult, disturbing and challenging, that has nonetheless continued ever since and which has aimed at Geertz's 'thick description'. More than just an attempt to describe or understand a given case like Fiona's, or any of the hundreds of individual stories of self-harm that I've heard in the years that followed, this has been the effort to describe and understand self-harm *itself*, as an idiom, as a distinct complex of meanings and values that, to paraphrase the anthropologist and psychiatrist Roland Littlewood (2002: 40), articulates a sense of personal predicament while at the same time representing broader issues of public concern and tension.

It has, necessarily, been an effort of interpretation or 'hermeneutics', as philosophers and literary critics prefer to call it (Gadamer, 1989), an attempt to understand and *make sense*, to, in the words of the cultural studies scholar Fred Inglis, 'catch hold of and shake into an intelligible version of itself the strange estrangements of other people' (2000: 2). Or, in other words, it has been an attempt to 'get it', to understand that self-harm, although it may be judged deviant by society, is nonetheless a practice that people engage in, become attached to or invest themselves in, take-up and use in particular ways *because it is meaningful to them*, because it is an expression of something significant, because it has something to say. It has been the effort, then, to try and work out what this 'something' is and so make sense of self-harm not just as a symptom but as a practice, and not just as a practice but as the product of a whole culture and pattern of life.

A Family of Practices

In truth, Fiona's facial lacerations were actually quite unusual, being far more demonstratively public than private, and a far more clearly enunciated act of defiance than most examples of that 'strange estrangement' that we call 'self-harm'. But that said, her actions that day were part of a broader pattern. Her case file was packed with more typical episodes of self-injury, which characteristically left medically superficial yet personally significant wounds cut into her flesh and a messy cross-hatch of scars that ran from her wrist to her elbow. A typical episode began for her with a kind of mixed cloud of toxic emotions—anger, anxiety and frustration—which she would feel build within her under the pressure of her isolation and estrangement from other people around her. With no one to talk to, no one to 'vent off' with and help her get her feelings out of her system she would only feel the pressure grow within her, threatening to overwhelm her and putting her sense of control at risk. Her failure to manage her emotions and her perceived failure to live up to her expectations of herself as the sort of person who ought to be able to manage them, to be happy and healthy and connected to others, would only add its own deep vein of self-loathing into the toxic mix and bring her closer to a psychological crisis point.

In these moments a sudden straight cut into her flesh would bring focus, release, relief and calm. The clouds would part and her mind would clear. She would be able to breathe, even if only for a few moments. Whatever bad feelings had been inside her would now seem to have been let out; expressed perhaps to no more a witness than the room or the universe, but she would have got them out of her system nonetheless. Now she would feel centred and in control, having transformed the intangible cloud of her psychological torment into a neat little wound, physical and touchable, that she could see, that she could understand and that proved that she really was in pain. This, she would tell herself, is what suffering looks like; it looks like a wound, it looks like blood, it looks *real*. But it wouldn't take long for the same wound to become a silent accuser and a source of guilt, bearing witness to her weakness and her inability to control her emotions in a more normal or healthy fashion, and these first moments of guilt that could appear even only minutes after she had cut herself would be the first signs of the cloud reforming and building back up into the familiar storm front.

This was the standard rhythm of Fiona's self-harm and it is also a fairly typical, although not exhaustive or definitive, example of the pattern of meanings and actions that most people understand as 'self-harm'. That it is this particular pattern that I want to explore here is important. As I will explain more fully in Chapter 1, 'self-harm' is a highly contested term and encapsulates a good deal of diversity and confusion. There are many different formulations of what self-harm means and what it does and does not include, but what most of these formulations have in common is that they tend to reflect, to greater or lesser degrees, the particular interests, concerns and prejudices of the institutions in which they were formed, prejudices that an exploration like this has no particular reason to share. For example, for the purposes of gathering statistics and compiling reports, the UK National Health Service (NHS) and the National Institute for Health and Care Excellence (NICE) use the term 'self-harm' to mean 'self-poisoning or self-injury irrespective of the purpose of the act' (NICE, 2004: 16); however, this definition captures not only what, in the common vernacular of UK culture, is called 'self-harm'—now 'nonsuicidal self-injury'—but also accidental self-poisoning through excessive alcohol consumption or drug use, and even attempted suicide. Predictably, this has led to some confusion in the media whenever self-harm statistics have been quoted. And, in fact, confusions proliferate where assumptions, institutional or otherwise, are brought to bear too strongly on what self-harm is and how we ought to go about making sense of it. Because of this our approach must be more empirical, concerning itself with self-harm as it can be found in people's lives rather than as it is imagined in textbooks and diagnostic manuals, and because of this it is the pattern of meanings and actions that these people, and more broadly the culture they are a part of, call 'self-harm' that stands as such in this study and that is our concern here.

As useful as Fiona's case is as a description of this pattern it is important to keep in mind that self-harm is not a narrow, stereotypical pattern but rather one of tremendous flexibility, diversity and variation. Indeed, one of the most basic areas of agreement within the research literature is that self-harm is 'overdetermined', meaning that it has multiple functions, numerous lines of contingency and connects with various states of mind (Nock and Prinstein, 2005; Klonsky, 2007; Klonsky and Muehlenkamp, 2007). If we look at how self-harm plays out in people's lives we certainly find a structure of continuities, shared themes and common meanings but we do not find a narrow, close-fitting form that shapes each individual case into a superficially different version of the same basic story. Rather, here we find the private and shadowed edges of people's lives refracted through the symbolism of self-harm into multiple shards of emotion, experience and sensation. We find more than just the iconic and expected razor blades, kitchen knives and broken glass, the cuts and scars on forearms and shoulders and lacerations on legs and torso; we also find flesh burnt by flames, friction and chemicals, the violent banging of head and limbs, and the deliberate breaking of bones. We find some, but perhaps not all, forms of skin picking, scratching and hair pulling. We find 'bloodletting' (the careful control of blood syphoned out of veins and sometimes into cups or jars) and the tying of ligatures around the neck and various forms of self-poisoning where the focus of the act is the experience of the harm it causes rather than the chance of death it affords. And we find the insertion of everyday objects from pens and pencils to needles and pins through the skin and into the body, and even the swallowing of such objects.

We find self-harm in those quiet, private places like bedrooms and toilet cubicles where our bodies can be dealt with without witnesses, mostly at home, sometimes at school or work, but also in the street and as many different places as you can think of. We find it in kits hidden under pillows, or in the backs of closets and even in the bottom of boots and shoes; kits that contain more than just razor blades and the tools of self-harm but which also often house the means of self-care—bandages and plasters, antiseptic and make-up. Contrary to popular opinion we find it among boys as well as girls, men as well as women, and among populations far removed from the stereotypical, although also genuinely demographically dominant, teenage white female.

We find self-harm within moments of desperation but also of defiance. We find it as a thin red line separating self-possession from overwhelming waves of emotion or from racing and negative thoughts. We find it in the lives of some people as a way to shock themselves back to reality after a dissociative episode; or as a means to validate their sense of self and testify to their authenticity; or else as the expression of an ascetic or stoical ideal and as a means to pre-empt and outmanoeuvre a world that it seems is only interested in harming them. We find it in moments of self-punishment and discipline and as a means of expressing self-loathing, guilt and shame. We even find it as a lifestyle and a form of identity—a body mark symbolising a personal and resistant pathos or else a subcultural ethos and therefore a shared symbol of belonging. Perhaps ultimately we find self-harm in people's lives at the limit of a sense of control in a world in which they feel they have no power except that which they can express and experience over the borders and boundaries of their own skin.

Whatever else it may be then, self-harm is not a narrowly prescribed or stereotypical behaviour, but rather a rich and diversely patterned complex of different yet related meanings and different yet similar actions. It is multiple, multifunctional, diverse and overdetermined; appearing more like a family of practices sharing clear social, historical, cultural and practical resemblances than a medical illness or a symptom of an illness (Wittgenstein, 1958). The overarching theme, in as much as there is one, that holds this diversity together as if in a force field and justifies the use of a single inclusive term is that it is always an act, normally a repeated, habitual act, which in some way causes direct harm to the body but one where the focus and purpose of the act *is this harm itself* and not some other goal such as decorative body modification or suicide. Whatever motivations, impulses or compulsions the person self-harming may feel they are tied completely to this act of harm and it is this harm, this wound, that holds significance and which signifies the meaning and experience of self-harm. It is a violent nonverbal speech act and the question of how to listen to it, how to understand it and make sense of what it is saying is the question that has driven my effort to understand it over the years and which now stands as the central question of this book.

The Challenge to 'Get it'

It is, of course, a difficult and challenging question, one that does not easily lend itself to common sense or conventional methods of understanding, and perhaps that is the point. The sociologist Jane Kilby notes that '[t]here is something particularly difficult to witness here... The act of harming one's own skin by cutting it up and tearing it apart speaks with a "voice" so sheer that it is virtually impossible for anyone to bear witness to' (2001: 124). And this is a paradox: we are supposed to hear, to listen, to understand and bear witness, but not in any kind of standard or trivial fashion. The 'bright red scream' (Strong, 1998) carved into Fiona's face was a challenge to 'get it', to bear witness, but to bear witness to something that she felt was normally excluded from communication, something that, as such, could not be expressed through a few words no matter how carefully chosen. Ultimately, I think this 'something' was herself stripped raw of the normative performance of social pretence and persona; a real, full and feeling person drowning in a profound despair and loneliness. And if, as we say, 'words are cheap' and 'actions speak louder than words' then how could she hope to communicate this sense of herself to others through ordinary language? In the end she didn't, she communicated it instead through a bloody rupture torn into the very fabric of ordinary communication itself; a speech act, then, but one that speaks of the limits and failure of language, a form of articulation but one that works by demonstrating the limits and impossibilities of what can be articulated, not something clothed in language but something made raw and naked by a more basic recourse to blood and flesh.

Perhaps this is why I felt so utterly confounded by Fiona; the frustration of unconventional communication mixed with the difficulty, the almost primal anxiety, of witnessing another human being and treating her as such rather than just as a platform of symptoms or the carrier of a disease the way you sometimes hear nurses refer to patients by their ailment ('the spleen in bed number two'). And perhaps this is why the standard interview schedule seemed so tempting and reassuringly safe; it's neat and orderly question boxes framed self-harm as something more or less like a medical and psychiatric symptom, not so much something to be understood or made sense of, let alone something to be witnessed, but rather a purely indexical sign to be processed, measured and explained away. It would have allowed me to shift my focus away from the person and the life before me and concentrate instead on the symptom, the clinical details and the imaginary metric of the risk assessment. What I learnt from Fiona was that such a medical, psychiatric or biopsychological perspective is simply too narrow, too reductive and too impersonal to cultivate a proper understanding, to make sense of something as expressive and ambivalent as self-harm. In trying too hard to confine human complexity within neat categories it renders the intricate living reality of someone like Fiona into nothing more than the case-specific clothing worn by a more material, impersonal and narrowly causal power; some hypothesised inner and pathogenic *thing* that produces acts of self-injury in the same way that the cold virus produces sore throats and runny noses. Whatever is left over, of either self-harm or the person themselves, whatever refuses to fit into this biopsychological and substantivist approach remains as a troubling and haunting trace or supplement (Derrida, 1976), an enigmatic presence that can only add to the already thick aura of dark fascination that attaches to self-harm. And there is much that is left over, much that slips free, from the standard substantivist frameworks.

By contrast, that self-harm *means* something, that it is something to be grasped and understood rather than simply explained away, has been the founding assertion of my ten-year engagement with it, the basis upon which it was begun with Fiona all those years ago and the basis upon which it has proceeded ever since. Throughout this book I have sought, in Littlewood's words, to 'understand personal experience as meaningful within a particular social and political context' (2002, xii) in much the same way that our speech acts and linguistic idioms can only be understood, and can only be meaningful in the first place, when placed within the context of a particular language. The point has been to make sense of self-harm, as a symbolic idiom signifying disorder, by grasping it as something characteristic of the culture that has created and nurtured it (Bordo, 2003), the culture from which it emerged and subsequently spread from country to country, namely, and for reasons that will be more fully explained in the first two chapters, the culture of late-modernity; a Western culture certainly but one that has proven quite successful at importing itself globally along with its common concern for and fascination with individualism, the medicalisation of distress and the psychologisation of social issues (Watters, 2011). It is only against this background of a broader conceptual world, the background system of meanings and values that has made it both a possible and a significant way to experience and express distress and estrangement, that self-harm can be described 'thickly' and thereby understood properly.

My approach, then, is perhaps best described as cultural sociology (Emirbayer and Goodwin, 1996; Jacobs, 1996; Alexander and Smith, 2001), which indicates a concern with mapping patterns of meaning as they are active across personal experience, the culture that embeds this experience and what the philosopher Ian Hacking (2002) calls the whole 'social ecology', the total and complex pattern of social structures and institutions, relationships and interactions, technologies and practices, historical events and political dynamics that surrounds, supports and encourages the emergence of a particular artefact of life, in this case self-harm. A cultural sociology, while it is not a study of individual life and experience as such, allows us to place the personal artefacts of particular thoughts, feelings and actions into the broader webs or circuits of meaning and processes of meaning-making within which individual people live, move and have their being, not to mention their significance. It offers the means by which we might understand and make sense of the personal because it appreciates the role systems and patterns of meanings and values have in the shaping of our minds, our experiences and our actions (Alexander, 2003).

The research that I conducted for this book consisted of a broad ethnographic study of representations of self-harm in academic and research literature, as well as those in self-help and popular psychology books, in the leaflets and websites of various charities and government bodies, in policy documents and official reports, in newspapers and magazines, biographies and autobiographies, and in film, television and radio. In addition to this I also conducted 30 interviews with 27 people, varying in age from 18 to 46, who self-harm in order to elicit their thoughts and feelings about it, as well as their individual experiences and valuable insights. These were unstructured interviews carried out either in person, or by email or by telephone so that people with social anxieties, people who worried about their ability to communicate or people who simply couldn't be available would still be able to participate. In addition to these interview data some of these participants also provided me with other materials such as diaries they had kept and even suicide letters that they had written during the darkest parts of their personal stories.

All but one of the people I interviewed were women, and this raises a final issue that must be dealt with as a matter of introduction to self-harm: the difficult and important issue of gender. Self-harm is often thought of and represented as being a distinctly female problem, a significant form of what the writer Leslie Jamison calls 'wounded womanhood' (2014: 212), but demographic studies tell a different if somewhat complex and even confusing story. For reasons that I will explore more fully in Chapter 1, the demographic mapping of self-harm, settling the question of how many people practise it and what kind of people they are, is muddled and ambiguous at best. With respect to gender, research estimates have varied wildly from stating that as much as 95 per cent of people who self-harm are female to suggesting an even split between the sexes, although it should be noted that most studies do find females outnumbering males, even if the margin varies greatly (Adler and Adler, 2011). Consequently, self-harm cannot simply be thought of, as it so often is, as a problem only affecting women; a particularly female issue in perhaps something like the same way that anorexia is, and that can only or exclusively be understood through a gendered and feminist analysis. There are a number of books that have overtly examined self-harm from an exclusively female perspective (Smith et al., 1999; Wegscheider, 1999; Miller, 2005), and even those that haven't have strongly tended to, albeit implicitly, treat it as a distinctly female issue. Of course, the reasons why individuals may experience distress and turn to self-harm may well be gendered and therefore require a gendered analysis but as our focus here is on self-harm itself, self-harm as a general complex of meanings that can mediate a number of stressors and that are put to use by both men and women, boys and girls, it will be necessary to take a less gender-specific point of view than has traditionally been adopted.

However, as will become clear in the pages and chapters ahead, and particularly in Chapter 6, this does not mean that self-harm is not an inherently gendered idiom nor that it is not a feminist issue. Quite the contrary. Self-harm is unquestionably coded as feminine in our culture. Consider, for example, that most public and media representations of people who self-harm are female,[4] that many people do not even realise that men, let alone a significant number of men, also self-harm and that self-harm is often explained through a logic supplied by popular gender stereotypes: that men externalise their negative emotions while women internalise them turning violence toward themselves (Miller, 2005). It may even be the case that some of the demographic confusion has been caused by an unwillingness among men to present with self-harm at clinics because it is perceived as a female problem, certainly much of the evidence for a higher percentage of males comes from nonclinical samples (Gratz, 2001; Muehlenkamp and Gutierrez, 2004). This cultural coding itself fits into a deeply ingrained tradition of representing woman as more prone to emotional volatility, psychological disturbance and mental disorder than men (Showalter, 1987; Ussher, 1991; Kohen, 2000; Appignanesi, 2008); an association that has been theorised in a number of different ways from 'naturalistic' explanations that rely on the pseudoscientific observation of biological and neurological differences between the sexes to more political and feminist explanations that understand illness as a means of symbolic and limited practical resistance to patriarchal power relations and the cruelty of a misogynistic culture (Showalter, 1987; Ussher, 1991). But whatever the truth of this our task here will be to map and understand self-harm as a general complex of meanings, many of which are gendered, and then to try and analyse why this complex has come to be coded as feminine, why there is a cultural tendency to see self-harm as a 'woman's problem' and an inherently feminine practice regardless of the biological sex of the people who may be practising it.

Chapter Summary

In Chapter 1 I argue that, contrary to popular opinion and against much that is asserted within the literature on the subject, self-harm is less like a natural kind, a definite and particular 'thing' in its own right with an intrinsic unity and a timeless essence (Young, 1997; Zachar, 2000), than a situated cultural practice; a pattern of meanings and meaningful actions making up a sort of distinct idiom of life through which people find a way to experience and express feelings of personal distress and social estrangement. For this reason the standard 'objectivist' paradigm typical of medical and biologically inspired psychiatry and psychology is ill-equipped to make sense of self-harm and we must instead pursue understanding through an interpretation of the meanings that are coded into the practice, which is to say the very meanings that are being articulated and used by people whenever they self-harm. This still leaves us with the question of exactly how we should find and interpret such meanings and it is this question that I turn to in Chapter 2. Here I argue that, contra objectivism and its popular counterpart, subjectivism, self-harm can only be made to make sense within the context of its surrounding culture and 'social ecology' (Hacking, 2002); that is, in the words of the philosopher Susan Bordo, the characteristic expression of its society and 'the crystallization of its discourses and contradictions' (2003: 141). In other words, the meaning of self-harm is contingent on, and can be mapped through, broader cultural discourses that make it a possible, meaningful and significant way to experience and express distress. And it is just such a mapping that is the purpose of this book.

In the analysis that follows I map the meanings of self-harm by using Bordo's concept of an 'axis of continuity' (2003: 142), which refers to the lines of connection between the meanings and values that make-up self-harm as a distinct pattern of concepts and actions, and the meanings and values that are more broadly distributed through the milieu of late-modern culture. I use a model made up of three axes: the ontological axis, the aetiological axis and the pathological axis. Together they describe the cultural matrix from which self-harm emerges and so can also act as a net within which its meaning may be captured. In Chapter 3 I explore the first axis of continuity, the ontological axis, which organises ideas and beliefs about what kind of ontological structures must exist in order for self-harm to perform the function that it is generally thought to perform. Here we find the discourse of the 'expressive imperative', the idea that you have to express your feelings otherwise there will be an internal build-up of negative emotion, like steam building inside a pressure cooker, an idea that frames self-harm as a kind of emergency valve or vent. Behind this discourse we can also find the deep impact and effect of psychodynamic thinking on our popular folk and professional psychologies and behind this psychodynamic concept of self we can find the much deeper and broader discourses that make up the idea of the psychological individualism and the modernist emergence of what Emile Durkheim called 'the cult of the individual' (2008 [1912]).

If the ontological axis organises ideas and assumptions about the ontological structures that make up the necessary biological and psychological architecture of self-harm, depicting the kind of subject for whom self-harm can be a useful or meaningful mechanism, then the aetiological axis I explore in Chapter 4 organises ideas about what kinds of conditions and factors make it likely that such subjects will, in specific cases, come to practise self-harm. I explore the idea of 'traumatic estrangement' and the key late-modern concept of psychic trauma, which provides a powerful metaphor for thinking about self-harm as the all-too literal expression of an inner and invisible wound. Behind these concepts we find broader cultural concerns with the issue of control and self-control in particular. Self-harm is ambivalently positioned here as it can be framed as both a coping mechanism and agent of self-control on the one hand or as a symptom of impulse dyscontrol, impulsivity and addiction on the other. But we can push even further out behind this paradoxical complex of concepts to identify the key modernist concern with authenticity and the very motive force for our general concern with issues of self-control and agency.

In Chapter 5 I explore the pathological axis that describes ideas about what it is like to be a 'self-harmer', the psychological and emotional content of the practice as such. Here we find a focus on self-persecution and a moral and emotional economy of self-examination, judgement and punishment in the light of idealised standards, which are nonetheless taken as normative expectations. This helps code into people's experience both a deep sense of responsibility and the horrible inevitability of failure. Behind this theme of self-persecution with its constant self-vigilance and self-policing we find the discursive complex of what Michel Foucault (1991) called the 'disciplinary regime' and behind this the modernist obsession with the idea of 'project' and of making something of ourselves, an idea that has come to characterise late-modern selfhood as fundamentally 'belaboured' (McGee, 2005), which is to say a self that is under strain, a self that is belaboured with the business of being a self.

Having used culture to interpret self-harm, in Chapter 6 I turn to using self-harm to critically interpret late-modern culture in order to uncover the tensions and conflicts that underpin self-harm and its meanings. I argue that every disciplinary regime implies a concomitant economy of desire, which, in late-modern consumer culture, is focused less specifically on goods and services than it is on the sense of identity or authenticity that is marketed and associated with the commodity. But if authenticity is what we hope to gain then we will instead find ourselves trapped in a cycle of desire and dissatisfaction as authenticity will always recede from such efforts. The economy of desire in late-modern consumer capitalism is based on a fundamental *lack* and the ongoing cyclic drive to fill in this lack. It is based on a constant pedagogy of invalidation, dissatisfaction and insufficiency, which mirrors our cultivated desires and subsequent cultural fetish for authenticity and validation. And because of the structure of the belaboured self and the individualisation and psychologisation of social and political problems the consequences of this pedagogy of discontent are all focused back on the self. The self becomes a battleground and if self-harm is telling us something then it is telling us that the belaboured self, rather than being just another construction of subjectivity, is a self in crisis, one that has become far too belaboured and that is ready to crack.

1
What is Self-harm?

> And they came over the strait of the sea, into the country of the Gerasenes. And as he went out of the ship, immediately there met him out of the monuments a man with an unclean spirit, who had his dwelling in the tombs, and no man now could bind him, not even with chains. For having been often bound with fetters and chains, he had burst the chains, and broken the fetters in pieces, and no one could tame him. And he was always day and night in the monuments and in the mountains, crying and cutting himself with stones.
>
> *Gospel of Mark* (5: 1–5)

Introduction: A Question of Meaning

The disturbing effect of an 'unclean spirit' described in Mark's gospel raises an interesting question of meaning and categorisation, namely the degree to which we can recognise here exactly the same pattern of meaning and action that we now call 'self-harm' or 'nonsuicidal self-injury'. As a recognised pattern and category of disorder self-harm is relatively new, traceable at best to the 1938 book *Man Against Himself* by the great psychiatrist Karl Menninger. However, the prevalence and cultural pervasiveness that self-harm has gained since the 1990s has, unsurprisingly, provoked an obvious question: has it always been with us and we simply failed to notice? Or is self-harm more a product and expression of its particular time and place?

The significance of this kind of question typically lies in its perceived capacity to settle a fairly standard debate over the nature of 'minor psychiatric illnesses' or what the psychiatrist and anthropologist Roland Littlewood nicely describes as 'dissociations of our customary consciousness' (2002: xi). Are such categories of illness and disorder best understood as something like a natural kind (Zachar, 2000); a definite and particular *thing* in its own right with an intrinsic unity and a timeless essence (Young, 1997), which has presumably always existed even if it has only recently been recognised by medical science (De Vries *et al.*, 1983; Conrad and Schneider, 1992)? Or are they better understood as salient articulations of the tensions and dilemmas that are peculiar to a particular society; less a timeless *thing* then than a situated cultural practice, a sort of ritual or idiomatic symbol of distress and estrangement (Gaines, 1992)?

It's a well-rehearsed debate, of course, familiar from the study of hysteria, anorexia nervosa, and any number of retrospective diagnoses made by historically minded psychiatrists and medically minded historians (Showalter, 1991; Shorter, 1992; Bordo, 2003). But, as interesting as it may be, its answer is nonetheless more often assumed than argued, and Mark's gospel account typically stands as one of the evidential exhibits in the historical and ethnographic record invoked by writers like Linda Plante when she states that

> Whether carried out in the socially sanctioned context of tribal initiation rites...the modern piercings common to Western adolescents, or the self-cutter's visual proclamation of internal struggle, the damaging of one's skin has spoken a common language across time and culture (2007: 7).

Indeed, for many self-harm simply *is* a transcultural and transhistorical 'thing' that has everywhere and always been present and, as such, has always 'spoken a common language'. And, of course, there is a kind of intuitive logic to this, reflecting a deeply embedded prejudice of late-modern culture. When faced with the complex bustle and commotion of everyday life we have a tendency to reach down under this shifting empirical matter and grasp at some-*thing* we imagine to be hidden *below* the level of personal consciousness, cultural meaning and social context,[1] some-*thing* we hope will prove to be more simple and solid, more stable and less transient (Elias, 1978; Derrida, 1991; Ricoeur, 2004). It's a well-entrenched perspective, strongly associated with the authority of natural science, medicine and the more biologically oriented approach to psychiatry and psychology; an *objectivist* perspective succinctly described by the anthropologist Clifford Geertz as the idea that 'culture is icing, biology, cake...difference is shallow, likeness, deep' (2000: 53), and one that is clearly evident in the current professional and public appetite for grounding explanations of seemingly every facet and nuance of human life and behaviour in biology and genetics (Rose et al., 1990; Nelkin and Lindee, 1995; Martin, 2004; Tallis, 2011).

While the particular *thing* in question may be variously modelled as microscopic agents of genetic destiny, or as the somewhat capricious chemical and mechanical processes of biology, or as so many programmes hardwired into our neural architecture, or even as the structural dynamics of our psyches, however we imagine or hypothesise it, it always carries the same strangely attractive yet counterintuitive implication: that an unseen, hidden and sometimes entirely hypothetical entity can somehow be more 'real', more concrete and more significantly causal than the immanent collage of content, movements and surfaces that makes up our actual experience of life from one moment to the next, now relegated to a mere façade (Rose *et al.*, 1990). This objectivist prejudice then typically leads us to *look past* meaning in search of mechanism and past culture in search of nature. It represents an asymmetric binary that organises the natural and the mechanical on the one hand as being opposed to the cultural and the meaningful on the other, positioning them as the primary is positioned to the secondary, the necessary to the complementary, and as the facts of the matter are positioned to personal prejudice and local colour (Littlewood, 2002; Timimi, 2002).

Perhaps it is little wonder then that in discovering a pattern of practice and experience like self-harm, seemingly present in both contemporary and Biblical psychiatry, that we would automatically assume the presence of something more natural than cultural and something that, while subject to historical variation at the margins, nonetheless always remains the same in essence and as such always speaks a common language. In this way the basic question of what self-harm is has typically been posed in objectivist terms and subsequent research and discussion has automatically framed it as a pathological behaviour and a clinical problem, a symptom more than a symbol and something to be diagnosed and treated more than something to be understood and made sense of. This is not to suggest that the realm of meaning has been completely dismissed or ignored, rather it has been side-lined or *looked past* as something that is of interest but not of much consequence, and the objectivist logic, although not the only one at work in representations and talk about self-harm, as we will see in Chapter 2, has commonly been used to define the nature of self-harm, to set the terms of the debate and answer the question of what *kind* of a thing it is, and in so doing has set out and regulated the boundaries of what can be said and thought about self-harm with any sense or authority.

However, as culturally typical and socially authoritative as this standard objectivist logic may be it has nonetheless struggled to make sense of self-harm (Tantam and Huband, 2009; Chandler et al., 2011). In fact, far from submitting to this approach the phenomenon of self-harm has seemed to actively resist it; appearing less as a ready and transparent object of knowledge characterised by an intrinsic unity and a timeless essence than as a troubling supplement always carrying more meaning than can be accounted for (Derrida, 1991), spilling through accepted categories to place treasured assumptions under a deconstructive strain (Derrida, 1976), and producing the all-too-familiar troubling and uncanny air of otherness that shrouds self-harm and which I noted in the Introduction. Perhaps then we need to heed Kafka when he noted that '[a]ll human errors are impatience, a premature breaking off of methodical procedure, an apparent fencing-in of what is apparently at issue' (1994: 3), and if our objectivist assumptions have failed to contain self-harm then perhaps we need to question them and return to the question at the heart of that standard and familiar debate—is self-harm really something like a natural kind that has always been around even if we didn't realise it, the product of an individual psychopathology arising from some kind of biogenetic dysfunction or perhaps some deep mechanism buried in our basic psychological architecture? Or is it something less amenable to the objectivist logic, something more deeply tied into our particular time and place in the world, the characteristic expression of our culture and the 'crystallization of its discourses and contradictions', as the philosopher Susan Bordo put it in discussing anorexia nervosa (2003: 141); a package of meanings and actions that is practised and put to use in people's lives because of the ideas and values that are coded into it? Or, to put it another way: exactly what is it we are talking about when we talk about 'self-harm'?

A World of Self-mutilation

Of course, it stands to reason that if self-harm can be found across radically different cultures then whatever causes it must be equally pervasive. The transient realms of the cultural and the social would perhaps prove too contingent and too changeable to provide this kind of solid base and invariant anchor and so, instead, if this was the case, we would have to locate that vocal 'thing' that speaks its common language from self-inflicted wounds the world over within the only common denominator universally present: the human body. Or rather that basic package of innate tendencies in thought, feeling and behaviour that we popularly call 'human nature' and that we imagine to be the basis and default condition of all human beings, regardless of the context and conditions of their lives (Rose et al., 1990). In this way the contention of a universal self-harm leads inexorably to a search for explanations that can only be found by digging deeply into the objective and substantive cake of biology and medicine. However, it is also precisely here that we find Kafka's premature breaking off of methodical procedure.

The commonly accepted idea that self-harm is everywhere evident and always speaks the same language is typically made, by Plante and virtually every other writer who makes the same claim, not by reference to original research but rather by reference to a single, and singularly important, text: the American psychiatrist Armando Favazza's 1987 book *Bodies Under Siege: Self-mutilation and Body Modification in Culture and Psychiatry* (2nd edition 1996). Perhaps the most important and influential book in the history of self-harm literature, *Bodies Under Siege* has without question exerted a massive influence on the very fundamentals of how we frame and think about self-harm. After its publication it quickly established itself as, and remains to this day, *the* indispensable reference for anyone writing on the subject and, as such, it is not just a book about self-harm but an important moment in its cultural history and a part of its ongoing story.

It is a large rambling mansion of a book, an ambitious global and historical survey of self-mutilation the pages of which are packed with vivid and colourful examples drawn from across the full spectrum of human life, from ancient myths of dismemberment to gruelling shamanic rituals, from religious asceticism and self-flagellation to factitious surgical addictions, from traditional initiation rites and the culturally sanctioned scarification, branding and body-marking practices of beauty, status and identity, to extreme forms of psychotic self-amputation and, of course, the kind of 'deviant' self-harm or repeated nonsuicidal self-injury that is our subject here. Indeed, the book's great strength is that, in describing self-mutilation as 'an integral part of the human experience' (Favazza in Strong, 1998: x), we are reminded of the symbolic power and psychosocial significance of our bodies. That we live not just *in* but *through* our bodies, and these bodies are not just the natural, biological objects that we typically take them to be but are rather the objective extension of our subjectivity, the raw corporeal matter upon which we inscribe, and through which we experience, our culture, our social position, our identity and our sense of self (Butler, 1993; Turner, 2008).

What is clear from the global tour that *Bodies Under Siege* provides is that forms of self-mutilation and body modification, far from being deviant, are, in fact, part of normal, ordinary human life. From cutting hair, clipping nails and various other common practices of grooming and ordering, to tattooing, piercing, wearing high heels and tight clothing, to the systematic destruction of muscle tissue in the gym as we seek to remove fat and sculpt our bodies into culturally defined and socially sanctioned ideals, Favazza reminds us that our bodies are not naturally civilised but rather that we make them so on a daily basis with discipline, effort and sharp implements. It is, of course, an important point to make, and a kind of mental palette cleanser to be taken before getting too lost in the fascination of strange foreign rituals and the transgressive thrill of talking about pathological self-mutilations. But as important as it may be to begin by recognising this fact, and as useful as it may be to help us forge links of understanding across the uncanny divide of estrangement and deviance that otherwise keeps self-harm and the people who practise it at an enigmatic distance, it is also important to understand that this is not the same as establishing that *all* such practices of self-mutilation represent the same basic pattern of meaning and action, experience and expression; that in some essential sense they are all examples of the same *kind of thing* and ultimately all stand in need of one basic explanation.

Take the Sun Dance ritual, for example, which appears in Favazza's book and which describes an eight-day ritual of the North American plain Indians. A basically shamanic ritual that climaxes with its participants being suspended from wooden skewers that are dug deeply into their muscles. The expectation of such a public, religious ritual is a vision experience and while, as Favazza explains, the 'participants volunteer out of personal initiative, the entire tribe cooperates in its performance, for it is the entire tribe that benefits from the suffering and self-mutilation of the dancers' (1996: 12). While it is certainly a practice of self-mutilation it is demonstrably not the same pattern of meaning and action that describes, for example, a British schoolgirl sat lonely and depressed behind the locked door of her bedroom and reaching for her razor blades because she can no longer manage or express her personal thoughts and feelings in any other way.[2] Indeed, if Favazza's crowded miscellany of rituals, practices, rites and behavioural outbursts is a testament to anything it is human diversity.

But if this is the case then why do Plante and so many others take Favazza's diverse anthology as evidence of a single phenomenon? The problem at root seems to be with the way a set of observations is transformed under the influence of common, and so rarely questioned, objectivist assumptions. The book itself is explicitly about 'self-mutilation', which Favazza defines as 'the direct, deliberate destruction or alteration of one's own body tissue without conscious suicidal intent' (*ibid*: 225) and as far as this goes there can be little argument with the assertion that self-mutilation, *so defined*, really does appear across remarkably different cultures separated by both geography and history. However, we must be careful to keep in mind what this statement actually amounts to.

Given Favazza's definition, the term 'self-mutilation' works as a loose and highly generalisable category, built from what the philosopher Gilbert Ryle calls 'thin description' (1971), which is to say the kind of bare bones description of events and phenomena that could be made by a detached observer or perhaps even by a recording device; a log of no more than what was actually physically said or done devoid of empathy, interpretation, meaning or explanation (Geertz, 2000; Ponterotto, 2006).[3] So if a person mutilates or causes harm to their own body tissue without the intention of killing themselves then their actions qualify as 'self-mutilation' by Favazza's definition, regardless of what other motivations, meanings, ideas, values, concerns, contexts or intentions may have been woven into the experience, or how deeply these dimensions may differentiate one such practice from another. Indeed, such differences simply don't matter to a category like 'self-mutilation' because it is what we could call a thin or *observational category*; a category that does not collect examples of a single 'thing' with a single common nature and explanation but rather one that casts its nets widely and collects examples of various phenomena that fit a relatively superficial set of criteria without having to establish a substantial or natural connection between them.

The statement that self-mutilation can be widely found across different cultures then, while true, amounts to little more than similar statements using similar thin categories; that body adornments can be found across different cultures for example or 'running behaviour'. Imagine a Favazza-like book that catalogued various different examples of people running, from the morning jog to running in the Olympics to running from an axe murderer. If someone is observed running then it qualifies as 'running behaviour', regardless of *why* they are running, and, as such, it can be included in the book. As interesting as such an anthology might be it is hard to imagine that we would mistake the thin, *observational category* used here to collect these examples with a thicker, more meaningful and *explanatory category*. We would not think that just because running behaviour can be observed universally that it must be caused by some mechanism, some structure or some-*thing* that is also universal, something that not only compels running, but that can also explain it. To make this argument would be to overlook the significant qualitative difference between running for fitness, running to compete and running for your life. Those genuine physical mechanisms that do underpin running do not compel it or explain it but rather simply facilitate its possibility so that in varying circumstances different people in different times and places may find themselves running for considerably different reasons and it would be *those reasons* that constituted the explanation of their running and not the physical mechanics of their knee and ankle joints or their quadriceps muscles.

As unlikely as it is that we would commit this objectivist fallacy for a thin category like running behaviour it is nonetheless this exact fallacy, this conflation of the observational for the explanatory and the thin for the thick, that leads Plante and similar writers to assume that just because self-mutilation is everywhere present that all self-mutilation *must* be the product of a single causal structure or mechanism, one that crosses cultures and centuries more or less unchanged and that can therefore speak a common language because it is basically the same thing wherever you find it.

'Self-mutilation', then, is not a thing, but a criteria of observation, and Favazza's book does not zero in on a universal human trait but rather on the myriad and deeply divergent ways that people have, in different times and places, turned to their bodies as a material, existential and psychosomatic resource to mark and enact issues of great meaning and significance. Indeed, the close relationship between our body and our sense of self, along with the malleability of the flesh and the physical capacity we possess to effect, modify and mutilate our bodies renders them a unique canvas on which we can experience and express significant ideas, thoughts and feelings, and through which we make selves and claim identities and status (Mascia-Lees and Sharpe, 1992; Turner, 2008). Given this, it is hardly surprising that we can find as many different kinds of self-mutilation as there have been different peoples but this does not mean that all self-mutilation is the same *thing*, is caused by the same *thing* and can be explained by reference to the same *thing*.

That such diversity is all too easily overlooked is as blatant an example of the implicit asymmetric binary I mentioned earlier (that while life may be both cultural and biological, culture only expresses or presents things, while biology causes and therefore also explains them) as you will find. The thing is that in Plante's work and that of several others there is an acknowledgement of and even a fascination with culture, with meaning and with social context; these factors are not denied at all. But in practice this fascination somewhat distracts from and covers over, even I suspect for the authors themselves, the persuasive effect of the asymmetric binary that is all the more powerful for being implicit. This binary does not reject or deny the sociocultural as such but rather simply *looks past* it as it encourages us to acknowledge the realm and influence of the symbolic but only as a façade, and only as long as we don't ever use it as an actual explanation for some pattern of life. What this objectivist-leaning binary struggles to conceive of is that meaning is consequential for human beings, that people do things for reasons that matter to them and that as such these different practices are not only differently interpreted within different cultures, but also differently lived; not only differently construed, but differently constructed.

That said, while we can identify Plante's mistake as a misunderstanding of Favazza's categories we must nonetheless admit that Favazza also seems quite confused. Indeed, there is little better evidence of the implicit nature of the asymmetric binary and the contradictions that it produces than Favazza's book itself. It is a text that is deeply interested in culture and the importance of meaning in human life, and even goes so far as to state that self-mutilation 'can be understood most fully by examining the cultural context... in which it occurs' (1996: 84), and yet Favazza nonetheless defines self-mutilation as a 'distinct disorder of impulse dyscontrol' (*ibid*: 287), which is to say that he defines it as a psychiatric illness relating to the failure of the individual's biopsychological system. An illness that he sees as being 'unleashed' by 'neurophysiological mechanisms' and that he maintains will, when discovered, be found to be basically the same in animals as in humans (*ibid*: 76). He even believes that it will eventually be possible to treat self-mutilation by medication (*ibid*: 70). Culture and understanding then are indeed interesting for Favazza but not really consequential, diverting but not truly significant, and the contradictions that are built-in to this position go unremarked upon because they don't seem to occur to him.

Perhaps the biggest of these contradictions, however, is the way that, having argued that deviant or pathological self-harm is just a culturally local expression of a more basic impulse to self-mutilate, Favazza nonetheless reverses this hierarchy and understands the broader and more universal category through the lens of the more specific category, casting it in explicitly medical and objectivist terms. In other words, his ethnographic sensitivities are somewhat overwhelmed by his psychiatric instincts (Scheper-Hughes, 1989), reductionistically diagnosing

Moroccan head slashing as 'castration anxiety' (Favazza, 1996: 92) and explaining away Aboriginal subincision as a *folie communiquée*, a kind of pathological practice that spreads through a culture from a single psychotic innovator (*ibid*: 186). It is the same confusion of meanings as if we interpreted all cases of self-starvation (a similarly thin and observational category as 'self-mutilation') within the terms appropriate to anorexia nervosa (a specific, Western and deviant form of self-starvation), so forcing us, among other misunderstandings, to re-evaluate Gandhi's political acts of food refusal as poorly understood symptoms of anorexia.

Self-mutilation then may be both important and prevalent but there is little or no real reason to think that it is a near-universal mechanism and that self-harm is simply a culturally specific interpretation of it. Indeed, we have little reason to believe that we can simply open the ethnographic record and find any evidence of self-harm in radically different cultures at all. But if it is a pattern of meanings and actions that is more specific than this then perhaps our next step should be to look in the historical record and attempt to track it back to its roots; however, this is also easier said than done.

A Short History of Self-harm: Part One

As already mentioned, it is generally accepted that the first clinical formulation of self-harm was made by Menninger in his 1938 book *Man Against Himself*. It's true that the Polish psychologist Casimir Dabrowski had published a short monograph in 1937 entitled 'Psychological Bases of Self-mutilation' but here 'self-mutilation' is given a broad definition and allowed to include everything from mostly unconscious and compulsive forms of pinching, nail biting, hair pulling and scratching patches of irritated skin to the factitious mimicking of organic symptoms and even 'tactless awkward behaviour... lead[ing] to self-accusation' (1937: 6), 'exposure to humiliation' and 'deliberate cynicism' (*ibid*: 54). In fact, there is little, if anything, in Dabrowski's short book that suggests the pattern of action that we would now recognise as 'self-harm' or nonsuicidal self-injury, although interestingly enough there is perhaps something of the same pattern of meanings. For example, Dabrowski describes a variety of reasons why people 'self-mutilate', including several concepts that would later become important dimensions of self-harm. He notes, for example, that acts of self-injury can be used to vent states of 'overexcitability' (*ibid*: 11) or 'unbearable tension' (*ibid*: 12) and so help regulate and manage problematic emotions.

He also argues that such acts can represent a form of self-punishment and an attempt to purify a sense of guilt exacerbated by an excessive tendency to self-reproach (*ibid*: 22–3). And he mentions a case from the famous psychiatrist Pierre Janet concerning a man who used to let drops of boiling water drip onto his palm and who explained that '[o]nly this can bring me back the feeling of myself' (*ibid*: 13). Indeed, it is difficult to read Dabrowski without getting the sense that he is unaware of self-harm as we now know it, but that he is nonetheless picking up on significant aspects of the cultural and psychological matrix of self-harm as they are manifesting in his particular time and place and giving rise to phenomena that are similar yet not identical to it.

In truth, however, much the same can be said for Menninger's book, although it has had a much more significant impact on thinking about self-harm than Dabrowski's. *Man Against Himself* is an attempt to map and classify different kinds of self-mutilation and it allowed Menninger to make the crucial observation that not all kinds of pathological self-mutilation can be understood as the secondary effects of suicidal desire but that, in fact, some may serve a purpose and a sense all of their own. For Menninger this nonsuicidal self-mutilation stood as a particularly raw expression of a basic defence mechanism mobilised against suicidal impulses, a mechanism that channels the urge to self-destruct away from total bodily annihilation and toward a far more limited and local act of violence; a wound in place of a death, a kind of symbolic or partial suicide. This act then, as conceived by Menninger, allows for a neat symbolic victory: the capacity to kill yourself and yet survive, 'a victory... of the life instinct over the death instinct' (1938: 285), self-mutilation as a paradoxical yet effective kind of morbid 'self-healing' (*ibid*: 271).

The problem is that although the basic insight of a life-serving self-mutilation distinct from suicide does indeed provide the basic foundation upon which the idea of self-harm would later be constructed he nonetheless, like Dabrowski, does not describe the pattern of meanings and actions that we have come to call self-harm, nor do any of his examples match this pattern either. The case he uses to develop his crucial insight concerns a 30-year-old high school principal who managed to amputate one of his arms by thrusting it into some machinery at the psychiatric institution where he was resident, an act of revenge or atonement focused on the arm that had brutally murdered his own two-year-old child with a hammer (*ibid*: 203–4). Menninger hypothesises that the arm was offered up as a substitute for suicide, the patient perhaps feeling that he owed a life for a life. But such psychotic self-mutilations and amputations hardly map on to contemporary nonsuicidal self-injury and, again like Dabrowski, the closest that Menninger gets to this pattern is his description of obsessive nail biting, trichotillomania (hair pulling) and skin excoriation (skin picking). But while self-harm may include forms of biting, hair pulling and skin picking, these specific forms and the cases described by Menninger are obsessive–compulsive actions and differ a great deal from the pattern of practice that we would ordinarily call self-harm. Indeed, Favazza himself takes note of this distinction, preferring to term these conditions 'compulsive self-mutilation' (1996: 242–3), and by doing so distinguishing them from both the kind of 'stereotypic self-mutilations' that describe monotonously repetitive and even rhythmic acts of self-assault such as the head-banging typical of, for example, autism and Tourette syndrome (*ibid*: 237–42), and from what we are more specifically interested in here, self-harm or nonsuicidal self-injury (which he terms 'moderate/superficial self-mutilation', although he also uses the category 'episodic self-mutilation' for those who self-harm only occasionally).

Perhaps people were self-harming in the way that we have come to know and recognise the practice during this period, and in their own ways Dabrowski and Menninger are somehow picking up on this but without fully tuning into it. The problem is that we cannot simply assume this, and what attempts have been made to find examples of self-harm prior to their observations have, Favazza-like, generally turned up various examples of self-mutilation that do not adequately fit the pattern of contemporary self-harm at all. So, for example, some have suggested that the celebrated eighteenth century man of letters, Dr Samuel Johnson, stands as just such a historical case on the evidence that he apparently picked and bit at his nails, would somewhat compulsively hit and rub his legs and perhaps most suggestively, and according to his biographer Boswell, 'scraped the joints of his fingers with a penknife, till they seemed quite red and raw' (quoted in Parry-Jones and Parry-Jones, 1993: 395; Farber, 2002). But this is meagre evidence and does not really describe a pattern of self-harm as such unless, that is, we use the contemporary pattern to flesh out this sketch of behaviours in our imagination. But caution must be exercised here; it is easy to project retrospectively onto a historical collection of facts a contemporary pattern of meaning, and in this vein Johnson has, in fact, proven a fertile lure for those who would pay their money and take their chance at a retroactive diagnosis of his famously eccentric behaviour, curious ticks and odd movements and mannerisms, all of which have been used at different times to diagnose everything from obsessive–compulsive disorder, to bulimia, borderline personality disorder, bipolar disorder and Tourette syndrome (King et al., 1999).

We move to firmer ground the closer we get to Menninger's period and in examining the late nineteenth and early twentieth centuries we begin to snatch suggestive glimpses of the cultural and psychiatric milieu out of which self-harm evolved and perhaps even detect traces of patterns which, like Menninger's examples, may provide evidence of the developmental process by which self-harm formed as a meaningful idiom and emerged as a significant practice. In 1901, for example, in Gould and Pyle's second volume of *Anomalies and Curiosities of Medicine*, we find a brief observation regarding '[a] peculiar type of self-mutilation [which] is the habit sometimes seen in hysteric persons of piercing their flesh with numerous needles or pins' (2003: 735). Indeed, there are several cases reported during the late nineteenth century of women inserting needles into parts of their body. In 1872 a Dr J.B. Andrews of the Utica Asylum reported in *The American Journal of Insanity* that he had removed 300 needles from a hysterical woman's body (reported in Changing, 1878), while an 1863 case describes how a 26-year-old woman awaiting trial killed herself by using a prayer book to hammer pins and needles into her chest, some of which stabbed through the walls of her lungs and heart while others travelled through her body to her liver (Favazza, 1996: 156). These so-called 'needle girls' represent a short-lived pattern of self-injurious behaviour, which, while clearly not of exactly the same pattern as contemporary self-harm, nonetheless provides a provocative suggestion that Western culture was moving toward the idea of self-injury as a meaningful way of expressing distress and estrangement. Perhaps then they represent something like an archaeological layer or embryonic precursor to self-harm. Favazza notes that the most proximate and likely explanation for the needle girls was the popularity at the time of 'human pincushions' (*ibid*: 157)—entertainers who specialised in inserting sharp objects into their bodies, often with a seemingly miraculous absence of pain or injury.

Perhaps the earliest, nearest case to contemporary self-harm can be found in a paper published in *The American Journal of Insanity* in 1878 by a Dr Walter Changing and concerning one Helen Miller, an energetic and flamboyant 30-year-old woman who had been arrested for multiple thefts and sent to prison before being transferred to a New York asylum for 'insane criminals'. While resident in the asylum Miller, who had been diagnosed as a hysteric, took to using broken glass to self-mutilate. As Changing records, she became enraged because she was refused opium, [and] cut her arms to avenge her wrongs.... The skin and superficial fascia were cut in a straight line and as cleanly as if done by a surgeon, but the muscular tissue below was hacked in every direction and nearly to the bone (1878: 370–1).

They subsequently discovered that she had thrust fragments of glass and splinters of wood into her wounds, a technique that would become a consistent feature of her self-injury and one that clearly connects her with the 'needle girls'. Dr Changing notes that over the full length of her two-year period at the asylum he and his colleagues removed from her wounds

> ninety-four pieces of glass, thirty-four splinters, two tacks, four shoe nails, one pin, one needle... the whole number of objects removed amounted to one hundred and fifty.... The smallest pieces were the size of small cherry stones. The longest splinter was nearly six inches long, the shortest less than one-fourth of an inch (*ibid*: 374–5).

Indeed, Miller's self-injury settled into a cyclic pattern in which, following a period of quiet cooperation during which her previous wounds would heal, she would increasingly become 'discouraged', as she put it, or 'depressed, irritable and suspicious' as Changing clarifies (*ibid*: 370), before engaging in a more or less identical act of self-injury after which she would calm down, make her apologies and begin the cycle all over again.

Certainly on the surface of it this description does quite closely reflect the idiomatic pattern of nonsuicidal self-injury, and the case of Helen Miller has been referenced as such (Strong, 1998), but on closer inspection there are some significant differences between contemporary self-harm and Miller's self-mutilation. Her criminal behaviour had consisted of the kleptomaniac theft of objects from the various doctors' offices that she had visited, objects such as a stuffed canary and microscope lenses, and the background information Changing provides, in part from one of these very doctors, suggests a woman somewhat obsessed with attracting medical attention. Indeed, this doctor is quoted by Changing as stating that Miller 'had a habit of boasting of all the physicians who had attended her and was fond of claiming acquaintanceship without much ground' (1878: 369).

The case study describes a cycle of increasing tension and then relief marked by self-injury, similar to the case of Fiona I mentioned in the Introduction and indeed to many people who self-harm; however, Changing gives us good reason to believe that it is not the injury itself that brings relief but rather the medical attention that follows. He notes, for example, that she was happiest when 'she was an object of surgical interest... [and] took a special pride in having the attention of the physicians directed toward her' (*ibid*: 375). He openly speculates that she had faked a case of *haematemesis*, or blood present in the vomit, notes that it is only when the medical concern and attention paid to her wounds wanes that she begins to experience her 'discouragement', and describes how she would wrap some of the glass fragments she inserted into her wounds in cloth so that they would be harder to find and probing for them would take longer, presumably extending her desired goal. Indeed, he states that 'she apparently experiences actual erotic pleasure from the probing she was subjected to' (*ibid*: 374).

In today's language we would probably describe her compulsive desire for medical care and concern, and therefore her self-injurious attempts to gain it, as evidence of a factitious disorder or the active production of symptoms and performance of illness in order to gain sympathy, attention and nurturance, and indeed a recognition of this dimension of her problem seems to have been behind her diagnosis of 'hysteria'. While there are enough echoes of contemporary self-harm in the case of Helen Miller to recognise something like a close precursor to the practice it is nonetheless the case that much here does not fit the idiomatic pattern of self-harm. Visits to the accident and emergency department are an inevitable risk with self-harm but almost always one that a person self-harming tries to avoid. Indeed, most people who self-harm try to avoid attracting any kind of medical attention and often become quite adept at cleaning, dressing and treating their wounds themselves. By contrast, Helen Miller's desire seems not to have laid within her injuries or the act of injury at all but rather in the connection to medical care and concern that it would afford her, and indeed it was the periods of such care that marked her happier, quieter and better days.

Closer yet is a case reported in the *Psychoanalytic Review* between 1913 and 1914 by a psychiatrist, Dr L.E. Emerson (reproduced in Reis, 2001). 'The Case of Miss A' tells the story of a 23-year-old American woman who had been cutting herself for three years by the time she presented herself at Emerson's clinic. She had discovered self-injury when, while cutting bread in the family kitchen, she had been sexually assaulted by her cousin. In the scuffle that followed she accidentally cut herself and found that it not only scared her attacker away but also provided some relief from one of the painful headaches that often tormented her. In Emerson's paper she is quoted as saying

> Before I cut myself I had what I called a crazy headache, and after I had let blood my headache went away, and I thought that the cutting of my wrist, and letting the blood flow had cured it (in Reis, 2001: 192).

But following this therapeutic success she soon began to find other reasons to self-harm. As she explains:

> [one night] I had gone to bed very much discouraged. I slept badly, and had horrible dreams mostly of a sexual nature.... I woke about 4:30 o'clock, and lay there and thought about everything, everything disagreeable that had ever happened to me especially about what happened when I was a child, and about my cousin. At last I could not stand it any longer, and in a manner almost frantic I went into my brother's room and took his razor—he was working nights—and slashed at my arm. I did not do it slowly. I did it quickly, because I hated myself, and some other people, and in a way I felt that by hurting myself I was hurting them and also I was wishing I could do it to them (*ibid*: 192–3).

What had happened to her as a child, and the reason she felt that dreams of a sexual nature were 'horrible', was a history of sexual abuse suffered mostly at the hands of her uncle who had forcefully masturbated her for some years under the protection of blackmail and the fact that all but one of her brothers had tried to have sex with her. The anxiety and self-loathing that she experienced as a result was only exacerbated when, as an adult, she confessed her history to a man she hoped to marry only to have him blame her for her own abuse and brand her a 'whore', something that she then quite literally did to herself by running home and using her brother's razor to cut the letter 'W' into her calf (*ibid*: 191–2).

But while there is much here that clearly reflects contemporary nonsuicidal self-injury, and certainly in her story of sadness, anger and personal tragedy there is much to remind us of modern people who injure themselves to help alleviate mental distress, again, as with Helen Miller, there is nonetheless also much that does not quite fit the contemporary pattern of self-harm and that suggests more a stage in the evolution of the practice than its fully developed presence in the second decade of the twentieth century. Perhaps most striking is the fact that, although Miss A first began self-harming because it helped alleviate her headaches, she believed that these headaches were themselves caused by irregular menstruation and so she began to cut herself every four weeks as both a symbolic and, according to her own understanding, a practical way of regularising her periods. In other words: if her body wouldn't bleed naturally then she would make it bleed manually so that she was at least losing blood when she was supposed to. Indeed, this became her principal motivation for self-injury and much of her remaining motivation, aside from using self-mutilation as strategy for 'reducing her obesity' (*ibid*: 194), was similarly symbolic and bound-up with issues of sex and reproduction. For example, believing that she would never be able to have a child she once took her brother's razor blade to her breasts in miserable anger 'thinking that if she could have no babies her breasts were useless' (*ibid*: 191).

Perhaps because of this tendency to symbolism and the connection between her self-mutilation and issues of sex and reproduction, Emerson, like Changing, also talks about his patient through the technical term 'hysteria', although deployed here less as a diagnosis than an interpretive lens that shapes his understanding. And this repeating connection with hysteria and early forms of self-harm, evident in Helen Miller, the case of Miss A and the 'needle girls', is itself important and tantalisingly suggestive. Hysteria may be an outdated psychiatric category with a 'fascinating and tortuous medical and cultural history' (Scull, 2009: 6), but it is also a complex of ideas, images and values that have continued to live in the cultural and psychiatric unconscious surfacing here and there in literature, film, feminism, folk psychology and popular prejudices about female mental health (Showalter, 1987; Ussher, 1991; Appignanesi, 2008). It is like the archetypal mad woman in the attic representing something we thought we had put well behind us, or at least hidden away, which nevertheless continues, frustratingly, disturbingly, to rattle its chains and bang on the ceiling, reminding us that it, she, is still there and still needs to be dealt with. As will become clear throughout this book the figure of the hysterical woman haunts the many representations and conceptions of self-harm that circulate through our culture. More than just an evocative Victorian image, the hysterical woman remains with us as an unconscious template through which we see and think about self-harm in particular and about female suffering, distress and mental disorder more generally.

Hysteria bears this weight of signification because for centuries it represented an illness category that framed women's distress as the result of their supposed constitutional weakness and that diagnosed women as suffering as much from their gender as from any kind of a disease (Micale, 1994; Scull, 2009). This blend of medicine and misogyny took on a new dimension, however, in the classic age of hysteria, the *fin de siècle* period of Jean-Martin Charcot's *Salpêtrière* psychiatric hospital in Paris and the publication of Freud and Breuer's *Studies in Hysteria* in 1895. Hysteria now came to be more exclusively framed as a purely psychological phenomenon rather than as some kind of organic nervous disorder. More precisely, it came to represent the psychological, and irreducibly psychodynamic, concept of *conversion*: the idea that 'an affliction of the mind' can be 'expressed through a disturbance of the body' (Slavney, 1990: 1–2), that when the self is silenced the body speaks on its behalf and that unexpressed mental distress may be translated and transformed into physical symptoms symbolically indicating the thoughts, feelings and conditions behind it. Understood in this way hysteria could be thought of less as a disease and more as 'an alternative physical, verbal, and gestural language' a kind of 'iconic social communication' that spoke of female suffering (Micale, 1994: 182).

Again the diagnosis of hysteria was associated with women, despite the number of men who apparently presented with its symptoms (Mitchell, 2001), but now less for the perceived weakness of their bodies than the imagined instability of their emotions, the volatility of the female mind and their inability to police the borders and boundaries of their own bodies without problematic leakages of thoughts, feelings and bodily fluids (Showalter, 1987; Ussher, 1991; Grosz, 1994). But if hysteria was now the acting out of a psychological stress then it also became a contestable issue as to why women were so stressed. Was it because women are constitutionally more vulnerable to disorder than men, or was it, and is it still, that in a society of gender asymmetry such experiences and expressions of illness and disorder provide women with both an alternative language and a limited means of, if not escaping, perhaps negotiating their predicament? By reflecting this question hysteria became an essential medium through which a rapidly transforming society discussed, struggled to understand, and sought to control and regulate the changing roles of women and the changing structure of female identity (Micale, 1994; Appignanesi, 2008). And this of course represents the primary familial connection between hysteria and self-harm. That in taking on a less symbolically veiled and metaphoric late-modern model of psychological conversion self-harm has, along with anorexia, also taken on the burden of representing female experience in as much as it is articulated through suffering 'wounded womanhood' (Jamison, 2014).

In this connection it is interesting to note that as hysteria became less popular as a diagnostic category and eventually lost all psychiatric credibility at the end of the 1970s, some of the diagnostic slack that it left over was taken up by precisely those categories of disorder, namely borderline personality disorder, dissociative identity disorder and histrionic personality disorder that have traditionally been associated with self-harm and which prior to 2013 had provided self-harm's only mention in the diagnostic literature (Bollas, 1999). There is at least one book, Merskey's *The Analysis of Hysteria* (1979), which appeared late enough in the day to recognise and discuss self-harm but still early enough to think of it explicitly through the lens of hysteria. Perhaps then we can speculate that self-harm is rooted in and grew out of the cultural and clinical milieu of hysteria but the picture we have of this process is opaque and clouded at best, and finding the 'patient zero' of self-harm is perhaps too contested and contestable an endeavour to bear fruit. However, the concept, the idea, of self-harm is easier to trace, although we can only really pick up the trail sometime after Menninger's first observations. It's true that there had been faint echoes of interest in the 1950s (Hendin, 1950; Schmidt *et al.*, 1954), and in 1964 a psychiatrist called Stengel had observed under the general label of 'attempted suicide' some behaviours that we would now perhaps more readily recognise as self-harm; however, this quiet period in the formation of the concept of self-harm was soon replaced in the mid-60s by something more like a moral panic (Cohen, 1972), with reports emerging from some American clinics of a 'wave' or 'epidemic' of self-mutilation.

It began with just a few papers in psychiatric journals detailing a rise among inpatients of repeated cutting to the wrists (Offer and Barglow, 1960; Graff and Mallin, 1967; Grunebaum and Klerman, 1967; Pao, 1969); however, soon the Philadelphia psychiatrists Graff and Mallin felt confident enough to claim that such 'wrist-slashers' had replaced schizophrenics as the new chronic patient of American psychiatric hospitals. Significantly, and recalling Menninger's conceptual breakthrough, many of these clinicians noted that this behaviour appeared quite distinct from suicide and subsequently began to formulate the idea of a separate 'delicate wrist-cutting syndrome' (Pao, 1969). This syndrome, as they reported it, could typically be found among women who were generally young, attractive, intelligent, even talented, and on the surface socially adept.... Invariably their early lives and family relationships have been unstable.... In many cases the father has been seductive and unable to set limits. He is intermittently indulgent, often inadequate at his occupation, and frequently alcoholic. The mother is usually cold, punitive, and unconsciously provocative.... Generally it can be said that these patients slash their wrists when they face the loss of a meaningful person or encounter an impasse in their interpersonal relations (Graff and Mallin, 1967: 528).

Tellingly, this description tends to illustrate the lingering and seemingly unconscious influence of the stereotypical construction of the female hysteric (Showalter, 1991). As sociologist Liz Frost notes,

This stereotype resonates with all the contradictory demands of what a young woman should be under psychiatry—attractive and available but virginal; intelligent but indiscriminate and lacking social competence, out of control and in need of help from the masculine science of medicine (2001: 26).

Such stereotypes are, of course, more than just abstract descriptions, they are the very means by which real people are interpellated and fixed into particular social roles or positions (Althusser, 1971), and the very conditions under which their lives are inscribed with a certain kind of identity—in this case an identity that seems to have used diagnoses of deviance and even madness to drag at the process of changing gender roles. One person who was interpellated, fixed and positioned in this way was Susanna Kaysen, an intelligent and precocious teenager who, in 1967, found herself referred to a psychiatric hospital following a 15-minute assessment with a doctor partly because, as he put it in his referral, she lived a 'chaotic unplanned life' (Kaysen, 2000: 13). Her autobiographical account of this experience, *Girl, Interrupted* (2000), conjures a troubled young woman into a dynamic and transitional society struggling between changing cultural values and the more conservative impulses of traditional social institutions. Her confusion about what it means to be a woman in this energetic period in history became subject to, and made her the *subject of*, a medical and psychiatric discourse that found it easier to deal with a patient with an illness—borderline personality disorder—and a tendency to harm her own wrists than a young woman negotiating fast changing personal and social expectations (*ibid*: 152). In considering the blatantly sexist rules that regulated her workplace before her institutionalisation she asks: '[w]as I crazy or right?' and responds 'In 1967, this was a hard question to answer' (*ibid*: 132).

It is a point that hits powerfully and depressingly home as she describes the process by which she was eventually released from the hospital. The institution's authorities were reluctant to release her without a job waiting for her and could not understand and would not accept her stubborn insistence that she wanted to become a writer. 'Luckily', she writes, 'I got a marriage proposal and they let me out. In 1968, everybody could understand a marriage proposal' (*ibid*: 133). Her discharge summary reads under 'prognosis': 'the patient may learn to make more wise choices for herself within the boundaries of her personality so that she is able to achieve a satisfactory dependent relationship if necessary which will sustain her for a long period of time' (*ibid*: 145).

This stereotype deployed by Graff and Mallin, and the very subjectivity that Kaysen found herself transposed or interpellated into, holds with surprising consistency within this wave of 1960s 'wrist cutting', or at least among its official recorders and analysts. Kaysen, in her memoir, suggests that this is hardly surprising as American psychiatric inpatients in the 1960s could, as a general population, be characterised along similar lines—those troubling society being in turn diagnosed by society as being troubled. But either way the enchantment of the stereotype didn't last much beyond the end of the decade and by 1971 research by Clendenin and Murphy (and then Weissman in 1975) had looked outside of the psychiatric hospital and found that 40 per cent of their wrist cutters were men, only a minority of the females were single and ages varied throughout both genders. But as short lived as the wrist-cutting epidemic had turned out to be it did significantly develop the idea of a discrete condition of 'self-harm', and help fix the popular prejudices associated with it into the well-established background provided by traditional hysteria, and, in particular, its connection to young women.

In 1975 the psychiatrist H.G. Morgan and his colleagues proposed a 'deliberate self-harm' syndrome, describing this in 1979 as

> Non-fatal episodes of self-harm [which] may be referred to collectively as problems of self-poisoning and self-injury.... We have used the term 'non-fatal deliberate self-harm' as ... a way of describing a form of behaviour which besides including failed suicides embraces many episodes in which actual self-destruction was clearly not intended. The general meaning of self-harm is also well suited to

cover the wide variety of methods used, including drug overdosage, self-poisoning with non-ingestants, the use of other chemicals such as gases, as well as laceration and other forms of physical injury (1979: 88).

The contemporary concept of self-harm is clearly recognisable in this description, although still clearly struggling to free itself from the category 'suicide' and claim a meaning of its own. One reason for this may have been the general reluctance of psychiatry to include seemingly fuzzy psychological concepts like 'intention' as part of the demarcation criteria for diagnostic and aetiological categories (Gardner and Gardner, 1975; Jones et al, 1979; Morgan, 1979). This was a period when psychiatry was trying to shrug off its psychodynamic heritage and become more biomedical in its self-identity and orientation, leading to a general desire to work more with the physical facts of a case than the interpretation of any subjective experiences and private mental states that may be associated with it (Shorter, 1997; Luhrmann, 2001; Horwitz, 2003). Psychiatrists R.R. Ross and H.B. McKay argued at the time that proposed classification schemes for self-harm needed to

> avoid the complexities and problems in attempting to examine the mutilator's motives or intentions or to determine the environmental or interpersonal conditions which may have preceded the act (1979: 15).

As such, research had continued to work toward a definitional distinction between self-harm and suicide but pursued this through an appeal to nonpsychological characteristics and variables. During the 1970s studies focused, for example, on the degree and type of physical damage done during different acts, or their level of 'lethality' (Clendenin and Murphy, 1971; Weissman, 1975; Morgan, 1979; Ross and McKay, 1979; Farberow, 1980), or else the frequency of episodes of self-attack, with self-harm being characterised as 'chronic repetition' (Bachy-Y-Rita, 1974; Gardner and Gardner, 1975; Morgan, 1979; Ross and McKay, 1979). Another proposal was the methodology of self-attack, with people who self-harm being distinguished by the variety of methods that they employed (Ballinger, 1971; Morgan, 1979; Ross and McKay, 1979). But in the end such technical developments were just so many avoidance strategies and soon the issue of intention would re-emerge as *the* major component in any adequate diagnostic conceptualisation or description of self-harm as a phenomenon in itself. This, in turn, meant that self-harm was no longer the exclusive property of psychiatrists and soon clinical psychologists and psychotherapists were developing their own approaches.

The most significant move in this direction was M.A. Simpson's 1976 formulation of self-harm as a kind of 'antisuicide', which is opposed to total self-destruction not only at the level of psychic process and physical action, but also in the most fundamental and definitional sense. Acts of self-mutilation are, according to Simpson, the means by which feelings of depersonalisation and psychic distress may be combated through galvanising the body's sense of being alive and the mind's sense of being unified and focused. As Ross and McKay were to put it (despite their professed lack of interest in intentional states), '[t]here is in the action of the self-mutilator seldom an intent to die and often very little risk of dying.... His behaviour is actually counter-intentional to suicide rather than suicidal' (1979: 15).

By 1983 the research of E.M. Pattison and J. Kahan had led to a differential classification system for self-harm behaviours that could support a call to recognise a distinct 'deliberate self-harm syndrome', which was markedly different from Morgan's original use of this phrase and which, unlike Morgan's version, excluded attempted suicide, drug and alcohol overdoses, and chronic, indirect self-attack. Although these calls were unsuccessful, two major works of the 1980s further established and consolidated the position of self-harm in the minds of the clinicians, researchers and the public at large as a separate and distinct classificatory and diagnostic entity. The first of these was Walsh and Rosen's *Self-Mutilation: Theory, Research, and Treatment* (1988), which connected self-harm with a number of disturbances and conditions suffered in childhood and adolescence, and theorised that in acts of self-harm people have 'acted out all the familiar roles from childhood: the victim, the (dissociated) witness to violence and self-destructiveness, and finally, the aggressive attacker' (quoted in Strong, 1998: 34). The second major work was, of course, Favazza's *Bodies Under Siege* (1996 [1987]), which, as I have already pointed out, currently stands as *the* canonical authority in the world of self-harm literature, with a quote or reference from this book being an almost invariable convention of texts on the subject. Indeed, more than any other it is this text that has helped raise public awareness and professional interest in a separate and distinct diagnostic category and form of mental pathology that came eventually to be called nonsuicidal self-injury or 'self-harm'.

Defining Self-harm in a Culture of Objectivism

Of course, it could be, and often is, argued that despite the story of self-harm's opaque and gradual emergence during the twentieth century it may nonetheless have been with us all along, confused perhaps with suicidal behaviours and sadomasochism, or else an orphan of people's embarrassed attention. But while this might be possible it ought also to be acknowledged that it is very unlikely and, more importantly, the sheer and uncompromising dearth of observation leaves us with little reason to think so. That said there is one other area that we might want to explore. The story leaves us at the end of the twentieth and beginning of the twenty-first centuries with a rough concept and a clear recognition of self-harm but if self-harm is a natural kind of a 'thing' then, now that we have noticed it, we ought to be able to define it precisely and in purely objectivist terms. Indeed, if it was something like a disease or a symptom of a disease then the objectivist paradigm suggests that defining it ought to be a relatively straightforward matter, something like 'cutting nature at the joints' and finding the right formula of words and ideas that can map its natural structure and so distinguish this universal and essential *form*, which would be true in all places and times, from the various surface details or incidental *content* (the icing on the cake) that may vary from one case to another, or one culture to another or one time to another (Littlewood, 2002; Timimi, 2002). Pathologies being, after all, objectively pathological and not merely judged to be so because of public opinion. However, in practice, self-harm has utterly confounded medical and psychological taxonomies, slipping easily through their classificatory nets and unsettling their standard and traditional assumptions, insisting, as we saw in the history of its development, that it be defined, at least in part, on grounds of meaning and value and not just thin descriptions or objectivist biopsychology.

Take, for example, a typical act of self-harm, say cutting the back of the forearms with a razor blade, and compare it with a more general and relatively normative practice like smoking cigarettes. The former is framed as self-evidently pathological and categorised as 'self-harm', while the latter is considered relatively normal, perhaps an unfortunate if popular habit but certainly not 'self-harm' and even less so evidence of mental illness. But in terms of mortality and morbidity smoking is by far the greater example of someone inflicting actual physical harm upon their body and, of course, the same argument may be made for drinking alcohol or even eating sugary and fatty foods. These behaviours, although not normally categorised as 'self-harm', are generally responsible for a greater degree of actual physical harm even at relatively normal levels of consumption and so cannot be distinguished from it on the basis of some natural boundary or medically objective calculus of harm.

We could look to psychological function to help us make this distinction but again a great deal of normative alcohol consumption could be framed as an act of deliberate self-poisoning indulged in at the end of a stressful day as a habitual technique of emotional management (Goudriaan *et al.*, 2007), mirroring the influential 'affect regulation' theory of self-harm that models it as a kind of pressure valve that lets off and so crisis manages high levels of negative emotions (Suyemoto, 1998; Crouch and Wright, 2004). Many people drink, smoke and eat to achieve these same goals but without their level of consumption, or reasons for doing so, being considered psychopathological and this is not even to factor in the complex feelings of guilt, shame and self-hatred that can be caught up with particular patterns of food and drink consumption and which can appear to be significantly similar to the psychological complexes characteristic of self-harm (Frost, 2001).

The point is that purely objectivist measures and terms like an abstract calculus of harm or the psychological logic of the emotional pressure valve cannot be used as definitions of self-harm without, at the same time, including quite normative forms of self-damage that we usually want to keep outside of this label and indeed beyond clinical authority. It has been a more or less standard feature of attempts to define self-harm that they have been subject to a kind of definition creep in which the attempt to ring-fence a desired target group of 'deviant' behaviours (while leaving out normative behaviours no matter how harmful they may be) causes categorical boundaries to break down and the meaning of 'self-harm' to seep through, implicating social locations and cultural practices not normally coded as deviant let alone pathological. This, for example, has happened with practices like tattooing, piercing, wearing high heels, cutting finger nails, going to the gym and even staying in dysfunctional relationships (Farber, 2002). The literature, both professional and public, has typically responded with a remarkable fetish for producing new definitions and terminology, as if taking multiple swipes at its target, hoping that each new attack will net the prize (Kilby, 2001: 126; see also Gratz, 2001; Sutton, 2005).

The clinical psychologist Jennifer Muehlenkamp (2005), for example, has counted over 33 different terms currently in use, each implying a slightly different definition, a slightly different way of answering the question of what self-harm is, and a slightly different selection of those practices that should be included and those excluded (Sutton, 2005; Chandler et al., 2011). The result has been a general public confusion and a deeply dissatisfying professional muddle in which different researchers have in effect been looking at slightly different patterns of phenomena, and the consequent patchwork of frequently incommensurable data has failed to link-up and provide a general picture or meta-analysis of self-harm at a social or epidemiological level. As such, for a long time, and to a large degree to this day, virtually any answer given to demographic questions had to be met with either measured uncertainty or else definite suspicion (Eisenkraft, 2006; Claes and Vandereycken, 2007).[4]

But in order to avoid this problem we have to abandon the attempt for a neat, precise definitional cut made by a purely objectivist scalpel and instead embrace the messiness of psychological intention, personal and cultural meaning, and social norms and public values; indeed, the very things that, in reality, decide what is classed as normative and what as deviant. And this is the nub of the issue. Typically objectivist definitions avoid using such things as a means of mapping the significant features of self-harm but how do we objectively distinguish between the normative and the deviant where no objective criteria seems to make sense? Or put another way: how do we make a value judgement without reference to values? Part of a successful definition for self-harm must include the fact that it is a subcategory of actions that are harmful to one's body and that are tied to a particular pattern of personal and cultural meanings, and that *simply are* socially evaluated as deviant and commonly recognised and labelled as 'self-harm'. As such, while cutting your forearms counts as self-harm, drinking, comfort eating and smoking do not because they do not carry this meaning personally, culturally or socially.

Perhaps this is why self-harm is so frequently represented as something irreducibly 'other' and uncanny, something almost uniquely disruptive to our ability to make sense. Its refusal to be contained by the objectivist paradigm carries a deconstructive capacity to disturb us and our typical assumptions (Derrida, 1976, 1991). The asymmetric binary works to make us *look past* meanings, norms and values on the assumption that they cannot be part of the essential, or 'natural', form of self-harm but this is to place the cart of definition and categorisation before the horse of empirical observation and description. It has, of course, only been assumed that self-harm is a pathology or something like a pathology, and therefore something that must be at root defined in objectivist language, an assumption that increasingly seems like a poor one. But it is also assumed in the culture at large that the language of objectivism is, indeed and in fact, objective, and that norms, values and cultural meanings play no essential role in constructing and filling out categories like 'deviance' and 'pathology' (Rhodes, 1996; Kleinman, 1991; Littlewood, 2002). But in its refusal to be defined on seemingly objective grounds self-harm reveals itself to be constructed on social ones instead and so undermines this 'aura of factuality' (Geertz, 1973) that attaches to biomedicine and prevents people from seeing that it is not only a system of knowledge but also a cultural system encoding power relations, social norms and public values (Kleinman, 1991; Rhodes, 1996; Foucault, 2003a; Lupton, 2003); that in self-harm we have an example of a public evaluation of deviance translated into a medical fact and so apparently cleansed of any political, social or historical significance (Taussig, 1980). It is perhaps not surprising then that rather than face the realisation that such categories of psychopathology are, as medical anthropologist Arthur Kleinman argues, 'the outcome of historical development, cultural influence, and political negotiation' (1991: 12), it becomes easier to create a fetish of continual re-definition and deferral of meaning.

But understanding that self-harm cannot be adequately modelled as a natural 'thing' or adequately mapped using purely objectivist language must be balanced against an appreciation for the contribution that such objectivism, understood precisely as a cultural system of signs, symbols, ideas and values, makes to the structure or package of meanings that make up self-harm as a concept and as a practice. What the survey of Favazza's confused categories, the history of self-harm and the problems of defining it on objectivist grounds makes clear is that the objectivist paradigm, and, in particular, its embodiment in medicine and psychiatry, have from the very beginning set the parameters within which self-harm has been defined and represented, and so have also shaped the criteria by which anything that is said about it will be recognised and understood as more or less sensible, meaningful and authoritative, or else ignored as nonsense and falsehood. This is not to say that medicine sits in sole control or possession of self-harm, that it has claimed it as its own and jealously guards against anyone else having a say. Seven and a half decades passed between Menninger's clinical observations and the *Diagnostic and Statistical Manual of Mental Disorders, 5th Edition* (DSM-5). But while it is certainly true that until now biomedical institutions have been somewhat ambivalent about laying claim to special authority over self-harm, or privileged knowledge about it (Favazza, 1996), the point is that we, as a culture and a society, have always framed it in more or less biomedical terms as something that is self-evidently a pathological behaviour, a category of illness and a clinical problem.

And this, of course, should be of little surprise. We live in a highly medicalised culture where objectivist ideas, institutional logics and symbols enjoy a great deal of social power and authority (De Vries *et al.*, 1983; Horwitz, 2003; Scheff, 2007; Lupton, 2003), and our distress is typically 'seen through a lens which encourages us to experience, and indeed shape, individual concerns in medical ways' (Littlewood, 2002: 1). This authority of the medical, its 'aura of factuality', influences the way we see and make sense of the world, ourselves and our patterns of action and practice (Kleinman, 1991; Conrad and Schneider, 1992; Johnstone, 2000; Littlewood, 2002), and this is really what I mean to indicate here through the idea of the objectivist paradigm: less a discrete school of thought or group of people with a distinct agenda then, than a particular *style* or *tendency* of thought that exerts a powerful influence on how we think and talk about things like self-harm. So even though almost everyone who talks about self-harm mixes objectivism with other styles of thought and representation it nonetheless bears the considerable gravitational marks of objectivist ways of thinking and setting the basic terms and concepts of debate, and even the basic rules of debate.

In trying to understand this idea of objectivism as a tendency of thought and representation, the concept of *discourse*, as it has been given a special, technical meaning by the radical French historian and social theorist Michel Foucault (2001, 2002), will prove particularly useful. For Foucault the word 'discourse' refers to the statements we make about a given subject (in this case self-harm) but it also refers to the conventions of meaning or grammars of sense that organise and regulate such statements (calling it an 'illness' or a 'pathology', for example, and assuming this to be the proper and correct, *the authorised*, way of talking about it), as well as the kind of knowledge and values these conventions express ('illness', for example, implies the 'medical' and the objectivist paradigm), and also, finally, who has the social authority to make such statements (the 'medical' by extension implies the patient's need for expert help where 'expert' implies both professional training and institutional authority). For Foucault and for 'discourse' these things are all connected, all patterned, and the significant point is that although they pattern each other it is the issue of *power* that really organises this patterning, that provides the rules of the language game so to speak. So when we try to understand our ways of thinking, speaking and representing the world we also have to understand power and, in particular, we have to understand the way that power can be more about convention, values and influence than naked aggression or threats (Foucault, 1991 [1975]; Rose, 1998).

'Discourse', as a theoretical key that we use to unlock and understand social processes, gets at the way that the systems of meanings and values that make up so much of our social and psychological worlds are not, in fact, neutral but are rather structured, and that this structure is managed and regulated mostly by the pervasive idea or set of rules that insists that some ways of thinking and talking are legitimate, while others are to be condemned as nonsense, folly or falsehood (Laclau and Mouffe, 1990). So whenever we make statements we are also implicitly invoking a whole background 'regime of knowledge' that includes not just particular ways of thinking, saying and representing, although these are the most obvious manifestations of it, but also a whole complex of cultural conventions, social norms, public values and patterns of power relations, as well, of course, as the institutional structures that tend to underwrite and provide the infrastructure for these power relations (Cousins and Hussain, 1984; Hall, 1992). For Foucault then, our social conventions and institutions, no matter how necessary or useful, must also be understood as political institutions which reflect our values as surely as they reflect our knowledge, because values and knowledge are not separate but rather irreducibly enmeshed, and constantly made manifest in both our dominant beliefs and in the ways in which we choose to organise and conduct our lives.

This is why the disciplines and social institutions that typically lay claim to authoritative knowledge about self-harm, disciplines like clinical and much general psychology, psychotherapy, counselling, social work and, of course, psychiatry, what we might call the 'psy-complex' (Ingleby, 1985; Rose, 1985), conventionally draw upon the cache of social authority invested in biomedicine precisely by adopting its discourses—its styles and ways of talking and thinking, its symbols and codes, its implicit rules of what is allowed and what is not. And in this way they have all too easily become satellites orbiting a biomedical core of paradigms, terminology, organisational logics and technologies (Stainton Rogers, 1991; Hook, 2007; Rose, 2007). And it is because of this gravitational effect that most representations and understandings of self-harm tend, implicitly or otherwise, to reflect and reproduce the assumptions and prejudices of the biomedical and objectivist paradigm. It is difficult, in fact almost impossible, to even talk about self-harm without calling it an 'illness' or a 'condition', and by so doing slip into the whole order of medicalising assumptions and objectivist language. Indeed, we are culturally ill equipped to talk about idioms of distress in general without engaging in medical discourse of some kind (Johnstone, 2000; Scheff, 2007).

In saying all of this, of course, it is important to stress exactly what the concept of discourse allows us to model so well—the fact that such objectivism stands as a broad discursive *tendency*, strongly influencing representations and understandings of self-harm, helping to shape and mould them, but by no means constituting a concrete authority or a discrete school of thought. There are attempts at understanding self-harm which are very strongly objectivist, as, for example, when researchers have tried to explain it away with reference to serotonin deficiency (Simeon *et al.*, 1992), abnormal psychophysiological response (Haines *et al.*, 1995) and even disturbances in glucose metabolism (Westling *et al.*, 2009), but most attempts to understand it and most texts that talk about it are more influenced, and not wholly controlled, by the objectivist paradigm. Other paradigms do exist, and hegemony is not homogeny after all. Although the strong objectivist approach has been subject to a robust critique for its social, political and personal effects (Breggin, 1993; Tew, 2005), as well as its empirical veracity and truth (Horwitz, 2003; Rapley *et al.*, 2011), my aim here is not to cast it as an ideological bogeyman but rather only to point out the scale and reach of its influence, its pervasiveness and its persistent tendency to limit ideas and restrict debate (Kleinman, 1991; Parker *et al.*, 1995; Johnstone, 2000). Indeed, for all the criticisms and caveats that have been voiced from within the health disciplines (Tew, 2005), the fact remains that it is *hegemonic* in the true and technical sense (Gramsci, 1992), which is to say that it gravitationally influences even those who are critical of it, and remains a convention of understanding and representing self-harm (and mental disorder in general) that is assumed a lot more often than it is questioned.

This influence then is felt not just at the naturalistic and overtly biomedical and reductionist end of the objectivist spectrum, as represented by theories of serotonin deficiency or glucose metabolism, but also at the more personalistic and psychological end of the spectrum where a focus on thoughts and feelings has often, and mistakenly, been thought to protect us against the blunter impacts of objectivism (Claes and Vandereycken, 2007). The fact is that psychological functions are often modelled not in terms of consciousness, meanings and values (Bruner, 1990), but rather according to the same core objectivist and substantivist assumptions that are typical of more naturalistic models; *that there is some inner mechanism at work on a more basic level than that of the total, socialised person*. Indeed, in both, the essential project remains the same: track down and identify that 'thing', disease or dysfunction, which sits at the core of the behaviour, and work out its mechanism—how *it* produces self-harm.

Take, for example, the 'affect regulation' theory mentioned above. Here the basic idea is that emotions dam-up in the individual's psychological system because they are not being properly expressed and so self-harm kicks in more or less automatically as a kind of emergency mechanism of expression, releasing the negative emotion and returning the individual to a more peaceful state of mind and body. Now, although we do seem to have here more of a focus on the person, their experiences and feelings than is typically found in many strongly objectivist models, this focus nonetheless obscures the fact that here again we have a more or less mechanical system, albeit a psychological system, and an explanation of self-harm as a kind of mechanism within that system. Personal meaning and context are included in this model but only as secondary factors, after the fact of the basic system of circulating emotions and the causal mechanism of emergency emotional expression, or 'letting things out'. The actual thoughts and feelings of the person who has self-harmed then stand only examples of the kinds of thoughts, feelings and personal biographies that can operate through this system and activate this particular mechanism. So, despite the emphasis on psychological function and a greater attention to the more personalistic elements of specific cases, this model is still fundamentally objectivist; meaning is still secondary to mechanism and self-harm is still formulated as a physically determined behaviour rather than a complex pattern of action.

Self-harm as a Symbolic Act

The Gerasene demoniac that inhabits Mark's gospel account and that opened this chapter wanders around a cemetery crying and cutting himself with stones and so appears, in the minds of some, to provide evidence of self-harm in ancient Biblical psychiatry. However, knowing what we now know, this assertion seems a little simplistic. Cutting oneself was an ancient Jewish practice of mourning that had apparently become at some point associated with magic and was subsequently forbidden by the writer of Deuteronomy (14:01; see also Segal, 1976: 17), and so describing the stricken man in this way may have been, in part, a way of explaining how he came to be so distressed and so possessed (that he was driven mad with grief; he was 'dwelling in the tombs' after all), and, in part, a way of indicating his connection with unclean spirits and that which is abominable to God. The assertion that this is self-harm seems to fall under the fallacy we have noted several times of imposing a contemporary, medicalised pattern of meanings and actions onto a historical or ethnographic example that does not really fit it. Indeed, if anything, such examples emphasise, as at times does Favazza, the cultural embeddedness of practices of self-mutilation.

Self-harm then, as we recognise and understand it as a distinct and particular pattern of meanings and actions, and contrary to much that has been said otherwise, does not seem to be a transcultural and transhistorical behavioural constant that has always and everywhere spoken the same language and that can be adequately mapped and modelled by purely objectivist language. Rather it seems to be something far more specific to its particular location in time and society; an idiomatic expression of disorder, distress and estrangement that makes up a powerful and increasingly significant part of our contemporary personal and cultural symbolism. Something more like a tool that people use than an illness that they catch. In fact, considering the many different methods of self-harm that are used (Favazza, 1996; Farber, 2002); the diversity of tools and props involved (Sutton, 2005); the different motivations experienced by different people (Claes and Vandereycken, 2007); the variety of emotions and thoughts preceding, accompanying and proceeding the act (Muehlenkamp, 2005); the assortment of resulting sensations and effects (Klonsky, 2007; Horne and Csipke, 2009); the range of psychological states achieved (Hass and Popp, 2006); and the miscellany of contingent factors that may or may not accompany the act in various mixtures from case to case, including the background situation, medical history and personal biography (Babiker and Arnold, 1997; Tantam and Huband, 2009), the overall picture seems to be less one of a singular natural kind of 'thing' with an intrinsic unity and a timeless essence than a family of related practices and experiences that are highly interconnected and configured into a vague but particular pattern in the same way that multiple and diverse threads are interwoven to make up a solid rope (Wittgenstein, 1958).

None of which, it must be made clear, is to suggest that self-harm is not 'real', or to doubt the seriousness of the pain that is associated with it. As Middleton and Garvie put it:

> People call self-harm all kinds of things—a phenomenon, a 'mental health problem'—I have even heard it referred to as a 'maladaptive tool for emotional regulation'. But what I know most of all is that self-harm is a real thing that affects real people (2008: 6).

To question the objectivist hegemony in framing self-harm is only to question whether or not our current ways of representing and understanding self-harm are capable of doing full justice to all the aspects of a 'real thing', and indeed all the forces that make up and operate through 'real people'. The tendency of the objectivist paradigm is to understand 'real' as meaning biomedical—the product of physical disease or structural dysfunction, whether this is understood to be genetic, biological or psychological in nature—and 'not real' can only mean factitious, malingering, hysterical or indulgent (Showalter, 1991; Hacking, 1995). But understood from a more sociological and anthropological perspective, 'real people' are always complex, enculturated, meaning-oriented, socially sophisticated and intersubjective beings (Crossley, 1996), and 'real things' are always a combination of both the physical and the symbolic, the material and the discursive (Kleinman, 1991; Butler, 1993). It may not be wrong to describe self-harm as a symptom as such, but only if, with Karl Menninger, we can ask '[w]hat is behind the symptom?' (1967: 325). As he explains:

> No man steals a watch for the sole purpose of obtaining a timepiece. No man cuts his throat merely in order to die. No man interrupts a successful career from the sheer wish to loaf. Human motivation is not that simple. There are easier ways to attain the objectives of these examples than to buy them at such great price. What do stealing or throat-cutting or loafing *mean* to these individuals in the totality of their experience and life and personality and environment? Why had they become so highly prized? Why were they so necessary? (*ibid*: 325–6, my emphasis).

For Menninger what is behind a symptom is not and cannot simply be some unknown inner and substantive *thing* that operates through purely physical mechanisms but, rather more profoundly, what is behind a symptom is a person and a life, something of meaning and significance. Self-harm appears in the actual lived reality of people's thoughts, feelings and actions as what Kim Hewitt, one of the first sociological voices to talk about self-harm, and from personal and research experience, described as 'the language of blood and pain' (1997: 58), or what Fiona Gardner describes as 'a system of signs marking statements about the self', about relationships and about experiences; 'a gesture, a representation and an action, involving paradox, metaphor and symbol' (2001: 4). And if self-harm is, as Hewitt and Gardner describe, a kind of radical and idiomatic speech act or significant symbol then we must approach it such and try to make sense of it as we would any other idiomatic expression or symbolic action.

To understand a symbolic action, or what the literary theorist Kenneth Burke elegantly described as 'the dancing of an attitude' (1989: 31), means going beyond thin description and the assumption of underlying mechanisms, the inner substantive 'thing', and working instead toward thick description, toward asking about the 'why' of human action; its meaning and significance (Cameron and Frazer, 1987). Of course, a growing chorus of voices is making this argument generally within the field of mental disorder or mental 'illness'; arguing that we must take the symptoms of such disorders as meaningful if we are to provide more effective services and develop a more reflexive and critical approach to psychiatry (Tew, 2005). But I want to argue here that alongside this work there is an important and supplementary task for social science: namely the exploration of the broader cultural meanings that attach to such idioms of distress and estrangement and that help shape them as symbolic actions and patterns of practice that people can use under certain circumstances so as to meaningfully experience and express their suffering. To look at not only what the term 'self-harm' means then, but also at what meanings are actually caught up in it, implied by it, necessary for it to mean what it actually does mean to people. To approach self-harm in this way then, which is the intention of this book, is to understand, to make sense.

This is not, however, it should be noted, and as many on both sides of the natural–social scientific divide have assumed, to oppose explanation to understanding, rather it is to recognise that the work of explaining human life includes the art and science of making sense of meaning. People, unlike geological strata or chemical processes are, as Max Weber memorably put it, 'suspended in webs of significance' (1962), and they live and move and have their being within such webs, which represent patterned systems of meanings and values, or, otherwise put: culture. As people do things because these things hold significance and meaning for them, to understand the background web of significances that provides the conceptual and cultural context of these such actions simply *is* to understand the action and its significance to the actor; it is to understand *why* she acted in this way, indeed *it is to explain* the action. For Weber, the philosophical and sociological tradition of *verstehen* (understanding) implied what he called 'explanatory understanding' (1962: 35) or an 'interpretive understanding of social action in order thereby to arrive at a *causal explanation* of its causes and effects' (*ibid*: 51, my emphasis). Johanness Weiss makes this point quite unequivocally when he states in his book about Weber that '[v]*erstehen* is a method of explaining and explaining only' (1986: 68). But even so, establishing that meaning is centrally important to a true understanding of self-harm and that understanding here counts as a kind of explanation is still to leave the hermeneutic question open: how is one to find these meanings? And how is one to actually go about making sense of self-harm? These are the questions that we will turn to in the next chapter.

2
The Problem of Good Understanding

Introduction: Strange Verses

On a May evening in 1991, after the indie rock band the Manic Street Preachers had played a gig at the Norwich Arts Centre and during an interview with *New Musical Express* (*NME*) journalist Steve Lamacq, the band's lyricist and rhythm guitarist Richey Edwards created one of contemporary rock music's most infamous moments and one of its most challenging images. Lamacq had been publicly unimpressed by the band and was particularly unconvinced by their attempts to identify with the punk music of the late 70s and early 80s (Lamacq, 2000). He went as far as to suggest that their slogans of social outrage and youthful rebellion were little more than a cynical marketing strategy, an exercise in identity consumerism that wrapped resistance in a pop package, and it was in response to this accusation that Edwards produced a razor blade from his back pocket and proceeded to cut '4REAL' into the full length of his forearm. The photograph that was taken of him only moments later shows his thin pale figure gazing steadily at the camera, his wounds open and fresh, a cloth wrapped around his hand to catch the blood.

The injury was severe enough that Edwards was taken to hospital where he received 17 stitches, but soon it had been treated, cleaned and dressed, and he was discharged and sent home to recover. By contrast, the picture of the injury was to demand attention well beyond that evening, transforming the '4REAL' incident from a passing if somewhat outrageous moment of public self-injury into a text recorded in words and pictures and written and re-written through years of subsequent controversy and speculation. It became the subject of a heated debate within the offices of the *NME*, a debate which was recorded and published as a bonus track on the Manic Street Preachers' EP cover of

'Suicide is Painless'; it was subsequently published by the *NME* amidst great controversy; became a popular image on the internet; was voted number 16 in Q magazine's '100 Greatest Rock Photographs of All Time'; and eventually even became a t-shirt. Shortly after its publication young women began attending Edwards' concerts with '4REAL' written on their forearms in marker pen (Jovanovic, 2010: 115), and, in the time since, the picture has become a kind of fetish for what can only be described as the cult of Richey Edwards; a cult that only gathered pathos after his mysterious disappearance in 1995 and his later being pronounced dead as a suspected suicide.

The picture is challenging in both senses of the word: it is difficult to look at and yet demanding of attention and understanding. It is a kind of speech act after all, even if it is written on the body in blood rather than expressed in more conventional terms (Hewitt, 1997; Gardner, 2001; Kleinot, 2009). But although it is a speech act and a kind of message it nonetheless carries something of a transgressive refusal to communicate, at least in more normative fashion, and so frustrates our conventional ways of understanding and making sense. On first inspection the picture may seem quite straightforward, a testament of authenticity and a visceral, if somewhat literal, enactment of McLuhan's famous dictum that 'the medium is the message' (1964); it nonetheless presents a much deeper hermeneutic challenge than this. It is not at all clear, for example, why *this* particular message should make sense within the context of *this* particular medium rather than some other, which is to say: why should lacerations and blood amount to a testament of authenticity? What is the homology between the pattern of this medium and the pattern of this message such that they act together to create a single and significant symbolic act, and represent Burke's 'dancing of an attitude?' Or, otherwise put: how does a wound like this carry meaning? And what meanings does it communicate?

Such acts can be taken as examples of what Dante calls 'strange verses' when he breaks the narrative of *The Inferno* to comment to the reader 'Ye that are of good understanding, note the doctrine that is hidden under the veil of the strange verses!' (1961 [1320]: canto 9, verses 61–63). They represent a kind of esoteric text, one certainly made up from the common signs and symbols of the culture that surrounds and embeds it but which nonetheless presses them to the edges of common use and forces them into a liminal expression; an existence at the edge of the semiotic system that creates something familiar yet alien, something Freud called 'the uncanny' (2003 [1919]). Making sense of such strange verses presents a peculiar hermeneutic problem because it is not just a question of checking the meanings of actions with the actors who performed them, asking why they did what they did and whether or not there may have been more thought or felt than just this conscious intention. And it is not just a question of mapping the structures of meaning that make-up the idiomatic or symbolic action onto the homologous structures that make up the surrounding culture, as if cultures were simple and utterly cohesive monoliths and their products miniature, cookie-cutter versions of themselves. More than just these, although they are certainly involved, it is the question of tracing how the idiom reflects and crystallises its culture's discourses, dilemmas and values *as these have been distorted* into an estranged and deviant modality, an exaggerated symbol both familiar and strange, meaningful yet confusing, a part of the cultural system and yet a transgression of it (Kenny, 1978; Showalter, 1991; Littlewood, 2002; Bordo, 2003). It is the question of how to read a text that seems almost to have been deliberately composed as difficult, disturbing and oblique; a text that calls on us to be understood, that challenges us to 'get it' and that *should* make sense, but which nonetheless seems to resist all attempts to understand it. In short, it is not a hermeneutic question located purely within the *identity* of idiom and culture, but rather one located in the liminal and transgressive space between them, in the *relationship* that they articulate.

Of course, typically, in looking for the meaning of a strange verse like self-harm, and in trying to understand the resonant yet deviant relationship it has with its sociocultural context, we have a tendency to follow Dante's epistemological recommendation and search for a 'hidden doctrine' that will reveal the logic that unites medium and message, and that will embed Burke's sense of 'attitude' within the particular pattern or 'dance' of action that serves as its symbol and vehicle. It's a tendency strongly evident in the framing of self-harm as the symptomatic product of some inner and pathogenic problem, requiring us to reach inward to find the hidden doctrine in the 'thing' that is taken to be both cause and explanation. But as I argued in Chapter 1, the questions that a search for an objectivist hidden doctrine raises far outstrip the answers that it typically supplies, and although we may now appreciate the need for understanding self-harm as a meaningful action, as something in need of interpretation and not just mechanical explanation, we still need to establish how this 'good understanding' as Dante puts it, the understanding that will reveal the meaning hidden within the strange verse of self-harm, should be arrived at. And it is to this question that I now turn, the question of exactly *how* the meaning of self-harm should be interpreted, and to begin to answer this question I want to return to the history of self-harm and how it may help us to understand Richey Edwards' infamous actions.

A Short History of Self-harm: Part Two

Of course, the experience of celebrities hardly justifies generalisations, and Richey Edwards' '4REAL' incident, like Fiona's facial lacerations, is by no means a typical example of self-harm. Yet, like Fiona, Edwards' actions sit within a broader personal history of more typical nonsuicidal self-injury and in many ways crystallises this background into a single and dramatic public performance, making explicit through exaggeration what is perhaps ordinarily left quietly implicit. Beside which, the most interesting thing about the '4REAL' incident is the fact that it was and has always been read as an example of self-harm, where self-harm is understood to imply a medical and psychiatric illness or problem, something indicating psychological vulnerability and mental distress. This wasn't inevitable; the '4REAL' incident could just as easily have been framed within a well-established tradition of public, transgressive, punk self-mutilation, a citation of Sid Vicious or Iggy Pop (Hewitt, 1997); indeed, this would have made perfect sense as a counter to Lamacq's accusations. In the late 70s, perhaps inspired by the broken glass used to cut Pop's bare chest during performances and other similar on-stage mutilations, a subtrend of punk known as 'emotional core', 'emocore' or just 'emo' emerged as a personal style and subcultural ethos that 'was notable for its obsession with feelings (as opposed to politics, anger, and smashing stuff up)' (Greenwald, 2003: 2), and its association with the 'mutilation of the body with razor blades' (Lack, 1995: 1). But despite this, Edwards' self-injury was not interpreted with reference to this tradition but rather from the beginning it has been framed as psychopathological self-harm; not simply a signifier of a rebellious or outsider identity then, but also a sign that he was a deeply troubled individual. So what happened between the time of Iggy Pop's career and the time of Richey Edwards'? What happened to change the way that a society would attach meaning to acts of self-mutilation?

In fact, there had been little growth in public awareness about self-harm since the dire warnings of an 'epidemic' of wrist-cutters in the 1960s. Before it could fully 'come of age' and take up its position as what the writer Ethan Watters describes as 'the lightning in the zeitgeist' (2011: 3), it would have to find a home in the broader social and cultural milieu and a resonance within the lives lived and suffered within that milieu. This seems to have happened largely via a percolation through popular music, subcultural motifs and celebrity culture; a process that took self-harm as an idiom that had been slowly and quietly forming through the twentieth century amongst more or less hidden populations of distressed people and their clinicians, and launched it into the popular cultural imagination, allowing it to become a recognised, and as such a *valid* and more widely *available*, way to experience and express feelings of personal distress and social estrangement, adding to what Watters, in describing anorexia, calls the 'gravitational pull of the disorder on the unconscious minds of the population' (2011: 53).

In truth, this process probably did begin with emocore punk and the use of self-mutilation as a statement of an outsider identity and a way of claiming the cache of 'cool' that comes with such an identity (Becker, 1997; Adler and Adler, 2011). It stood as a raw symbol of emotional depth; a declaration made in blood and pain that the person cutting themselves would rather suffer the world than compromise with it, rather cut their flesh and show their feelings ran more than skin deep, than be shallow in the way they imagined everyone else to be (Young *et al.*, 2006; Wilkins, 2008; Adler and Adler, 2011). It was a symbol of brash stoicism, a defiant statement of individual authenticity and, by extension, a condemnation of social superficiality, but it was not 'self-harm' as we understand this term, not self-harm *as* a mental disorder. In order for it to become such it would take a new and more introspective subculture, emerging from emocore in the early 80s in the aftermath of punk and marrying the tradition of transgressive self-mutilation with the suggestion, more commonly coded into the medical and psychiatric conception of self-harm, of psychological sensitivity and personal pain.

These were the goths, who, with their horror-show theatrics of white painted faces, black pseudo-Victorian clothing and vampire aesthetics (Wilkins, 2008), evoked the eighteenth-century Romantic movement and its influence on nineteenth-century gothic fiction. Their style typically referenced angst, personal authenticity and emotional depth on the one hand and an implicit critique of the soul-crushing effects of the bureaucratic and machine logic of modernity on the other (Day, 1996; Gergen, 2000). Trapped between the dullness of normative existence and the failure of the flower-power revolution, goths turned to a playful celebration of all things dark and sublime, and within this context self-harm, now consciously understood and practised as psychopathological self-harm, came to act as a symbol and validation of their romantic ethos; the medical legitimacy of the symptom acting as a certificate of authenticity for the feelings that it represented. In this way, self-harm became popularly associated with goths and for some even acted as an important marker of group identity, although perhaps this has been somewhat amplified in the imagining of public stereotypes.

By the 1990s goth had given rise to more broadly popular subgenres like 'death rock' and 'doom rock', whose stars, people like Marilyn Manson and Trent Reznor, used self-harm as a significant motif within their lives and lyrics. Manson even dramatically and controversially revived the tradition of on-stage self-mutilation but presented it not simply as a theatre of transgression in the style of Iggy Pop, but rather as the artistic mirroring or even therapeutic processing of a more personal sensibility and a more private practice (Manson, 1998). For his part, Trent Reznor wrote about self-harm in the 1994 Grammy-nominated song 'Hurt', which was subsequently covered by Johnny Cash in 2002 to much critical acclaim. The song opens with an evocation of dissociation and the estrangement often connected with self-harm as the narrator tells us that he has hurt himself so that he can 'see if I could feel', to 'focus on the pain' as this is now the only thing now that is 'real' to him. In Reznor's song, then, self-harm gives form to the solipsistic theme that all that is real is the realm of the inner, the realm of the emotions, the realm of personal pain and suffering, and that, by extension, the outer world is somehow unreal and superficial, an 'empire of dirt' as the song later puts it. Themes that speak to teen angst and alienation certainly, but which also in truth speak far more broadly to late-modern society and its prevailing culture of individualism, distrust of society and government, and its near overwhelming concern with the psychological.

Although Manson and Reznor can be understood, musically, stylistically and culturally, to have come out of goth they were also perfectly positioned by the mid- to late 90s to be included in the next generation of this subcultural family. This generation took punk, goth and doom rock and turned them into something more broadly popular, packaging them in a somewhat watered down and more commercially appealing form; more referencing an outsider identity than representing one. While both punk and goth had at various times been described as 'emo', the term was often used derisively 'to dismiss something that's overly weepy, self-indulgent, or unironic' (Greenwald, 2003: 2), but this new movement more or less claimed the term as its own and used it to represent an overt, even proud, concern with emotional depth, self-reflection and personal authenticity (Simon and Kelly, 2007). The emo subculture is what the music publicist Tristin Laughter sums up as the 'connection between twentieth-century American punk and nineteenth-century French romanticism' (quoted in Greenwald, 2003: 3). It has enjoyed a far greater following than punk or goth could ever boast, and is stereotypically linked to a personal style characterised by emotional sensitivity, shyness and angst, and like its parent trends has been linked to self-harm for these same reasons. In an interview in 1999 with *Mademoiselle* magazine emo icon and actress Christina Ricci commented that 'sometimes the idea of self-destruction is very romantic'.[1] While in an interview in 2000 with *SPIN* magazine emo rock singer Courtney Love talked about her own history of self-harm and commented:

> I think self-destructiveness is given a really bad rap. I think self-destructiveness can also mean self-reflection, can mean poetic sensibility, it can mean a hedonism and a libertarianism and a lack of judgement.[2]

Whatever the actual demographic truth of the link between emo and nonsuicidal self-injury it is undeniable that self-harm stands as a significant symbolic motif in emo music and culture representing the symptomatic expression of a sensitive soul in a less than understanding world. Indeed, while the the Manic Street Preachers are not exactly an emo band as such, Richey Edwards stands as a notable icon of emo and the embodiment of its style, ethos and attitude. Emo's combination of broad popular youth appeal and interest in self-harm has, of course, led to the all-too-depressingly predictable tabloid moral panic, with the the *Daily Mail* asking in 2001 'Is Rock Music Destroying Our Children?', a headline that was placed next to Edwards' '4REAL' picture (Jovanovic, 2010: 100), while in 2008 they described emo as a 'sinister cult' (Rawstorne, 2008), and the *Telegraph* called it a 'self-harming youth cult that glamorises death' (Alleyne, 2008).

It is perhaps all too easy to be carried along by such overreactions or, alternatively, dismiss the role of self-harm in such youth subcultures as nothing more than an affectation, a fad and the very definition of inauthentic for that very reason. But it would be as wrong to dismiss the role of self-harm within these subcultures as something that cannot serve as a genuine and potent vehicle for deep-seated thoughts and feelings as it would be to believe with the tabloids that it is music, style and peer pressure alone that leads to prolific or problematic self-harm and even suicide. But in either case the role of young people and youth subcultural media is only part of the story of how self-harm 'came of age'. It was also in the mid-90s that a number of high-profile celebrity confessions outside of the music industry were to help secure broader public attention and recognition for self-harm, and none was more high profile than that of Princess Diana who made her confession on a BBC *Panorama* interview in 1995. Apparently feeling trapped by her public role and her dysfunctional marriage to Prince Charles, she had resorted to acts of self-injury both in front of him and in private. Her biographer, Andrew Morton (1998), later elaborated on these events, reporting that she had thrown herself into a glass cabinet at Kensington Palace, had thrown herself down a flight of stairs, and that she had at various times cut herself using razor blades, a penknife and a lemon slicer. On one occasion, during an argument with Charles on an airplane, she locked herself in the bathroom and cut deeply into herself, smearing the blood over the walls and seats. During the interview she explained

> When no one listens to you, or you feel no one's listening to you, all sorts of things start to happen. For instance, you have so much pain inside yourself that you try and hurt yourself on the outside because you want help.... So yes, I did inflict upon myself. I didn't like myself, I was ashamed because I couldn't cope with the pressures.[3]

Diana's 'confession' undoubtedly stands as a seminal moment on the self-harm timeline and it's no exaggeration to say that it produced a shock wave, suddenly and considerably raising public awareness about self-harm, with various clinicians and experts consulted on the issue by radio, newspaper and television. But there was also a sense, much reflected on since, that Diana's revelations changed people's attitudes toward self-harm (Harrison, 2006). It became something that people could admit to on the logic that if she, a princess, celebrity and one of the most loved and popular people in the world, could self-harm then perhaps other people could also admit to the practice without feeling that they were irredeemably deviant, and it has even been claimed that both her confession and her death in 1997 were met with recorded increases in levels of self-harm (Harrison, 2006).

Not surprisingly, as it began to emerge into the public consciousness as a serious issue of social concern so self-harm also began to appear in newspaper and magazine articles. In 1993 Marilee Strong published an article entitled 'A Bright Red Scream' in the *San Francisco Focus* magazine, which she later elaborated into a book with the same title and which represented the first in-depth investigation into the subject by a journalist. In her book she describes self-harm as 'the addiction of the 90s', which, while it is certainly an exaggeration, does help to capture some of the sense typically evoked at the time of a hidden problem suddenly, urgently and disturbingly coming to light, a mental health epidemic. Other journalists soon followed suit, with several important articles appearing in the mid- to late-90s such as 'Scars are Stories' by K. Harrison, written for *Vogue* magazine in 1995, 'The Thin Red Line' by Jennifer Egan, which was a *New York Times* cover story for July 1997, and 'The Unkindest Cut' by Sylvia Rubin, which appeared in the *San Francisco Chronicle* in 1998. It was also during this period that self-harm began to appear more frequently as a theme in films such as *Female Perversions* (1996), *Secretary* (2002) and *Thirteen* (2003), as well as in television programmes like *Buffy the Vampire Slayer* and *Six Feet Under*. In fact, self-harm has become so recognisable on screen that in February 2005 the British Board of Film Classification included it for the first time in its age classification system. Self-harm is now listed as a theme that raises concern under its 'imitable behaviours' category, explaining that such are 'dangerous behaviours... which children and young people are likely to copy'.[4]

But while the emergence of self-harm into public awareness and cultural consciousness has been importantly tied to music, movies, television and journalism, it is undoubtedly through the internet that the biggest impact has been felt and that the largest social vector for this 'epidemic' can be traced. Since the late 90s a distinct self-harm 'community' emerged on the net, active across a range of different sites from video uploading sites, to discussion groups, bulletin boards and personal blogs. Indeed, the number of websites dedicated to self-harm increased by as many as a 100, from 400 to 500, within just one year from 2004 to 2005 (Whitlock *et al.*, 2007). The tone of most of these sites is supportive, and self-harm is almost ubiquitously represented as a 'coping mechanism' and as what Favazza (1996) termed a 'morbid form of self-help', although on many sites the contributions made by people who self-harm can become somewhat conspiratorial and for this reason sites like these are often closely regulated to make sure that hints and tips about harming or keeping one's harm a secret from parents, for example, don't get passed through the forums. That said, a small but significant proportion of the sites dedicated to self-harm imitate the better-known 'pro-ana' (pro-anorexia) sites in maintaining an almost militant connection to self-harm, proudly declaring its practice as an alternative way of life and refusing to frame it as either an illness or even a problem.

Tracing a trajectory from the late 70s to the second decade of the twenty-first century then self-harm seems to have reached a cultural saturation point. In the age of the internet it has become a complex or package of ideas, images, meanings and values that have found their time and come of age, and, of course, it is this process, this coming of age, that has intervened between Iggy Pop and Richey Edwards, allowing the former to be read as a transgressive punk performer and the latter as a troubled soul with mental health problems. Indeed, Edwards could even be described as a famous self-harmer; both in the sense that he was a celebrity who self-harmed and in the sense that he owed at least part of his fame to his self-harm and the public controversy that followed it. Self-mutilation in the age of Richey Edwards not only came to symbolise an illness or a symptom of an illness, but also came to symbolise a kind or category of person characterised by emotional depth, a concern with feelings and personal authenticity, psychological vulnerability, and a sense of isolation and estrangement from a world this person does not understand, at least in part because they feel that the world does not understand them. In other words, self-harm has come not only to represent a mental health issue, but also a lifestyle and an identity. As 'Erica', a participant in Adler and Adler's cyber-ethnography of online self-harm, explains regarding the importance of the online self-harm community:

> Just the fact that there were other people doing it. Maybe like it really is, there's a group of people. I *am* part of this group, obviously. That helped me connect my identity to a self-abuser. Whereas before I was just, like, one of two people doing it so it wasn't really an identity, it was more of a problem. I didn't really think it was a problem, just a habit. Whereas on the Internet it's a lifestyle almost, the way you are, instead of just a habit (2008: 41).

Subjectivism: The Ghost in the Machine

While the history of self-harm is a story told from within an objectivist framework, with the practice itself almost always defined as a basically pathological behaviour and a clinical problem, what this second part of the history makes clear is that this is not the full story, that, as I pointed out in Chapter 1, hegemony is not homogeny and that self-harm is a complex symbolic package made up of many different meanings and values woven together, not all of which are objectivist in nature. In fact, almost every text, representation, theory and model of self-harm is shaped by the gravitational influence of at least two different, primary dimensions or discursive tendencies; the objectivist tendency on the one hand and the somewhat contradictory, somewhat complementary *subjectivist* discursive tendency on the other. This latter stands for our ongoing cultural interest in people's personal thoughts, feelings and experiences, and while the medical framing of self-harm allowed it to become a recognised and thereby legitimate way to express mental distress, it is what Christina Ricci here calls the romance of self-harm, its capacity to evoke a spirit of personal meaning, emotional depth and the ethos of authenticity into the biological machine, that has allowed it to become a profound and pervasive one.

Despite our strong social commitment to objectivism, reflected, for example, in the popularity of genetic and neurological reductionism or the framing of social sciences such as psychology and economics as more like natural sciences, there is a general unwillingness in the public and cultural imagination to give up what Gilbert Ryle pithily called 'the ghost in the machine' (2000 [1949]; Guignon, 2004): the attachment we have to ideas of personal significance and psychological meaning. In trying to avoid the full implications of the objectivist vision of ourselves as the machine-and-nothing-but-the-machine we have tended to settle for an awkward dualism that haunts this machine with the ghost of a more or less unique essence, a personal spark of authentic selfhood trapped within it. And this, of course, is why we have the asymmetric binary. It acts as a kind of conceptual chaperone protecting this cherished dualism from the indissoluble tensions and cognitive dissonance that it necessarily implies, allowing both objectivist and subjectivist motifs, ideas and values to co-exist, even within a single model of self-harm, but only by keeping them strictly organised into primary and secondary, essential form and variable content; the necessary, 'real' and substantial on the one hand, and the ephemeral and nonmaterial on the other. Aspects of the subjectivist paradigm may qualify the objectivist one then, but hardly ever question or undermine them. They exist together and what we see is almost always a mixture of the two, although not an equal mixture and certainly not a blended one, by which I mean that there is no theoretical assimilation of the one to the other, no solution to the tension and dissonance of the dualism, just a commitment to overlooking it, to having your cake and eating it, icing and all.

The relative strengths of these gravitational influences also allows us to grade different representations and texts of self-harm on a spectrum from the strongly objectivist to the strongly subjectivist. Where the influence of objectivism is at its strongest—in medical, psychiatric and academic psychological texts—the effect of subjectivism may amount to little more than an acknowledgment that acts of self-harm, while basically biological or neurological in nature, are nonetheless clothed in thoughts and feelings that may be important to the person who is self-harming and so may have to be dealt with in clinical settings. Less a ghost in the machine then than the simulacrum of a human face placed over it, but as we move through the spectrum of objectivist models from the more naturalistic and biologically oriented to the more personalistic and psychological, we obviously find this ghost increasingly present and materialising more fully. That said, it is important to understand that even here, where subjectivist elements are more pronounced they are *not* normally integrated theoretically into the objectivist-style mechanisms that are still used at root to explain self-harm. Or, if they are integrated to some extent, then as I noted with respect to the affect regulation model these personalistic elements are typically understood as providing nothing more than the specific but nonconsequential content and background details of a given case. Indeed, contrary to a strain of popular belief most psychology is not subjectivist in nature but rather understands subjective experience to be the product of objective structures whether these are conceived of as brain structures or mind structures (Bruner, 1990; Danziger, 1997; Tallis, 2011).

But moving further through the spectrum toward an increasing subjectivism we find a class of texts where the influence of both tendencies is strongly felt, even if they are still not equally valued with respect to cause, nature and explanation, and this typically describes books of popular psychology, self-help and psychotherapy. Here we find a reliance on objectivist psychomedical models of self-harm to define the issue and set out the basic terms of debate, as well as invoke the necessary expert authority, but we also find a good deal invested in the personal feelings and individual backgrounds of people who self-harm. We find, for example, the frequent use of the word 'understand' or understanding' in the titles of these books (see, e.g., Alderman, 1997; Levenkron, 1999; Smith *et al.*, 1999; Miller, 2005; Sutton, 2005; Clark and Henslin, 2007; Hollander, 2008), as well as the common stylistic device of peppering the text with case studies and short vignettes allowing a more human face and name to be hung onto the otherwise abstract and technical ideas that are being explained. We also frequently find poems, written by patients or clients of the author.

Take, for example, 'The Silent Scream' by 'Sian', which appears at the end of the preface to Jan Sutton's book *Healing the Hurt Within* (2005: xxii–xxiii). In describing her self-harm, Sian pictures herself as an 'artist' who 'painstakingly, and with much giving of herself, creates a masterpiece' of mutilation; a portrait of a 'silent mouth' whose 'blood red lips' nonetheless utter a 'silent scream' voicing the pain trapped within the artist. But, interestingly, although she notes that she paints this portrait to be understood by those who 'gaze on it', she also acknowledges that they, and especially those 'who seek to help her', may not understand it.

Here then, a poem that actively makes the point that the poet's strange verses may not be understood by those who 'seek to help her' is used to preface a popular psychology book, a book that enthusiastically takes up the theme of the emotional and personal lives of people who self-harm, even as it translates these lived realities into the standardised terminology of psychomedical objectivism, and searches beneath personalistic content for the structure of naturalistic form. But by this strategy of poetic inclusion texts like this are able to acknowledge and to some extent assimilate the more subjectivist reading of self-harm, using it to provide a dimension of human engagement but no essential information about the nature of the issue being dealt with. The asymmetric binary is clearly at work and while the shaping force of both discursive tendencies is powerfully evident their relationship to one another is not fully drawn out, nor are their inherent tensions properly thought through.

But if poetry is often used to lend flavour rather than substance to texts that have a basically objectivist framework then it is nonetheless the case that these poems, along with some other texts, mostly those produced by people who self-harm, move us much further along the spectrum and stand in themselves as examples of a strongly subjectivist text. Ricci is right, there is something very romantic about Sian's depiction of herself, not romantic in the contemporary saccharine sense but as the goths and the emos understand, in the sense of the tragic, the authentic and the sublime. Sian conjures the person who self-harms as an artist, their corporeal sculpture of blood and pain presenting some of the same challenges as Richey Edwards' infamous picture—namely that such acts are an attempt to express and communicate something intensely personal and meaningful, something authentic and '4REAL', and yet paradoxically are expressed through a refusal to communicate, at least in more conventional terms, and stand to some degree as acts of defiant nonarticulation. Sian knows that hers is a strange verse and says as much when she acknowledges that others may not understand her, and yet despite this there is a sense that because this woman is 'trapped' or imprisoned within a suffering body that she feels does not belong to her, and because her pain is so great and she feels so estranged from her world, that self-injury is the only means of expression and communication left open to her, the only way to break through the prison walls that keep the ghost of her selfhood from the world beyond her skin. It is as if ordinary communication has failed, or perhaps is simply incapable of expressing the depth of feeling that Sian evokes, unable to act as a vehicle for the inner self and cross the ontological divide that separates one person trapped in their body from another person trapped in their body. As Richey Edwards describes his own self-harm he reflects that

> it's also, I think, really connected to the fact that you almost feel, like, silent, you have no voice, you're mute, there's just no, you've got no option. Even if you could express yourself nobody would listen anyway. Things that go on inside you, there's no other way to get rid of them.[5]

This feeling of being rendered 'silent' or 'mute' then is a major subjectivist theme. A condition in which, as Kim Hewitt, explains 'gesture replaces language' and '[w]hat cannot be said in words becomes the language of blood and pain' (1997: 58). The poet and activist Jerry Rubin gives us some idea of why language has failed in this way when he laments that '[n]obody really communicates with words anymore. Words have lost their impact, intimacy, ability to shock and make love. Language prevents communication' (1970: 109). For Rubin, ordinary language has been colonised by the interests of the powerful and the agenda of social management, the by-line of the advertiser, the false promises of consumerism and the spin of politics. In an age of social media and the proliferation of language across new spaces and mediums words have lost their poetic power and subversive capacity.

This, of course, was much the same observation that Lamacq was making regarding the style and music of the Manic Street Preachers. He contended that punk was being marketised and rebellion branded, and it was this very accusation this provided Edwards with little left for authentic communication other than his body. The sociologist John O'Neill (1972) points out that when the use of ordinary language by regimes of social control leaves little opportunity for dissent and resistance through words then all that is left is just such a 'nonverbal rhetoric' of the body. The flesh becomes the site for a more authentic and less compromised communication, something more 'real' or true to self, which lies beyond the norms and conventions of society, beyond its artifice and superficiality. It is this sense of a corporeal 'resort to the real' (Žižek, 2000) that is well illustrated in Brian Patten's offbeat love poem 'Meat' (1971) in which the expressive failure of language, even poetic language, is lamented and the poet vows in frustration 'I don't want to give you these things, I want to give you meat...something that by its rawness, that by its bleeding, demands to be called real'.

Self-harm mobilises the same sentiments and symbols, it, too, is raw and bleeding and it, too, demands to be called 'real'. In this way it takes over the 'failed promise' of ordinary language (Kilby, 2001: 125), and restores through its recourse to urgency, desperation and sacrifice something of the values of authentic communication, of individual self-expression and resistance to social pressure. If Edwards felt 'silent' and that he had 'no voice' it would seem that it was not because he lacked the power to communicate whether through songs, poetry or self-harm but rather that he felt that others, society and the world 'outside' himself, outside his body and beyond his skin, weren't listening: 'even if you could express yourself nobody would listen anyway'. In speaking of the 'afflicted', which is to say the disempowered and alienated, the philosopher Simone Weil argued that this failure of language resides not in the power to speak but rather in the question of who listens. For her the afflicted 'are like someone whose tongue has been cut out and who occasionally forgets the fact.... [They] soon sink into impotence in the use of language, because of the certainty of not being heard' (1977: 332–3). Or as the poet Adrienne Rich powerfully asserts '[i]n a world where language and naming are power, silence is oppression, is violence' (1995: 204). Self-harm, subjectively construed, is intensely personal and private, but it is a privacy that results from a sense of estrangement and alienation from society at large; it is a bruised insular and silenced privacy that implicitly entails a social critique. In this sense, self-harm is the answer to a difficult question: how do you communicate when you cannot use words? How do you express yourself socially, reach out from within your meat machine to touch another human soul, if it is social norms, and the moral and spiritual bankruptcy of society that have sealed you within it in the first place? The only answer must be something transgressive, something like a strange verse.

For his part, Edwards showed a great deal of interest in strange verses, in discovering critical texts of angst and alienation, and through them like minds with similar sentiments to his own. Dante was a favourite and he even had religious images inspired by the poet's work tattooed on his body. Another favourite was the modernist poet T.S. Eliot and indeed Edwards' biographer Rob Jovanovic (2010) makes much of his sense of connection with Eliot in general and his masterpiece 'The Waste Land' (2009 [1922]) in particular. Perhaps we can see a connection here between one of the most difficult and esoteric poems ever written, the very epitome of strange verse, and Edwards' own corporeal poetry of self-mutilation, but in any case Edwards and 'The Waste Land' certainly shared a vision. Jovanovic, for example, seems to be speaking about both poet and rock star when he observes of Eliot that '[h]e wasn't just writing of personal hopelessness but also of the wretchedness of modern society and the loss of order and faith' (2010: 17). Eliot and Edwards both regarded and reviled this world without order; a world in which people's lives seem to be curiously posthumous, overwhelmed by the mechanised and the rationalised, and without any rejuvenating moral or spiritual impulse. Theirs was an undeniably critical vision articulating a fundamental sense of estrangement from both themselves and their world, a vision characterised by the famous sentiment of drug advocate Terrence McKenna that '[t]he cost of sanity in this society is some level of alienation'.[6] This vision expressed the sense in which neither man could 'bear to live such a life' (Jovanovic, 2010: 18), and within which both appeared as ghosts, or 'ruins', as Eliot might have it, trapped within the machine and 'shored' by the 'fragments' of strange verse that they drew strength from (Eliot, 2009: from 'The Waste Land' line 430).

Of course, since the '4REAL' incident, Edwards' own life, his lyrics and comments on self-harm, and the '4REAL' picture itself, have all been endlessly debated in biographies and internet forums, and as such have become texts available to other people exploring similar sentiments and outsider identities, just as Dante and Eliot were available to Edwards. As such, he has taken on an iconic status, his name cropping up frequently on self-harm websites, while a visit to these websites, as well as those that are dedicated to him alone, will show that many of the members of his cult were just a few years old when he went missing, strongly suggesting that, somewhat like Kurt Cobain (who also self-harmed), his ongoing relevance lies less in the remembrances of a generation that grew up with him in the 90s than in the iconic function of the enigmatic and romantic image that has shaped his memory in the years since. An image and a memory that is an instantly recognisable, even stereotypical, archetype of tragic introspected youth and the misunderstood romantic poet. An image that is significantly crystallised in his self-harm, both private and public, although it is important to realise that none of this means that his thoughts, feelings and actions were any the less genuine for it.

Still, as strong a subjectivism as we find here with Richey Edwards and Sian, the framing power of objectivism is still present and informing, and perhaps this is all we can expect in such a psychologised and medicalised culture (De Vries *et al.*, 1983; Conrad and Schneider, 1992; Horwitz, 2003; Furedi, 2004). Why, for example, is flesh and blood, 'meat', so 'real'? How has it come to represent a kind of ground zero reference point and guarantor of authenticity? Perhaps this is, in part, the physical cost of self-harm: surely no one would cut themselves unless they had a reason that was at least important to *them*, it's just too damn painful to indulge in as a form of meaningless play. But the association of the flesh and the real goes much deeper than this in our cultural imagination. As remarked upon earlier we have a culture in which the 'real' is understood as the physical and the material, where physics and biology are our ground zero of truth and where 'real' problems are biogenetic in nature, 'real diseases', or else they are 'all in the head' and not to be trusted. The body is available to us as a 'recourse to the real' because it carries this significance and valuation. The irony is that it is only because the objectivist construal of the body as an organic machine carries so much social legitimacy that it can consequently become an available symbolic resource for expressing the authenticity, the validity, of one's highly subjective feelings.

And, of course, the very idea of a ghost *trapped* in the machine demonstrates the degree to which the romantic and tragic dimension of subjectivism depends on the construal of the body as an organic machine. Sian's inner self is a profoundly powerless spirit, less the animating principle of the body than its passive prisoner; conscious within but unable to project itself outward except through the somewhat extreme measure of self-harm. Her body is undeniable, the objectivist 'natural body' (Shilling, 2003) of anatomical maps, medical statistics and postmortem examination (Hahn and Kleinman, 1983; Freund and McGuire, 1999), the dumb flesh that the German philosopher Edmund Husserl argued lacks 'communicative intent' and can 'only mean in the sense of indicating' (1970 [1901]: 275), the way that a lump may indicate cancer or a sore throat may indicate the cold virus. For Sian and for Edwards self-harm cannot be read like a lump or a sore throat; it is not a mechanism of the body at all, something that lacks 'communicative intent', but rather it is an expression of a trapped and indwelling spirit, which, if anything, suffers from *too much* communicative intent, an excess of emotional and psychological meaning that overwhelms ordinary language and leaves them trapped within the body as machine, the body as dumb, meaningless flesh. But it is only because the ghost is trapped within the machine that it, and by extension self-harm, can carry this meaning; it is only because the self is wrapped in dumb flesh that authentic communication requires a violent tear in this silencing and suffocating flesh, or its symbolic equivalent in burns and bangs.

Finally, it is only because self-harm carries the legitimacy of objectivist medical and psychiatric discourse that it can be effectively used by Edwards, and by the goths and emos and many others, as a way of meaningfully experiencing and expressing deeply subjectivist concerns, in particular a sense of emotional depth, psychological vulnerability and social estrangement, while simultaneously using this symbol of objectivism to validate and legitimise these concerns, to say that they are indeed 'real' and not just 'all in the head'. After all, if these feelings lead directly to the raw and dripping 'meat' of self-harm then how can they be anything but 'real'. Here then, between objectivism and subjectivism and within the legerdemain of the asymmetric binary, we have a play of dualism in service to a form of life. If we were constructing a system of logical propositions such play would be fatal, but we are not; we are mapping a cultural system of meanings and values, and such systems do not need to be utterly consistent, cohesive or even particularly rational so long as there is a means by which the cognitive dissonance that is produced as a by-product can be effectively repressed.

The Ghosts in the Paradigms

If the objectivist paradigm offers little help in understanding self-harm as a meaningful practice and not simply a mechanical one, then perhaps it is tempting to fall back on the subjectivist paradigm instead as the other major influence in how we think and talk about it. It is utterly focused on meaning after all; the depth of meaning and the weight of meaning, the burden of meaning and the need to express it, the need to connect meaningfully with other people. But if the objectivist paradigm falls short because of its unwillingness to account for meaning as a formative influence on practices like self-harm, then, if anything, the subjectivist paradigm also falls short but precisely *because* it puts too much emphasis on meaning and frames self-harm as an essentially private and privately generated force characteristic of the ghostly subject, the trapped plenitude of inner selfhood. It represents the logical opposite of self-harm as Plante's 'common' or universal language, which is to say self-harm as the very epitome of a completely private language; a representation of something utterly specific and unique, the intensely personal, emotional and spiritual signature of the individual who is self-harming.

The idea of a private language might seem strange, a language after all, for it to even count as a language, has to be a shared and common communicative resource. But, in fact, this idea of a language which, as the philosopher Ludwig Wittgenstein explains, represents 'what *can only* be known to the person speaking; to his immediate private sensations. So another person cannot understand the language' is quite recognisable (1958: 89, my emphasis). We tend to think that everything we say, do, think and feel comes from deep within us, from within some private inner space, inner self or inner presence—'an enduring, subjective nucleus' as the psychologist Jerome Bruner describes it (1990: 107)—and that because of this meaning is generated from within us, from within the individual person, and exists in the first instance as the completely private possession of the inner self *before* subsequently being clothed in the shared and conventional apparatus of ordinary, public language. It's a popular belief and one that shapes our conscious experiences as much as our psychological ideas, but it has several rather unfortunate and important consequences. Firstly, if it was true, it would seal each person into their own individual mind and realm of experience, and create what Wittgenstein's mentor Bertrand Russell called the 'egocentric predicament' (2009), the problem of how an inner mind can know anything of the outer world or of another's inner mind. Secondly, this would mean that the study of people, the business of social science, would be severely limited as we cannot get inside people's heads to know their intentions, thoughts, feelings and the reasons why they do the things they do. And, thirdly, whether it is literally true or only ideologically so, it helps creates the felt sensibility, exemplified by Richey Edwards and the subjectivist paradigm, that whatever we say and communicate to others will inevitably be a shadow and pale imitation of what we actually think and feel in the depth of our being.

If we accept this popular view, that meanings originate from within us, and therefore also accept along with it the possibility of a private language—the forms these meanings have in our minds before their more or less adequate translation into a public language—then these problems become intractable, and, in fact, much Sisyphian labour in philosophy and the social sciences has been poured into overcoming them over the years but with little success. But Wittgenstein did not aim at overcoming them, turning a Sisyphian labour into a merely Herculean one, but rather at freeing us from this labour all together, at showing us that the whole thing is based on a misunderstanding, which itself is based in language, and at undermining our reasons for logically and linguistically privileging the private over the public and the 'inner' over the 'outer' in the first place.

Of course the dualism is attractive and influential, appearing as it does to be obvious: we have *inner* thoughts and sensations, and we articulate these through a language that by virtue of its being shared, common and public belongs to the *outer* world. But, as Wittgenstein points out, if this dualism was correct then I would have no way of knowing that what I call anxiety, for example, is also what you call anxiety. If our particular private sensations of anxiety are locked away within our minds and cannot be directly compared then as long as we both keep to the rules of language, the rules of talking about 'anxiety', there is no reason for any discrepancy between my anxiety and your anxiety to get in the way of us holding a conversation on the topic. In fact, you could be lying about experiencing anxiety and I would not know; again, as long as you used the right rules in talking about it. More than this: you could be a cleverly programmed artificial intelligence that knows how to talk about anxiety, which follows the right conversational rules, but that never actually experiences it. How would I know? The problem is that under such circumstances exactly what it is that is inside our heads, or even whether there is anything inside our heads, becomes irrelevant to the operation of the outer language. As long as the rules are followed for talking about a particular sensation then the referent of that talk, the sensation itself, falls away and we are left with only the language.

A true dualism of inner thoughts and outer language, then, cannot work and, in truth, we are generally able to compare our anxieties and even know when someone else is genuinely anxious. Contra such dualism there must be a basic connection between mental states and processes on the one hand and language and semiotic processes on the other. What the idea of a private language, and Wittgenstein's celebrated battery of arguments, similes and thought experiments against it, really shows is not that there is no such thing as mental processes, something that would render Wittgenstein a kind of behaviourist, which he staunchly denies, but rather that this basic connection cannot be contained in the inner and private realm of individual selfhood; that it is not so much language that is 'inner' but the mind that is in some sense 'outer'. The fact is that the words we actually do use to express our thoughts, feelings and sensations are quite indifferent to our inner mental states, so we cannot say with Lewis Carroll's (2013) Humpty Dumpty that words mean just what we choose them to mean and that we can each be the 'master' of the language and meanings that we use. Words are not simply spontaneous eruptions springing from whatever we are feelings at the time;[7] we have to match our 'inner' sensations to the words that describe them, and should we mismatch them this has no impact whatsoever on the meaning of the word we have used. 'Happy' does not mean 'sad' no matter how 'sad' I am when I say it. Otherwise put: words do not depend for their meaning on the mental state of the individuals who use them and so are not simply the innovations and products of some inner plenitude.

But to be meaningful words do depend on the whole system of rules, grammar and syntax that governs a language, and as Wittgenstein reminds us such must be anchored in social interaction. Rules require independent criteria without which 'whatever is going to seem right to me is right. And that only means that here we can't talk about "right"' (1958: 92). We can imagine a Robinson Crusoe type of character without anyone to talk to for decades thinking and believing that he has kept his language skills sharp only to be rescued and discover that the shape of his grammar has softened and slid over the years, and that the rules he thought he was following had been decaying without anyone else to talk to and keep his grammar observed and correct. As Wittgenstein argues 'to *think* one is obeying a rule is not to obey a rule. Hence it is not possible to obey a rule "privately": otherwise thinking one was obeying a rule would be the same thing as obeying it' (*ibid*: 81). In short: there cannot be a private language, and the basic connection between language and thought cannot be a connection between an inner self and its private products.

Even the very idea of an inner space or mental realm is deeply problematic for Wittgenstein. Because of the way we use language we tend to conjure this dualism of inner and outer into our sensibilities, imagining two distinct spaces containing two distinct kinds of 'stuff': physical stuff like books and wallets, and mental stuff like thoughts and feelings. But despite this dualism we use the language of outer knowledge to talk about the inner world, framing the mind as if it is a box that can only be looked into by the person it belongs to and therefore giving the contents of this box a secret, private and unique quality. But knowing what is in a box and knowing what is 'in' your consciousness are not really the same thing. As Wittgenstein points out: '[i]t can't be said of me at all (except perhaps as a joke) that I *know* I am in pain. What is it supposed to mean—except that I *am* in pain?' (*ibid*: 89). If someone asks if I'm in pain I don't have to turn my inner eye into the box of my mind to discover if it contains the sensation of pain, I am either in pain or I'm not. But this is how our language encourages us to talk and think about our minds, and it is as a consequence of this kind of inner/outer schema that the egocentric predicament and the idea of a private language can become problems for us. We find ourselves talking about the intractable problem of getting 'inside' someone else's head without realising that we have largely created this problem for ourselves in the first place precisely by talking and thinking about it in this way. It is not so much an issue of getting *inside* the person then but rather of dealing *with* the person.

Of course, analytic philosophy aside, what is empirically obvious but perhaps all-too-rarely contemplated is the fact that the meanings we actually do use in real life are not invented within ourselves at all but rather implicate our minds in vast and complex circuits of meaning that connect the social with the cultural with the linguistic and the material. Whenever we experience and express our individuality, our identity and our uniqueness by the way we speak or what we say, by writing notes, letters and emails, or by writing journals and diaries, poems, stories and songs—in fact whenever we use language—we are not using meanings that we have invented ourselves but rather ones that we have picked up and put to use according to well established and conventional schemas or scripts. We may modify them, fit them to our needs and circumstance, articulate them in more or less unique ways, but we do not create them *ex nihilo* from within. And this is true not only of language defined simply as words written and spoken, but also that broader field of language or semiotics that includes everything from music, clothes and food, to movies, television and art, literature and architecture, religion, politics and sport, and even the grand triad of social stratification, gender, class and ethnicity: all are public, social systems of meaning that we have found ourselves in, and through which we build, inhabit and articulate a sense of self. The truth is, as the psychoanalyst Paul Verhaeghe puts it, 'we are a lot less original than we think' (2014: 39).

We inherit a language from the community that we are born into and we learn to inhabit our world by inhabiting our language. Indeed, in a very fundamental sense our experience of the world depends on the system of conceptualisation, categorisation, classification, definition and judgement coded into our language; a system that maps the continuum of empirical experience, divides it up, organises it and lends it shape and structure (Geertz, 1973; Gadamer, 1989; Bruner, 1990). A private language wouldn't just imply a unique system of signs then, but also a unique perspective and experience of the world, one that would probably strike the rest of us as an extreme form of psychosis. Even the self, the very experiential basis for believing in Bruner's 'subjective nucleus', is itself dependent on social and symbolic interactions. Sociologist Peter Callero notes that 'personal thoughts are never quite real until they are exposed to the reaction of others and tested for truth and legitimacy in symbolic communication' (2009: 51), and certainly the same can be said for our roles and identities and the entire infrastructure of selfhood such that without this recognition we lose our sense of self and we are forced to admit, with the poet Arthur Rimbaud, that 'I am an other' (White, 2009). The sociologist Erving Goffman put it this way:

> [the self] does not derive from its possessor, but from the whole scene of his action.... A correctly staged and performed scene leads

the audience to impute a self to the performed character, but this imputation—this self—is a product of a scene that comes off, and is not a cause of it (1997: 23).

It seems, then, that systems of meanings and values, and of conventions and institutions, and the entire network of relationships and interactions that embody these, in short both culture and society, provide the frameworks on which, and in which, we live, move and make sense of our world. As the historian E.H. Carr puts it, '[t]he individual apart from society would be both speechless and mindless' (quoted in Younge, 2011: 17). This is not to deny the individual person, or the individual and even private nature of personal thoughts and feelings, if 'private' is used here in its vernacular sense rather than its extended philosophical meaning. Wittgenstein himself maintained that '[i]t is important for our approach that there are human beings about whom someone feels that he will never know what is going on inside them. That he will never understand them' (1980: 74). But as the psychologists Rom Harré and Michael Tissaw point out, 'the core psychological phenomena are patterns of meaning' (2005: 18), and while these patterns may be more or less individual and perhaps even unique they are nonetheless reflections and refractions through the lens of personal temperament and individual perspective of the much broader, shared patterns of meaning that make up culture. As Geertz explains:

> [t]hinking consists not of 'happenings in the head' (though happenings there and elsewhere are necessary for it to occur) but of a traffic in what have been called, by G.H. Mead and others, 'significant symbols' meaning anything that is 'used to impose meaning upon experience' (1973: 45).

Thoughts and ideas then are not the 'unobservable mental stuff' of individual minds but rather 'envehicled meanings' (Geertz, 1980: 135), psychological speech acts that exist as articulations of a given cultural language. We have personal inclinations, yes, but these do not warrant a dualism between inner and outer; our inclinations arise from within complex sociocultural contexts, they are shaped and moulded by these contexts, they reflect and bear the stamp of these contexts, and they are really only intelligible to us or to others against the background of these contexts. Our inclinations, our thoughts, feelings and psychological processes may be facilitated by our brains and basic mental architecture just as our verbal language is facilitated by our lungs, larynx, tongue and so on, but our speech is founded in the conventions of our particular language and not in the physical apparatus of speech, and likewise our minds are founded in the conventions of our culture. What Wittgenstein wants us to appreciate is that there is no sublinguistic or subsemiotic realm of thought and feeling where meaning is generated before it is translated into the conventional forms of a shared, common and public language. Rather we learn to think, feel, speak and act, we learn to be a person, within the circuits of meaning and intelligibility that make up our culture and not by looking within ourselves to find a private inner truth locked away from all others. Or as sociologist Charles Lemert puts it, 'society gets under our skins' (2008: xiv).

For Wittgenstein, and for us in our pursuit of good understanding, the point of all this is that there is nothing about you that is intelligible to you that is not also, in principle, intelligible to me. Of course you can keep secrets from me, or lie to me, and in this sense what is 'inside' someone's head *is* private but keeping secrets and telling lies are uses of language, or what Wittgenstein calls 'language games'; they are secondary and derivative practices and rest upon the foundation of a learned public language. But the point is not that we can't have a private thought in this sense but rather that meaning and its forms are not private in origin and it is for this reason that if you were to tell me your secret I would be able to understand it; so even your secret thoughts are not utterly cut off from the rest of existence, locked into their own dimension of reality, rather they are simply part of that great vault of information, including your bank balance and underwear size, that I don't have immediate access to.

And it follows that if our secret thoughts are not private then neither is self-harm. If it was a completely private symbol annunciating an utterly private pain then there could be no hope of understanding it and it would not strike us as a deviant form of expression that we could, in theory at least, relate to, but rather as an impressively complete psychotic break, something utterly devoid of conventional meaning. As it is, we as a society, and not just an isolated 'I', can talk about self-harm and when we do we know what we mean by it even if we struggle with its definition; it is a *shared* part of our personal and cultural symbolism, a recognisable and meaningful pattern, a common idiom or figure of speech in our cultural language. It is only because of this that it is available to us, that it can be picked up by different people and put to use in slightly different but strongly related ways, and in so doing articulate significant issues, concerns and dilemmas to both the person self-harming and, in theory, fantasy or practice, to those others who they wished knew how they felt.

But to understand self-harm as a cultural symbol and a pattern of action, albeit personal, that is rooted in its social context is to do more than just undermine the private language pretensions of the subjectivist paradigm, it is also to undermine the basic approach of the objectivist paradigm and, in fact, the whole idea of finding 'good understanding' in a 'hidden doctrine' concealed within, or what the philosopher Jacques Derrida (1991) calls the 'metaphysics of presence'. By this term he means to indicate the broader pattern into which both the objectivist and the subjectivist paradigms fit and make sense; a commitment to finding the cause and the explanation of things within the things themselves, within some kind of inner substance, essences or 'presence', whether these are modelled as genetic, biological, psychological or spiritual in nature. As different as they are, both paradigms are the product of the same post-enlightenment Western culture, and both are the expressions of this metaphysics of presence.

At root, they represent two perspectives on the nature of the individual, what the sociologist Robert Bellah and his colleagues call 'utilitarian' and 'expressive individualism' (Bellah *et al.*, 1985); they both imply a commitment to explaining self-harm on the basis of some inner *substantive*: biopsychological structures and functions on the one hand, and an essential psychic plenitude of selfhood on the other. Objectivism and subjectivism then, as forms of a broader substantivism, necessarily lead to a kind of centripetal explanatory logic, or what the philosopher Paul Ricoeur (2004) calls the 'hermeneutics of suspicion': a dismissal or suspicion of outer, manifest phenomena coupled with a belief that the unclouded truth always lies behind or beneath, resulting in an inward push in search of a hidden doctrine. But in the light of Wittgenstein's arguments and the failure of both paradigms to describe, explain, understand and make sense of self-harm adequately, perhaps it is this broader substantivism, this metaphysics of presence, that we need to be suspicious of. After all, as the philosopher Maurice Merleau-Ponty argues, it is precisely these outer, manifest phenomena that are 'the source which stares us in the face... the ultimate court of appeal in our knowledge of these things' (1962: 23). They are not the phantasms of assumption but rather the means by 'the sociologist returns to the living source of his knowledge' (Merleau-Ponty, 1964: 110).

The Hermeneutics of Context

Perhaps then, following Wittgenstein, Derrida and Ricoeur, it may be necessary to throw the substantivist subject, the metaphysics of presence and indeed the whole hermeneutics of suspicion into question. But what does this mean for cultivating the kind of good understanding we need in order to interpret strange verses, and what kind of understanding is this when the very substantivist idea of a 'hidden doctrine' no longer seems to make sense? If one of Edwards' heroes, Dante, can describe our initial hermeneutic challenge then perhaps another, Eliot, can point the way to a solution. Edwards' fascination with Eliot's 'The Waste Land' seems, in part, to have been based in its capacity to reflect some of the same attitudes and sentiments that he expressed through self-harm, sentiments Jovanovic describes as 'personal hopelessness', 'the wretchedness of modern society' and its 'loss of order and faith'. For his part, Eliot expressed these sentiments through a refusal to inform or shape the poem around the metaphysics of presence and the whole background of substantivist assumptions that run through our culture. Indeed, like the strange estrangement of self-harm, Eliot's 'The Waste Land' has been subject to any number of interpretations that follow a hermeneutics of suspicion and that have attempted to divine within its oddly fractured and fragmented lines and voices some unifying meaning or hidden doctrine but which have all faltered and been haunted and disturbed by a troubling remainder; an excess of meanings and references that simply do not fit the hidden doctrine that has been proposed—the poem always seeming to mean more. In 'The Waste Land', instead of a neat logical structure spun around a certain central and organising concept, the inner self of the poem so to speak, we find a miscellany of texts from the whole of the historical and literary culture that pervaded Eliot's life, stirred up into a witches brew of references, citations and fragments forming complex ensembles piled one on top of another until eventually the grand assemblage of the poem itself emerges. The point being that while the poem does, in fact, seem to have a sense of self it is one that arises as a product of this process and not one that prefigured or prescribed it.

This collage of citations are the 'fragments' of tradition and meaning that shore up the 'ruins' of a life Eliot could not quite bear to live, trapped as he was in a world that he could not quite understand. In other words, they were the 'traffic' of 'significant symbols', the very things that he drew on to make sense of himself and his experience, to build up a sense of self and identity. Because of this the meaning of his poem cannot be found through the typical *centripetal* push inward to an indwelling presence or essence of selfhood, but rather only by a *centrifugal* push outward *into the tradition, into the culture*, into the semiotic and intertextual weave and web that formed the background to Eliot's life and vision and constituted the living context in which his poem found its shape and meaning. What the quest to interpret 'The Waste Land' reflects then is the fact, already noted, that we build our individual selves and lives from materials that are far from individual, that are collective, social and symbolic, and it is only in trying to understand individual selves or actions within their particular contexts that they can make sense. This is not a hermeneutics of suspicion then but rather a *hermeneutics of context*.

Richey Edwards' '4REAL' picture then, no less than 'The Waste Land', is something that cannot be understood simply by looking within his individual body or mind for the core explanation. It only makes sense when you put it into the context of the culture, the tradition and the texts that circulated, surrounded and pervaded his life and actions; the texts that he drew on to make sense of himself and his experience. The prose and poetry that he wrote certainly, but also the transcripts of interviews that he gave. 'The Waste Land' itself as it was so influential on him, helping to shape and reflect his character and attitudes, and so also Dante's *Divine Comedy* and other favourite texts, texts that he cited and even had tattooed on his body. But as this nesting of the '4REAL' incident gets thicker and thicker we could also add to this list all the biographies, newspaper and magazine articles, the clinical assessments, reports, and evaluations, and, of course, the great volume of comments and contemplations about him on the internet. In this way, Edwards' life, style and actions would be put into ever larger sociocultural contexts supplying more and more of the background of significant symbols, concepts, sentiments, meanings, values, events and social structures that fed into that one incident and so help describe it thickly and make sense of it.

These form what the philosopher Ian Hacking (2002) calls a 'social ecology', the complex ensemble of contingent factors and forces, the rich system of relationships and interactions, that pattern people's lives, their forms of life and their particular actions just as an organism is patterned by its ecosystem. And so as we map this rich ecology surrounding, embedding and supporting Edwards' self-mutilation we would find not only the contexts of punk rock, of late-modern subjectivist and romanticism, but also the context that explains why authenticity is connected to the body, is connected to 'meat', and that helps us to understand the symbolic power of the medical and the psychiatric, the expressive value or sense to someone like Richey Edwards of being ill. Eventually, as we pushed ever outward from the crystallised specific to the general forces acting upon it, and using the one to help us make sense of the other in a constant interpretive iteration (Gadamer, 1989), we would come to some useful limit, the total and complex social and cultural background, the complete *ecology* of significant meanings and sentiments, that were drawn upon, that fed into and that helped produce the infamous event of that May evening in 1991.

But our interest here is not so much in the biography of a rock star as it is in the question of good understanding; the question of how we make sense of self-harm as a symbolic idiom and a complex of sentiments, ideas, feelings and values. Geertz tells us that such complexes imply more than just 'happenings in the head' but rather involve the 'traffic' of 'significant symbols', and Mary Douglas, another of the grand doyens of anthropology, notes with characteristic clarity that '[a] symbol has meanings from its relation to other symbols in a pattern' and it is '[t]he pattern [that] gives the meaning' (1973: 11, my emphasis). So just as a word needs to be placed into the pattern of a phrase in order to make sense, and just as a phrase must be placed into the pattern of a sentence, a sentence into a chapter and a chapter into a text, and, at the very limit, the text itself placed into a whole language, community of language users and the entire complex structure of their culture, so we will only understand self-harm if we also place it into its proper context. This means the rich and complex social ecology of meanings and discourses that provide the conditions within which a symbol like self-harm can be recognised and understood by us *as* a meaningful symbol, as a meaningful way to experience and express personal distress and social estrangement. Or, in other words, and as Douglas has it, the whole pattern of symbols that surrounds and embeds it, its culture.

In a famous borrowing from Max Weber, Geertz (1973) describes culture as the 'webs of significance' within which we find ourselves suspended but which we ourselves have spun. For Geertz, Ryle's 'thick description' is not about the interpretation of private meanings but rather the making sense of personal meanings, meanings that make up a person or a person's conceptual world, against the background of their culture as a speech act makes sense against the background of its language. Geertz points out that it is only within the context of their particular culture that 'social events, behaviours, institutions, or processes...can be intelligibly—that is, thickly—described' (2000: 14). '[C]ulture and the quest for meaning within culture are', as the psychologist Jerome Bruner puts it, 'the proper causes of human action' (1990: 20), and as such they are also the proper means of describing and explaining it.

Again it must be stressed that this is not to deny the existence or the relevance of the individual person or of psychology. The philosopher Ray Monk points out that one of the great advantages of Wittgenstein's approach is that it 'preserve[s] in all their nuances the rich variety of psychological descriptions of other people that we have at our disposal' (2005: 106). It is just that, following Harré and Tissaw, we must take these descriptions as individualised patterns of meaning, personal articulations of the broader system of meanings that make up a culture. These individual, psychological, articulations exist and are important, but the point here is that they cannot exist or be understood except in the context of the broader pattern of system that they are a part of. Self-harm stands as an idiomatic pattern, a kind of prepackaged pattern of meanings and meaningful actions that are available to people to use in slightly different though strongly related ways and across a range of different although somewhat similar circumstances. And, as with any idiom, the general meaning coded or prepackaged into it is a precondition for understanding its specific use and articulation. Psychology is important then, but it is the symbolic pattern of self-harm itself that we must understand and make sense of.

Wittgenstein leaves us with the same psychological individual that we always thought we knew and all the things that psychological language describes, but passed through a kind of grammatical correction or therapy in which he undoes the tendency to reify, to believe that because our language describes psychological objects, states and processes that these must exist as substantive things (Harré and Tissaw, 2005; Mulhall, 2008). After Wittgenstein, psychological language is largely not to be taken as an ontological or analytic language but rather a descriptive one. Similarly, even though both the objectivist and subjectivist paradigms have failed to explain self-harm they are still useful in trying to make sense of it because they describe different dimensions of the complex of meanings that make up self-harm's symbolism and represent a common cultural cosmology and mythology. And this is really the point, to be kept firmly in mind in the analytic chapters ahead of us, that for this kind of exploration and mapping of cultural meanings we must understand psychology less as an academic discipline or a legitimate epistemological approach to asking and answering questions about people, and more like a socially pervasive metaphysics or cultural cosmology: one of the dominant dimensions of our social ecology and a popular and pervasive way of describing our lives and ourselves, and of encoding late-modern concerns and questions.

This implies more than just the collected statements and discourses, institutions, experts, relationships, practices and technologies grouped in front of the prefix 'psy' (psychology, psychiatry, psychotherapy, etc.), the 'psy-complex' (Stainton Rodgers, 1991; Rose, 1985, 1998), but implicates a broader social and historical frame that takes the human subject as its primary object of knowledge (Foucault, 2001), and which understands the psyche more than anything else to be the essential and defining characteristic of this humanity. It reaches far beyond the covers of textbooks, the walls of consulting rooms and the halls of university departments, and finds itself reflected through numerous social sites, many of which have no overt connection to the psy-complex as such. A significant aspect of this spread of the psychological, especially in recent decades, is the spread of a general psychotherapeutic sensibility and adherence to therapeutic technologies evident in the media and public consciousness, but also in the work place, domestic sphere, services and government (Moskowitz, 2001). Through the second half of the twentieth century psychotherapy went from being a clinical to a normative presence in our society, something that was considered a general good and good for generally everyone, developing from elaborations of therapeutic techniques to a more widely established 'therapy culture' (Furedi, 2004). Indeed, as the historian Eva Moskowitz explains,

> We live in an age consumed by worship of the psyche...we share a belief that feelings are sacred and salvation lies in self-esteem, that happiness is the ultimate goal and psychological healing the means...Our world outlook has been profoundly shaped by this faith. Not only our personal lives but the entire landscape of human events (2001: 1).

In late-modern society 'psychology' has come to stand for more than just an academic discipline, or even a complex of social institutions characterised by fine-grained, although admittedly significant internal differences, but rather represents the 'the creed of our times' (Herman, 1995: 1), 'telling us how to work, how to live, how to love and even how to play' (Dineen, 1999: 3). More than this it tells us who and what we are, and why we do the things we do (Bellah et al., 1985; Rose, 1998, 1991). Indeed, the most powerfully influential dimension of the social ecology surrounding and pervading Richey Edwards and the '4REAL' incident is 'the psychological' and the very idea of self-harm and the category of 'the self-harmer' as a particular kind of person are irreducibly psychological ideas and can really only makes sense within the social ecology of a psychologised culture (Hacking, 1995). The analysis contained in the chapters that follow will contain much psychological language but it must be remembered that these are appearing here as structures of meaning and descriptions of experience. The experience is real and the psychological terms used are our common cultural labels and descriptions for experiences, but we must keep Wittgenstein in mind and remember that just because we describe and experience psychological phenomena in this way does not mean that we are making statements about causal structures within our minds, let alone revealing the hidden doctrine within.

Our task then is to describe and map the complex of meanings that make up the symbolic idiom of self-harm and trace them back along what Susan Bordo calls 'axes of continuity' (2003: 142) into the broader cultural milieu from which they emerged. The meanings we find will tell us why self-harm can stand as part of our late-modern repertoire of meaningful actions, why it is a possible and available way to experience and express personal distress and social estrangement. And the connections these meanings bear to the broader cultural milieu or surrounding social ecology will help us to identify the particular social dilemmas and problems that underpin it, and that are symbolically indicated by it in its capacity as, to paraphrase Bordo, the characteristic expression of its society and the very 'crystallization of its discourses and contradictions' (*ibid*: 141). The method we will use to accomplish this task, and which has been used before to explore and analyse idioms of mental disorder (Hacking, 1995, 2002; Bordo, 2003), is one derived from what Foucault called 'archaeology' (2001, 2002). Of course, here 'archaeology' is just another metaphor for the hermeneutics of context, referring to the fact that archaeologists interpret the meaning of a cultural artefact that they have dug up by placing it within the context of the overall site they are excavating, pottery in a temple perhaps meaning something different than pottery found in a private house.

Foucault's archaeology seeks to contextualise the cultural artefact of an idea or concept into the background of more general and largely implicit meanings and values, the discourses, which are active and influential in the social ecology and which allow this artefact to make sense, to be for the people within that culture part of the 'constellation of the thinkable' (Downing, 2008: 10) to which we might also add the repertoire of the do-able. Archaeology is a way 'of analysing and coming to understand the conditions of possibility for ideas' (Hacking, 1986), what makes them intelligible and meaningful in a given cultural context. That said, our interest will also be to consider the way that the constellation of the thinkable, animated by power relationships and manifested through particular kinds of technologies, practices and ways of life, helps to inform and shape subjectivity and people's sense and experience of self; an interest that Foucault (1998) considered a development of his archaeological method and which he associated more with what he called 'genealogy'. After all, the contingencies and conditions of possibility that are the matrix of a particular pattern of life are never only conceptual but also material and embodied.

Bordo's 'axes of continuity' then are threads on Geertz's webs of significance linking the specific products of a culture in the middle of the web to their broadest sociocultural dimensions and frames at its edges. Although remembering the concerns that I raised at the beginning of the chapter, we must keep in mind that these are not simply axes of identity between idiom and culture, but axes describing a relationship with the idiom standing not just as the product of its culture but as a distorted and exaggerated artefact of its particular problems and dilemmas. In what follows I have largely followed Bordo's approach to archaeology/genealogy; however, I have made a small adaptation to her technique. While she talks, in her archaeological analysis of anorexia (Bordo, 2003), about general thematic axes such as a 'dualist axis' that link dualist concepts central to anorexia with dualist concepts central to Western culture, I divide each axis up into three sections that represent different levels of discursive structure. Firstly, at the level of actual representations and understandings of self-harm, there is the structure of the *key thematic discourse*, which is to say a discourse that forms the substance of how we typically think about, talk about and represent self-harm. Secondly, and further along the axis pushing outward to the edges of the web, there is a *discursive complex* that underpins the key thematic discourse and provides the conditions for its possibility, which is to say that this complex provides the rules and conventions through which the thematic discourse is constructed and maintained as a meaningful and perhaps even an authorised representation. And finally at the most general end of the axis is the third section, which represents a very broad formation or *order of discourse*; this helps characterise our general cultural paradigm or what Foucault (2002) calls an 'épistème', and it is this that provides the conditions of possibility for the discursive complex, which, of course, in turn provides the conditions of possibility for the key thematic discourse. The three levels of discourse fit into each other like concentric circles of context moving from the middle of the web to its outer edges, although in Chapter 6 I shall reverse this movement and, having used culture to interpret self-harm, will then use self-harm to provide a critical interpretation of culture and the broad tensions, conflicts and dilemmas that underpin self-harm.

I have identified three principle axes, although obviously this represents the hermeneutic dynamics of this particular research and other axes could be used, or the material of the three axes I have used here could be divided up differently. I have called these three the *ontological axis*, the *aetiological axis* and the *pathological axis*. The names are not supposed to reflect any bias toward the biomedical approach to mental disorder but rather designate in the language of the culture that I am describing (a largely medicalised culture) categories that already exist as structures for organising meanings and values, categories that are 'native' to this culture. The ontological axis deals with those structures and mechanisms that are taken to be natural to the subject and that are implied by accounts of the nature and function of self-harm. The aetiological axis deals with those factors that are thought to be connected to the cause and origin of a person's self-harm. And the pathological axis describes the ideas and experiences associated with acts of self-harm, what happens when the ontological structures mix with the aetiological conditions and a distinct and diagnosable result emerges.

This tripartite division also maps nicely onto the three most common functions or reasons given for someone to self-harm; these are, respectively, to express and deal with problematic psychic forces (usually negative emotions, racing thoughts or disturbing memories), to overcome dissociation and a sense of not being real or not really present, and to express feelings of shame and self-loathing. As I move through the three axes and their internal structures over the next three chapters I shall describe and analyse each of these three functions, but as I have already pointed out it is not a particularly discrete practice and these three themes or functions are not mutually exclusive and as such neither are the axes themselves; rather, they should be thought of in dynamic and complex interaction; making up self-harm not in any additive fashion but rather between them. The next three chapters describe and analyse each of these three axes, moving from key thematic discourse to its underpinning discursive complex to its underpinning order of discourse. I begin with the ontological axis.

3
The Ontological Axis

Introduction: Picturing the Self of 'Self'-harm

The following is from my field diary:[1]

> I met Sally today outside a cafe in Brighton. It was a warm and sunny evening, lots of people sitting around chatting, making white noise, which drowned out individual voices and provided us with a bit of privacy. She was friendly and talkative, in her mid-20s, and smartly dressed in a dark trouser suit as she had just finished work for the day. We made our introductions, which were easy and relaxed, and I went inside to get us some coffee. We sat outside for the interview, which lasted about an hour. I didn't have to do much prompting as she was happy to talk about her experiences.... I noticed Sally using an expressive gesture; a sort of open-handed parenthesis with her palms facing inward so as to indicate herself, or to enclose herself, and alternately bracketing her head and chest. She leaned into this gesture, looking down into it slightly so as to create a space just big enough for herself; physically indicating her personal space and the only thing that occupied it—her. This gesture dominated her body language throughout the interview and now I think about it it's a gesture that has dominated the body language of everyone else that I've met and interviewed so far (early October, 2010).

Of course, it's a simple gesture, usually indicating that someone is talking about themselves rather than the world outside, although in its near rhythmic undulation between head and heart it also emphasises that this inner world is primarily one of private thoughts and private feelings. It is a gesture that physically brackets and isolates the self, stressing a sense of selfhood that is also bracketed in all its individuality and interiority. It becomes particularly pronounced whenever the conversation turns to feelings of isolation and the raw power of inner emotional life. But as common as this gesture may be, once I had noticed it I began to recognise it as part of a broader family of postures and gestures particularly characteristic of depictions of self-harm. For example, on the front cover of Dee Pilgrim's (2007) information booklet for teenagers a boy sits with a downturned head, looking into his lap, his hands palm inward and wrists resting on his knees. Virtually the same posture is depicted on the cover of Tracy Alderman's *The Scarred Soul* (1997), while a version of it can be found on Levenkron's *Cutting* (1999), where a woman is half turned from the viewer, her back arched as she leans slightly forward creating an almost fetal position and a highly private and personal space.

These are depressed introspective postures emphasising not only the lonely sense of estrangement and isolation that many associate with people who self-harm, but also the acute interiority and psychological nature of the practice, its connection to an individual's deepest and most private thoughts and feelings. On none of the books I looked at was the figure of the person who self-harms shown as anything but completely alone, and if backgrounds were included at all then they were vague, general and without detail. What is being emphasised in these depictions is the individual *as an individual*, which is to say Bruner's enduring, subjective nucleus or, in Geertz's famous formula, a

> bounded, unique, more or less integrated motivational and cognitive universe, a dynamic center of awareness, emotion, judgment and action organized into a distinctive whole and set contrastively against other such wholes and against its social and natural background (1983: 59).

In other words, the individual as our society, and, in particular, its politically conservative and economically neoliberal discourses, likes to think of the individual; the individual that Wittgenstein, Derrida, Ricoeur and Foucault warned us about, the individual of our cultural imagination rather than our actual human condition. The multiple and complex networks of social relationships and interactions that embed a person in their life and world, the cultural systems of meanings and values, and the whole living context of a person's existence and experience are all allowed to fade into the background when this conception of the individual is in the foreground, and appearing to us as a profoundly single, solitary and clearly deep figure. The figure in the centre of the frame, marking the place where surface appearance ceases to be all there is supposed to be and becomes instead the cover of a profound interiority, the raw potency of thoughts and feelings and the full naked intensity of a human life.

The one exception I found to this rule was the series of six cartoons in Louise Pembroke's *Self-harm* (1996), a book written by people who self-harm, where she depicts herself in tense relationships with various mental health staff in all but one, and even in this exception a disembodied speech bubble represents the voice of a doctor or nurse. In this book, and bucking the conventions of the literature, we find a description of self-harm as an experience that occurs within relationships, a fact underlined by Diane Harrison's poem 'See Me' (*ibid*: 9), which charts the emotional space between the self-harmer who is trying to hide themselves and the other who sees them and may judge them. 'Who do you see?' she asks, the calm 'surface' or '[t]he person beneath' who '[h]ides from you'. The self is still isolated then, but for Harrison her condition is less an extension of human nature as such, the ontological boundedness described by Geertz, than a product of the freezing up of relations between people, trapping the self within itself, leaving it feeling under threat and withdrawn. However, Pembroke and her contributors are the exception; everywhere else a picture of a person who self-harms is almost always a picture of a person alone—an individual self, lost in the internal drama of their mind and heart.

In this chapter I want to take this semiotics of posture and gesture and explore the contributions that an emphasis on the individual and the private, the psychological and emotional, may make to the meaning of self-harm. I want to explore the implication of the gesture I noticed in my journal, and the related posture used to depict people who self-harm in pictures, and indicate what is perhaps the most obvious yet deeply structuring dimension of discourse at work in the shaping of representations and understandings of self-harm, so obvious as to be virtually invisible, and perhaps so obvious that even when noticed it might seem inconsequential, namely the dimension of 'the self' itself.

Of course, the word 'self' appears as a prefix to the many different terms used for self-harm and in so doing it clearly designates the site of the act, and positions the self as both the victim and the perpetrator of violence. But Favazza's (1996) preference for 'automutilation' in animal cases of what would otherwise be classed by him as 'self-mutilation' suggests that 'self' indicates more than just the site of the violence and the grammar of its action. Rather, while animals may be understood to attack their own bodies under certain circumstances, the implication here, perhaps not fully thought through but nonetheless quite clearly present, is that, by contrast, people always attack their *selves* (Walsh and Rosen, 1988: viii). Perhaps, then, this is another example of the subjectivist tendency haunting a generally objectivist text. Although self-harm can be framed, as Favazza generally does frame it, as a mechanism of the biopsychological system, and conceptualised in a continuum with animal automutilation, it nonetheless appears to be significant that even within this framework such a system is understood to contain or constitute a reflexive, self-aware and human subjectivity.

By returning to the book covers we can see how important this sense of self is. In these pictures it is precisely this haunting presence of selfhood that provides what Barthes (1993) describes as the *punctum* or 'that which pierces the viewer'. Which is to say that element of the picture that moves beyond the mechanics or surfaces of depiction and that instead haunts us with a sense of human depth, of the naked intensity of something personal, and that draws us in with something tender and empathic, that reaches out to us and asks us to witness the pain that is being pictured. Paradoxically, it is this *punctum*, this call to empathy, that is signified by the closed down and introverted posture depicted on posters and book covers. The posture is not only a bodily arrangement of isolation, but also a bodily signifier of it, a message to others that this hunched figure feels unable to send or receive messages, unable to be social and connected. This posture, and therefore also these pictures, are telling us that within the fetal cocoon of this body there is indeed a self, a person, but one who is trapped within this body and this life and that for whatever reason has turned herself away and turned herself within. Perhaps, then, it is part of witnessing and of empathy that we as the viewer, or the reader if these postures are depicted in words rather than images, are drawn in precisely by the enigmatic punctum of a person who has turned away, who has closed down. It is because they have become enigmatic that our desire to understand is engaged.

Interestingly, in almost all of these pictures the eyes of the person, if visible at all, are directed away from the viewer, providing a kind of safety effect; we can look at them and empathise with them but without being challenged to witness them, remembering that Jane Kilby described acts of self-harm as speaking 'with a "voice" so sheer that it is virtually impossible for anyone to bear witness to' (2001: 124). Indeed, in the case of Fiona, the young prisoner with the facial lacerations, it was as much her steady gaze as her self-injury that I felt as a direct demand to 'get it'; I was left unable to play at empathy. Instead, I was being challenged to witness. And then, of course, there is the transgressive and challenging picture of Richey Edwards with '4REAL' carved into his forearm. He, too, looks directly at the viewer and so matches the defiant claim of his words with a demand to be witnessed, recognised, understood and accepted as being '4REAL'. But in most depictions this challenge to witness is diluted into a mere invitation to be interested; a request, or at most an appeal, that the viewer might reach out to this human enigma trapped within the bounded individuality of their body and find within it a self and a voice that is not being expressed, or rather is not being heard. But in either case, the challenge and the invitation, there seems to be the sense, crucially and centrally important, that there is a potently meaningful *self*, a dammed-up plenitude of indwelling spirit, trapped within the closed boundaries and enclosed posture of the body, and so unable to connect and express themselves, and that self-harm is a direct consequence of this condition.

The Expressive Imperative: The Key Thematic Discourse of the Ontological Axis

> I felt so strange that evening—numb but silently screaming in pain. Why couldn't I scream out loud? Why couldn't I show people how much pain I felt inside?... As the night drew in, I sat alone and in silence, holding back the tears I was too afraid to show. My mind was flooded with disturbing memories, most of which had been buried for a very long time. The wall that had contained these memories took many years to build, yet within hours it had fallen allowing the thoughts and images to torment me once more, I couldn't push them back to rebuild it.... My mind jumped from one event in my disastrous childhood to another—I had no control and the volcano inside me was growing dangerously close to eruption. I'd had an unusual thought the night before. It was a thought I didn't want to listen to, but a voice deep inside said it would calm the turmoil. My gaze drifted to the discarded plastic that once held four cans of beer together: as the melted plastic landed on the flesh of my forearm, the screaming inside suddenly stopped and I drifted off to sleep (Allie, email).[2]

Allie's account of an episode of self-harm vividly evokes what Conterio *et al.* describe as 'the pressure cooker theory'; the idea that you must 'get your feelings out' or else they will build up inside you and create a disturbing and dangerous inner pressure eventually risking a potentially volcanic 'eruption'. They note that

> [m]any of our patients... believe that people have to 'get their feelings out' or they will burst. This is the idea of catharsis, that you somehow have to release the unwanted tension into the environment... we directly challenge the belief that every emotion must lead to a physical action of some kind. Self-injurers tend to believe this deeply (1998: 219).

This, of course, is the same model that we encountered earlier under its more academic title, the 'affect regulation model', and as Conterio *et al.* (1998) point out it represents a popular-enough metaphor for self-harm to make their suspicion of it quite unusual. In fact, for many people the logic of the pressure cooker simply *is* what self-harm is all about and constitutes its working definition. The BBC online health magazine, for example, includes an entry on self-harm written by the Royal College of Psychiatrists, which explains that '[y]our feelings of anger or tension get bottled up inside until you feel like exploding. Self-harm relieves this tension'.[3]

This model has an appealing logic to it; it makes sense to us and so softens the otherness of an otherwise strange verse. But this aside it is important to note that it is a product of its culture, as indicated, for example, by the fluid metaphor of 'bottled-up' emotion, which, as the sociologist Deborah Lupton (1998) has made clear, stands as a central trope in Western conceptions of affect. Consider Allie's mind becoming 'flooded' with disturbing memories, or the 'volcano' building up inside her; or consider more generally the image of the pressure cooker conjuring emotions as things which 'seethe', 'bubble' and 'boil over'. This idea of the pressure cooker nicely ties the traditional fluid metaphor of emotions into an explanation of self-harm as working like a pressure valve, perhaps as an open wound breaching the boundary between the inner and the outer, venting off the built-up pressure and providing much needed, emergency relief. As Alyson describes this:

> Whenever I've self-harmed it's been whenever I've been feeling desperate, a really desperate mix of emotions, kind of sad and angry or really frustrated. I just feel like it's absolutely filling me up and it's about to burst out... it feels like I have to let these feelings out and if I hurt myself that will let these feelings out... it feels like a kettle about to boil and there's a lid on it and it's about to explode (telephone).

Indeed, for many of the people that I interviewed self-harm simply is this function of emotional expression and release, albeit with other dimensions of meaning embedded or attached. Karen, for example, describes self-harm as 'the physical outlet for emotional pain' (email) and Susan sees self-harm as fulfilling its function 'when emotions build-up too much and we have nothing else to turn to' (email), while Allie defines self-harm as 'a coping mechanism which is often used when people don't know how else to react to/cope with emotional issues and/or difficulties in their lives' (email). The metaphor of a fluid build up, then, is connected to another near ubiquitous metaphor for self-harm, that it is a 'coping mechanism', a kind of valve in the larger mechanical system of the 'natural body'. So behind this basic metaphor of self-harm as a pressure valve we find a whole background of facilitating ideas and theories that support it; ideas drawn from the Western cultural tradition and that fundamentally shape our notions about the nature of the subject, of emotions and of psychology.

Consider, for example, that the same conceptual logic is at work in the commonly held wisdom of 'get[ting] your feelings out'; a normative injunction of emotional expression and externalisation that is fairly pervasive in our culture from clichéd proverbs ('a problem shared is a problem halved') to advertisements for tissue paper (telling us to 'just let it out'[4]) to online health advice for children ('Sharing your feelings helps you when your feelings are good and when they aren't so good'[5]) (Taylor, 1992: 368–90). It is a concept so normative as to be naturalised and taken as a truism. It sits as the foundational logic of our immensely influential 'therapy culture' (Furedi, 2004), derived as it is from the very idea of a 'talking cure' (an innovation, it should be noted, of only the late-nineteenth century), and underpins its therapeutic confessional commandment (Foucault, 1978, 2003b; Hook, 2001, 2007; Moskowitz; 2001; Guignon, 2004). As the website for the charity The Mental Health Foundation puts it: '[t]alking about your feelings can help you stay in good mental health.... Talking about your feelings ... [is] part of taking charge of your wellbeing and doing what you can to stay healthy'.[6] Indeed, everywhere we turn in contemporary culture and society it seems we are being met with an injunction to talk, to share our feelings or otherwise express ourselves rather than 'bottle things up'. It is what I will refer to here as the *discourse of the expressive imperative*: a common normative prescription based on a particular model of subjectivity that describes the idea of a mechanical, biopsychological, *necessity* to express emotions if we are not to put our mental stability and well-being at risk. And it is this discourse of the expressive imperative that forms the first key theme in representations and understandings of self-harm to be dealt with here, and in order to explore this discourse I want to attend to two subdiscourses that help construct and support it: a pervasive vocabulary of emotions, and the framing of the subject as a deep psychic system.

A Vocabulary of Emotions

The discourse of the expressive imperative describes both a mechanism of externalisation and the category of things that must be externalised. And this latter component is, of course, made up of emotions. Indeed, our vocabulary of emotions is the very flesh and blood of how we think and what we say about self-harm, making up the substance of almost every representation of it. The words and sentences that we use to depict self-harm are fundamentally shaped by our particular cultural construal of the emotions and their dynamics, and so, in turn, representations of self-harm constantly refer back to this broader culture of emotion talk, even to the point of definition, as when Harrison and Sharman write in their information booklet published by the charity Mind:

> [self-harm] may help someone to cope with feelings that threaten to overwhelm them; painful emotions, such as rage, sadness, emptiness, grief, fear, loneliness and guilt (2007: 3)

Or when psychotherapist Michael Hollander writes that

> [t]he two most common reasons for self-harming are (1) to control the extremely painful and frightening experience of overwhelming emotions, and/or (2) to escape from an awful feeling of being numb and empty (2008: 7).

In both the cases stated here the central issue framed is the emotional life and dynamics of the person self-harming. That this also applies to the second point is brought out more fully in a similar statement made by the Cornell Research Program on Self-injurious Behaviour and quoted in the introduction to an information book entitled *Self-mutilation*: '[t]he act of self-injury provides a way to manage intolerable feelings or a way to experience some sense of feeling' (Williams, 2008: 14). One way or the other then, whether it is about managing emotions then or eliciting them, feeling too much or not enough, it is nonetheless clearly all about 'feelings'. While the depersonalisation and dissociation that characterises feeling too little is often defined in these terms as a lack of affect it is nonetheless typically represented as a problem because of the strong negative emotions that such a lack of feeling is paradoxically understood to evoke; feelings of fear, guilt, anxiety and estrangement from self and others. The basic point is, as Middleton and Garvie elaborate in their self-help book *Self Harm*, that

> Self-harm is part of an attempt to find a way of coping with extreme and painful emotions. Self-harm acts are often triggered by difficult emotions, and it is common to see a pattern of people harming in an attempt to bring an end to a horrible emotional experience (2008: 15).

People who self-harm are no less likely to frame and interpret their actions in this same affect-laden register. Karen, for example, describes her self-harm as a 'way of dealing with my feelings when I was upset' (email), while Sadie defines it as 'when people hurt themselves in order to deal with overwhelming situations and emotions' (email). For Katherine, who connects her self-harm to her experiences of childhood sexual abuse at the hands of her grandfather, self-harm expresses a deep seated pollution of her emotional life, as she explains:

> most of the things he did didn't harm my body—he proposed them all as expressions of love and my body couldn't have known anything different—it was my emotions that were corrupted and damaged (email).

In fact, throughout all the interviews emotions were consistently framed not just as the prime movers behind acts of self-harm but as the primary point of reference for *all* experiences, whether thought of as internal or external, and indeed as the most immediate and important context in which we have a sense of self and through which we live our lives. Emotions then, in these texts and in our culture more broadly, are given a privileged role in explaining people's intentions and motivations, whether these are related to self-harm or not. Something of this affective hegemony is illustrated by Karen as she began our interview by making some introductory remarks about herself:

> Today I am really positive and a generally happy person, really friendly and fairly confident but very shy...I get stressed very easily and worry quite a lot, and do feel very down at times...at the time [of self-harming] I had extremely low self esteem, I absolutely hated myself and that's difficult when you're stuck with yourself all day!! I didn't think I deserved anything, thought everyone hated me...so

yeah I think I was depressed and that's where the self-harm came in (email).

The landscape of Karen's life is painted here in the prime colours of powerful emotions. Other psychic objects, such as her thought that she didn't deserve anything, are mentioned, but even these have reference to emotion and seem to emerge as effects of her more basic emotional condition. She displays a strong identification with her emotions, which are used to frame a basic sense of who she is and what kind of a personality she possesses. More than just indicating that self-harm principally makes sense within an emotional register, Karen's words suggest that self-harm takes its place within a whole life-world that is principally framed and interpreted through the same emotional register (Shutz, 1967).

Of course, this primacy of emotion in the construction of life-worlds is hardly restricted to people who self-harm but rather articulates an axis of continuity connecting the structures of meaning characteristic of self-harm with homologous structures similarly characteristic of contemporary late-modern and 'Western' culture in general. Moskowitz's statement that ours is 'an age consumed by worship of the psyche' (2001: 1), meaning one in which 'feelings are sacred', contains the significant conflation of 'psyche' and 'feelings', the realm of the mind and the realm of the emotions, and reflects the hegemonic position that a vocabulary of emotions has taken up within the contemporary discourses of popular psychology, the self-help movement, psychotherapy and even much clinical psychology (Furedi, 2004). Today, for example, we can read in Daniel Goleman's hugely popular book *Emotional Intelligence* (1996) about the desperate need for 'emotional literacy' in our lives and about how failing to acknowledge one's 'true feelings' can lead to personal distress and social failure. Or we can read on the website FamilyDoctor.org that mental health means 'keeping your emotional health' and that 'people who are emotionally healthy are in control of their thoughts, feelings and behaviours. They feel good about themselves and have good relationships'.[7] Today our cultural worship of the psyche more or less means a cultural worship of the emotions (Craib, 1994); a fact that is well illustrated by the discourse of the expressive imperative as in this discourse it is our *feelings* that we must somehow get out of ourselves and that are at the centre of our mental well-being.

Lupton (1998) has argued that this contemporary valuation and even fetishisation of the emotions in late-modern culture is a result of their being understood as extensions of, or emanations from, some sense of a 'true' and 'inner self', that they are

> [G]enerated from within the self in a dark secret place that is somewhat mysterious. It is believed that individuals experience emotions internally first, and then may or may not reveal them to others (1998: 63).

And, as Lupton notes, this idea that emotions come from within allows them to stand for something more 'honest' and 'natural' than the 'artificiality' of culture and the social negotiations and personal compromises of the ego (*ibid*: 89). Because of this, emotions are understood to be the 'bearers of truth about the individual' (*ibid*: 27), the most 'Me' that I can possibly be (Lutz, 1985), and it is as bearers of truth and echoes of a true-self that emotions are represented as something of great inner value that we may have lost contact with and, as the expressive imperative urges us, we now need to 'get back in touch with', to accept rather than repress, and to allow to rise to the surface of our psyche and express rather than 'bottle up'. But if emotions are positioned as the primary reality of life and its constant reference point, and if such emotions are coded and understood to be essentially internal and individual forces, then our lives and worlds also necessarily become coded as internalised and individualised. This is an issue that I shall return to many times; however, for the moment, I just want to indicate this function of the discourse: that part of its work is precisely *to emphasise the internal and the individual, and to present these as primordial and dominant realities.*

But, paradoxically, while our culture has been led by its psychologised and psychotherapeutic values to demonstrate a predilection for the emotional, the general discourse on self-harm hints to us that there may be something more going on; that this fascination covers over a deeper ambivalence within this order of values. As we have already seen when talking about self-harm, emotions can be cast as a deeply powerful and deeply meaningful substratum of the self and psyche, as well as being the very substance from which our selves and lives are made up, but they can also be cast as raw, natural forces that can be 'overwhelming' (Hollander, 2008), 'intolerable' (the Cornell researchers), and 'extreme' (Middleton and Garvie, 2008). And in this latter sense they seem to be like an internal weather system, standing for the psychic climate of our inner world; a natural given that can either be temperate or tempestuous and that we do not create but that we must nonetheless weather.

Indeed, in this very connection to nature emotions are typically positioned as being forces that necessarily complicate the issue of rational agency, and the executive function of a conscious sense of self or ego as we will now explore.

The Subject as a (Deep) Psychic System

> [U]sually I could feel the pent up anger and sorrow building but I'd bury it down deep where I wouldn't have to think about it... when I would cut myself for 'blue' emotion, let's say depression, sadness, abandoned, those kinds of feelings, I'd be resisting the urge to do it, I hated what was coming and I knew I couldn't fight it off, I didn't have the emotional or mental strength to do it; I'd hate feeling the knife draw slowly across my skin and watch it rip apart, but then as the blood came out, it was a sigh of relief; once the blood was out it was done, I'd bled, and I wanted to bleed myself dry of all unhappiness (Susan, email).

Here Susan provides another powerful yet compact statement of the expressive imperative, describing, for example, the psychological suppression that leads to a failure of expression and that therefore also leads to 'pent up' pressure as she attempts to 'bury' her feelings 'down deep' and out of conscious awareness. She also deploys the fluid metaphor evident in the eventual relief that comes with expression and release with the blood symbolising unhappiness and consequently being let out and drained off. And, of course, here she also privileges an emotional vocabulary in modelling psychic forces and processes. Indeed, emotions are the primary palette from which Susan makes sense of and seeks to explain her actions, the foundation and principal mediators of her experience, but significantly also the prime movers of her actions. Notice, however, that Susan not only talks about her emotions as having a certain determinative power, as forcing her toward an inevitable act of self-harm, but that she also frames her capacity to resist this power through the conflation of 'emotional' and 'mental strength'. Consequently, in this statement it is emotion that leads her to want or even need to self-harm, it is emotion that makes her feel she shouldn't ('I hated what was coming') and represents her strength to resist, and it is emotion that constitutes the outcome of the act and the reason for doing it in the first place. The world of self-harm is clearly, first and foremost, a world of emotions, but as foundational as the concept of the individual's emotions is Susan's description makes it clear that this is not unambiguous or without ambivalence.

Of course, the idea that emotions can be a problem for people who self-harm is central to the discourse and ideas of the expressive imperative. All the people that I interviewed for this research would seem, ultimately, to resonate with Deborah's plaintive statement that 'I seem to feel emotions a lot more than other people do' (email). The same basic idea is conveyed by Hollander in his self-help book *Helping Teens who Cut* when he claims that

> By and large, adolescents who self-injure are extremely reactive people: they feel things very deeply and are prone to becoming emotionally overwhelmed quickly. They possess powerful emotional systems without the tools to manage them.... They have great difficulty harnessing their powerful emotions in the service of clear thinking and problem solving (2008: 17).

He builds on this theme in his book, building on and reifying a basic idea through the language of popular psychology to argue that people with high levels of 'emotional reactivity' (those that 'feel emotions a lot more than other people') can suffer from forms of 'emotional dysregulation' owing to their poor management of their 'powerful emotional systems' and, as such, can become subject to disturbing and potentially dangerous excesses of affect. An idea that betrays an ambivalence in the privileging of an emotional vocabulary and an acknowledgment that emotions are not just representative of a benign 'true self' but also possess a problematic dark side, that they can also be

> visceral and primitive, closer to our animal than our higher side. The emotions are associated with chaos, with excess, disorder, unpredictability and irrationality, and even with some degree of social or physical risk for both oneself and others (Lupton, 1998: 85).

As such, the general discourse on self-harm construes emotions as problematically dual in nature; being at the same time truth-bearing emanations of an inner self, and potentially disturbing, somewhat capricious and even pathological bodily forces. Frank Furedi (2004) has noted this same dualism at work in popular psychology in general where there is both a clear fetish for the emotional and yet also a wariness of 'raw unprocessed emotions'. He argues '[c]ontemporary culture does not simply applaud emotions it also demands that *strong feelings* be curbed and moderated' (2004: 33 my emphasis). It is an important observation as it suggests that the point at issue is not the individual *meaning* or significance of a feeling but rather its *strength*. As we have already seen, in self-harm discourse emotions that are framed as problematic are coded as 'overwhelming' and 'intolerable'. And in Susan's and Hollander's statements it is not the specific emotions themselves that seem to describe this dark side of affect but rather the qualities of 'reactivity' and 'dysregulation'. In other words, it is the level of excitation that the emotions are thought to produce in the psychological 'system' that is important, the fact, as Deborah put it, that people who self-harm feel emotions '*a lot more*' than most people, and not the particular emotions themselves; a fact well illustrated by the list of emotions that Susan indicates as contributing to her self-harm. And, of course, this is precisely what the expressive imperative warns us about; not particular emotions and their personal content or meaning but rather a general *build up* or 'dysregulation' of emotions and the risk it carries of disturbing and overwhelming the inner psychic system, thus threatening our self-control (presumably represented by the faculties of 'clear thinking and problem solving' that Hollander mentions).

This focus on the *power* of emotions supplies one sense in which the person who self-harms is commonly represented as someone who is 'deep', where 'deep' implies the almost tangible force or strength of the emotion, as, for example, when Harrison and Sharman write in their information booklet that '[s]elf-harm is a way of expressing very deep distress' (2007: 2). People who self-harm are often represented by themselves and others as suffering precisely because they are a 'deep' reservoir of just such powerful emotions, which they struggle to express and so control. Emotions are framed here as a kind of 'chaotic energy', which, in the absence of adequate control, can become 'dangerous to anyone in their vicinity and [which] weakens the person experiencing them' (Lutz, 1986: 291). As such, both the mechanism of the expressive imperative and the idea of the psyche as a system containing this mechanism can be seen to promote a concern with the rational order of the self and the control and containment of the body. Indeed, it reflects what Lupton following Heywood (1996) describes as

> the ascetic avoidance of excess, the quest for rationality, the transcendence of desire and the flesh. Emotional states, according to this logic, have the potential to disrupt this sense of self-containment. They are impure, defiling, animalistic, and disgusting (1998: 86).

Perhaps this is the reason why the psychiatric and clinical psychological literature describes self-harm as an 'impulse-control disorder' (Knock and Favazza, 2009), or, in other words, the result of a breakdown in the subject's civilised ability to control and contain the chaotic energy of her emotions; her 'reactivity' or inability to enlist her emotions 'in the service of clear thinking and problem solving', as Hollander puts it. Through the discourse of the expressive imperative then the idea of chaotic emotions overwhelming someone's self-control portrays the person who self-harms as an object lesson in what happens when rational management and regulation of the emotions is not maintained; when emotions are not 'processed', *which is to say turned into thought and language and subsequently expressed*, and the only strategy of externalisation left is the 'bright red scream' of self-harm (Strong, 1998).

But beyond the binary dynamic of deep-as-powerful and the processed-as-contained, there also appears to be another sense of 'deep' implicit in all of this. This is the sense of 'deep' that implies a vertical metaphor of the psyche and through which raw and chaotic emotions in their natural unprocessed forms *rise up* from the inner reservoir to threaten the rational mind and self-control. This is the sense in which '[self-harm is] a means of communicating what can't be put into words or even into thoughts and has been described as an inner scream' (Harrison and Sharman, 2007: 2); the sense of Allie's 'volcano' and the sense implied by Susan when she tries to 'bury [her feelings] down deep', the sense which explains why when emotions return from this unsuccessful burial they might be experienced not only as painful, but also as 'other' to the self, as something alien and intrusive. As Harrison and Sharman explain it '[e]motions that have no outlet may be *buried* and blocked completely *out of awareness*' (*ibid*: 3, my emphasis) and '[w]ith plenty of support... [people who self-harm] learn that they can cope with the pain, anger and rage, *which need to surface*' (*ibid*: 9, my emphasis). Emotions are understood, in this sense then, to be deep because they are powerful, and they are powerful because they come from the depths and represent the raw, natural forces of our being. The expressive imperative is not only a matter of inner/outer then, but also of depth/surface and requires the subject of self-harm to be subject to what used to be called 'depth psychology' and the psychodynamics of the unconscious.

Interestingly, then, it seems that the discourse of the subject as system has several functions. It balances the dual formulation of the emotions as both positive and problematic, and manages the potential contradiction, by positioning them within a dynamic system in which it is the power of the emotion and its capacity to disturb and overwhelm the system that is potentially problematic rather than the emotion itself or its meaning. Emotions generally may be seen as highly positive, but the dynamics of the emotions, the degree to which they are processed and regulated, is where the risk lies. In this way the discourse of the subject as a system locates the expressive imperative, and by extension self-harm, despite the privilege of a potentially quite subjectivist emotional vocabulary, within a biopsychological objectivism and works to focus our attention away from the subjective significance of the emotion and onto the mechanics of the system that processes it and the constant threat of 'dysregulation'. This is one way in which self-harm can be modelled and understood as a mechanism, serving as part of the system's strategies of rational management and regulation albeit as a desperate and emergency measure. But, of course, this again betrays a certain characteristic ambivalence. Just as self-harm is modelled as a mechanism in a rational system, an agent of rational self-control, because it is an emergency measure and is therefore positioned at the very limit of the rational as it vents the irrational force of unprocessed emotions, it can also be modelled as a symptom or form of mental disorder. Confusingly, then, it stands in our thinking as both a coping mechanism and an illness, and as the tension between these is not really acknowledged let alone thought through it usually stands as both in exactly the same texts at more or less the same time.

So apparently even when this deep psychological system is breaking down its dysfunction must be modelled along rational and mechanistic lines, once again betraying the influence of the asymmetric binary and the process of looking past. We seem to focus, fetishise and celebrate emotions in contemporary culture, and we often explain this to ourselves as a late-modern reaction to older and more repressive traditions of rational self-control and discipline (Foucault, 1978), a liberation from the kind of values we may associate with the Victorians, for instance, and yet part of this celebratory discourse is the idea that what we actually want is good emotions, which is to say controlled emotions, regulated emotions, emotions under a rational discipline. By casting the emotions as natural forces in need of rational management and regulation the asymmetric binary allows an overt discourse of subjectivist emotionalism to be used as a vehicle carrying the deeper organising logics of rational self-control and containment; continuing to influence and shape the way we think about ourselves, our minds and bodies albeit now under a slightly different semiotic style and emphasis. Under this style the actual meanings of emotions can be effectively looked past despite this general culture of emotionalism because they are framed through the objectivist paradigm as fluid energies or substances within a system, and it is *the management of the system* that is being prioritised and tied to mental health. As such, the person themselves is also looked past, even as their emotional life is being acknowledged, as this life is principally described as an issue of systemic management and psychic regulation.

The Psychodynamic Self: The Discursive Complex of the Ontological Axis

To understand the expressive imperative, which, importantly, stands as both a key thematic discourse organising and regulating what we think, say and experience about self-harm, and a key discourse similarly shaping and managing what we think, say and experience about selfhood, we have to look for the broader background of meanings and values that support and facilitate it; the cultural conditions of possibility that allow it to make sense, that allow it be a meaningful and influential discourse. In order to do this we listen to the philosopher Charles Taylor when he points out that

> [w]e are selves only in that certain issues matter for us. What I am as a self, my identity, is essentially defined by the way things have significance for me. And... these things have significance for me, and the issue of my identity is worked out, only through a language of interpretation which I have come to accept as a valid articulation of these issues... we are only selves insofar as we move in a certain space of questions (1992: 34).

So we must consider in what 'space of questions' and through what 'language of interpretation' is this conception of selfhood defined and constructed. To answer these questions is to identify and understand the discursive complex that underpins and organises the expressive imperative as a key thematic discourse, the language game, if you like, whose rules it follows. Of course, the space of questions that allows for the expressive imperative is perhaps that space opened up by separating the idea of the inner from the outer, and depth from surface, and which by so doing conjures the very presence of a private internal self and psychic system into the human enigma that lies within each face (Trilling, 1974; Elias 2000 [1939]).

The point, as Josh Cohen (2005) notes, can be illustrated with reference to Nathaniel Hawthorne's 1835 story *The Minister's Black Veil* (1986). Here, a New England reverend suddenly decides to conceal his face behind a black veil for no apparent reason and with no explanation given to his congregation. The effect is dark and dramatic. As one old woman says: '[h]e has changed himself into something awful, only by hiding his face' (*ibid*: 98). The veil interrupts the connection between the minister and his congregation, and represents 'a fearful secret between him and them' (*ibid*: 102); a secret which in its being a lack, like a vacuum, sucks in the darkest sins that exist in each townsperson's imagination to fill it. Eventually, on his deathbed, the minister reveals the secret of the veil: 'What, but the mystery which it obscurely typifies, has made this piece of crape so awful?... I look around me, and, lo! on every visage, a Black Veil!' (*ibid*: 106–7). What the minister had made obvious through the oddly trivial act of wearing a piece of crape over his face was the unnerving realisation that each living face can be framed or positioned as its own veil, hiding the inner truth and very essence of the person away from others. Indeed, by wearing the veil Hawthorne's minister had conjured into his own figure the effects of depth and surface and the space of questions, which is driven to ask: what is going on behind the veil? This effect rendered his words and actions into seemingly 'strange verses' the 'hidden doctrine' of which was veiled from the sight and understanding of others. The veil, then, had two principal effects: to suggest an ontology of secrets, an inner self that is completely private, and to suggest through the absolute condition of this privacy a basic interpersonal separation, a basic ontological distance between people, and the impossibility that follows from this of a pure and full communication.

It is precisely across the barrier of the veil that the expressive imperative becomes a necessary but problematic process. In becoming unknown to his congregation the minister also became unable to demonstrate the truth of his self; rather, this truth became a private and secret possession locked within him, and subsequently takes on the character of an essentially inexpressible plenitude. After all, whatever might be said by the minister his veil remains, suggesting that there is always more truth and more essence behind the veil. But just as the veil separated the minister from his congregation so our faces, our bodily surfaces, separate us one from another *but crucially only when they are framed in this way*; only when we think, as our culture does think, as Wittgenstein pointed out, of the face as covering over some inner presence, some inner and private self.

But even more significant than this is the suggestion also present in Hawthorne's story that even as the self who defines herself through this space of questions, as we typically do, becomes a highly private self which is unknowable to others, in as much as this self also *defines herself to herself* in the very same terms, she too may be become a mystery to herself. Not only an enigma of inner and outer, but also one of depth and surface. Indeed, we react to our own veiling through the process of enculturation and the psychology that it shapes, by 'cast[ing] ourselves in the role of helpless martyr, battling powerful and irrational forces within us' (Solomon, 2008: xv). As such, Hawthorne illustrates, decades before Freud published his first psychodynamic work, that the relevant 'language of interpretation' is that psychological language that deals with the hidden depth and plenitude of the self; the language of depth psychology and psychodynamics.

A Culture of Psychodynamic Opinion

Hawthorne may have been writing before Freud but there is something unmistakably psychodynamic in the veiling of the minister and the suspicions of dark motives and hidden desires that are assumed by his congregation. Indeed, the subdiscourses of the expressive imperative also point us toward the essential semiotic cornerstones of psychodynamics through their model of a deep and de-centred subject, their concern with the dynamics of an internal psychic system, the vertical metaphor and layered structuring of the mind that maps conscious and unconscious regions of the psyche, the idea of difficult and even disturbing truths emanating from the unconscious, the tension between the impulses of human nature and the executive control of a rational ego, the therapeutic value of self-expression and indeed the very idea of suppression itself. All of these threads that contribute to the semiotic weave that makes up the discourse of the expressive imperative, and that of self-harm, readily suggest the broader fabric of psychoanalysis and the cultural legacy of Sigmund Freud.

Perhaps the connection was there to see from the very beginning, as Conterio *et al.* use the psychoanalytic term 'catharsis' to designate the very idea of 'getting your feelings out', or as Freud himself put it to Joan Riviere (who took his words only slightly out of context as a good everyday language exposition of the core process of psychoanalysis),

> Get it out, produce it, make something of it—outside you, that is; give it an existence, independently of you (Freud quoted in Riviere, 1958: 146).

However, this is not to say that psychoanalysis is the key method for interpreting self-harm but rather that part of the key may be a more general background of concepts and ideas representing the developed and popularised echoes of psychoanalysis as they have helped shape contemporary conceptions of the self and psyche, and this is what I mean here by 'psychodynamic'. Psychodynamic ideas are those that have a central preoccupation with modelling mental processes as dynamic processes, as flows of energy through a system, and are historically rooted in psychoanalysis but which have evolved through their having been absorbed into the fabric of a general psychologised culture.

That such an important part of contemporary psychological ideology as the expressive imperative should have its roots with Freud should be of little surprise. It is commonplace now, especially in professional psychology, to dismiss Freud and his legacy. However, this symbolic patricide is somewhat disingenuous as, regardless of our personal disposition toward psychoanalysis, there is no questioning the mass of concepts and ideas that has been taken directly from the pages of its books and absorbed, although often under different names, into both professional psychology and our lives and thoughts more generally. Indeed, psychodynamic concepts and values constitute the core ideology of both therapy culture and the literature and social movement of popular psychology; they characterise much contemporary folk psychology and they are clearly evident throughout the general discourse on self-harm. Indeed, what the poet W.H. Auden famously called 'a whole climate of opinion' (2004) engendered by Freud has since become a more tacit collective inheritance, and is now perhaps better described as a whole culture of opinion, a culture that 'play[s] an important part in the way in which people in contemporary western societies now understand themselves' (Barrett, 1991: 115). So much so that the psychotherapist Michael Jacobs complains that

> [O]ne of the difficulties we now experience... is that we can never be sure whether what we observe is genuinely the same as that which Freud also identified, or whether people have been so influenced by his writing (even through the popular press) that they have unconsciously come to express themselves using his concepts (2003: 2–3).

Such concepts, of course, are not necessarily understood or used as Freud intended, so perhaps it is too much to claim that whether we like it or not we are all Freudians now, but as the psychotherapist Ernesto Spinelli notes

> [h]owever much the majority of lay individuals who employ such ideas may have overextended, trivialized or even misunderstood a great many of the terms employed in order to explain or make sense

of their own, or others', beliefs and behaviours, it remains the case that these ideas have entered common parlance, and, in so doing, have shaped, and continue to shape, fundamental views we hold about ourselves (1994: 12).

He concludes that '[l]ike it or not, we (particularly in the West) are the 'children' of Freud and all his many diverse followers, re-interpreters, rivals and detractors' (*ibid:* 13). As much as Freud's public standing and overt intellectual capital may have taken a tumble in the second half of the twentieth century, psychoanalysis has nonetheless emerged through processes of transformation as a general culture of opinion that helps mould and inform contemporary folk psychology (Gellner, 1985). It is this sense of a culture of opinion shaped by psychoanalytic ideas and concepts, rather than psychoanalytic ideology itself, which I intend by the term 'psychodynamic' here.

Of course, the developments and differences between the strictly psychoanalytic and the more nebulous psychodynamic are important and clearly evident in the subdiscourses of the expressive imperative. Perhaps one of the most important centres on the core and defining binary distinction at the very heart of the expressive imperative: namely that between expression and repression. It is the process of repression that tries to 'bury' thoughts and feelings, pushing them down into the basement of the mind and preventing them from becoming properly processed into thoughts and words, and it is repression therefore that is understood to cause unprocessed or only partly processed feelings to build up in the system so creating the pressure that self-harm seeks to vent off. Consequently, in contemporary psychodynamic discourse, as it influences therapy culture and popular psychology, and as it appears in the general discourse of self-harm, repression has become a dirty word and the very opposite of the therapeutic confessional commandment to 'get your feelings out'.

But this formulation of repression is different from Freud's original conception in three important respects. Firstly, Freud did not see repression as an unambiguously bad thing but rather considered processes of repression as a necessary and important part of healthy psychic function. Secondly, he restricted the use of the term 'repression' to the process of *unconscious repression* rather than the more conscious check on feelings implied by its more general contemporary use, which is, in fact, much closer to what Freud meant by *suppression* (Rycroft, 1995). Thirdly, exactly *what* it is that is understood to be repressed has also undergone an important transformation. While Lupton formulates the point of psychoanalytic therapy as 'facilitat[ing] the release of unconscious emotions through talking to the therapist, thus *relieving the pressure*' (1998: 94, my emphasis), the philosopher Richard Wollheim (1971) reminds us that for Freud it was unacceptable *ideas* that were repressed into the unconscious and not emotions; the affective charge connected to repressed ideas being redirected elsewhere as part of the process of repression.

Of course, Lupton's understanding is mediated by the developed discourse of the expressive imperative and its vocabulary of the emotions, and indeed it is this affective conceptualisation of the expression/repression binary that is at work in representations and understandings of self-harm. Nonetheless, the power of the Freudian conception is utterly present within this more general psychodynamics and the process by which the expressive imperative positions self-harm as a necessary mechanism is as easily and justly described in Freudian style as 'the return of the repressed' as by any other formulation. Perhaps it is also useful to think about the contemporary fetishisation of the emotions in the light of this psychodynamic inheritance. As I discussed earlier, the emotions stand as the representatives of nature and natural impulses within the psychic parliament of the mind, and so take over somewhat the role that Freud had allocated to the *id* and the *libido*. Indeed, the representation of the emotions as the *elan vital* of the psychic system and the dynamic natural force that underpins much of our thoughts and actions, suggests that the transformation of the emotions into the primary force of self and psyche may have been based partly in their capacity to re-package the Freudian libido for a supposedly post-Freudian society, being somewhat less abstract and less exclusively associated with sex.

The Psychodynamics of Self-harm

Even with these changes to the meaning of repression and expression, however, the traces of Freud's conceptual innovations can still clearly be found within representations and understandings of self-harm. Returning to Allie's account of self-harm, which I used to introduce the expressive imperative, we find evidence of repression ('most of which had been buried for a very long time'), the blockage in expressed emotion ('silently screaming in pain. Why couldn't I scream out loud? Why couldn't I show people how much pain I felt inside?'), the seemingly independent agency of psychic forces ('allowing thoughts and images to torment me...I had no control'), and their power or cathexis ('the volcano inside me was growing dangerously close to eruption'), ambivalence ('I'd had an unusual thought the night before. It was a thought I didn't want to listen to') and the inner division of the de-centred self ('a voice deep down inside said it would calm the turmoil'), and finally the process of a pathological conversion from a psychic pain to a physical one ('as the melted plastic landed on the flesh of my forearm, the screaming inside suddenly stopped') and the subsequent return to equanimity ('and I drifted off to sleep'). And, of course, reading back over this account, we can also add the importance of childhood experience and the power of psychic trauma ('[m]y mind was flooded with disturbing memories... [it] jumped from one event in my disastrous childhood to another'), both of which are central concerns of self-harm discourse but which are issues that I take up in the next chapter.

Psychodynamics, then, stands as an influential language of interpretation through which contemporary selves make sense of themselves and do so in a way that emphasises dynamism, multiplicity and ambivalence. This is important because like the asymmetric binary, and the general ambiguity and ambivalence that is a more or less pervasive part of how we think and talk about self-harm, the psychodynamic conception of the self allows for what otherwise seem like opposite ways of framing selfhood and subjectivity to coexist in the same model without the constant risk of fatal contradictions or cognitive dissonance. In other words, it allows for a fluidity and a plasticity in how we think about ourselves, a generous margin of vagueness that means we can somewhat alter our conception of selfhood to suit the needs of the context. This inclusive ambiguity has been evident so far in the framing of self-harm as both a rational mechanism *and* a symptom of irrational forces, as both a necessary part of the biopsychological system *and* as an illness, and as both a strategy of regulation *and* an emotional eruption.

But it has also been evident in what the psychologist Kenneth Gergen (2000) considers the key dynamic tension at the heart of late-modern subjectivity; the tension in each of us between a 'romantic self' who seeks in some sense to live through and not in spite of her emotions, and a 'modernist self' who is more concerned with self-control and emotional and psychological containment. Of course, we have already encountered this tension, briefly as it has been formulated by Robert Bellah and his colleagues as, respectively, 'expressive' and 'utilitarian' individualism, and more fully as it is represents not only conceptions of selfhood, but also broader discursive paradigms as subjectivism and objectivism. The romantic self and the modernist self may appear to be at odds by definition but in the psychodynamic model they are brought together through the mutually necessitating order of rational self-management and disciplinary self-control. In psychodynamics we find a language of interpretation that includes a romantic, subjectivist discourse of the emotions and the raw, natural forces that inhabit the psychic system, as well as a modernist, objectivist discourse about managing and regulating these forces and the necessity of doing so in order to maintain good mental health.

So here the asymmetric binary is at work again, allowing the romantic self to be included but only as long as it is governed by the modernist self. But, crucially, note that the modernist self is prioritised and allowed its executive position only because of the cultural value and emphasis that is placed upon the romantic self and its emotionalism. This emotionalism smuggles in logics of rational self-control, but these logics become culturally and personally valued only because they are associated with the vital energy of this very emotionalism. The consequence of this arrangement is that, as a result of thinking about emotions as dangerously raw forces in need of rational self-regulation, the individual self is constituted within our culture as a site of psychological self-surveillance and self-discipline and the discourses, technologies, experts and institutions of psychology are justified and legitimised through this constitution as representing a realm of authoritative knowledge about this site. But this is to move us on from the discursive complexes of this psychodynamic cosmology to the very broad order of discourse that makes it possible and meaningful.

The Psychological Individual: The Order of Discourse for the Ontological Axis

If the key thematic discourse of the expressive imperative is fundamentally embedded in the 'language of interpretation' that is psychology, and more specifically psychodynamics, then as Taylor makes clear we must, in turn, position this language of interpretation as itself being embedded in a broader background; a 'space of questions' or what I refer to here as an order of discourse that makes such a system of representation and cultural discourse both meaningful and significant. As I briefly indicated before, this space of questions seems to point generally toward that *sine qua non* of thinking and talking about both self-harm and psychology—the sense of a basic division between the inner and the outer and the way that the surfaces of the human body seem to us to cover over an inner depth, like the veil of Hawthorne's minister, and in so doing conjure the substantive presence of a private inner self. It follows then that just as the key thematic discourse of the expressive imperative is positioned and finds its proper context within the discursive complex of the psychodynamic self, so, in turn, this complex finds its proper context within the broad order of discourse that describes the idea and the ideal of the Western modern- and late-modern-bounded and utterly individual self that Geertz described at the beginning of this chapter.

Whether or not we emphasise the modernist or the romantic self, or whether or not we emphasise a biopsychological objectivism or a more personalistic subjectivism, what is absolutely foundational in describing, explaining and experiencing self-harm is the nature of the individual subject, the self who self-harms. This is what underlies what we mean and signify in self-harm, and although implicit in the discourse it nonetheless holds the logical position of key site, core and cause of the practice. It is the individual self that is the constant frame within which representations and understandings of self-harm take on their meanings and make sense. Perhaps in one sense it is too obvious a point but it is also an utterly central one: that to understand 'self'-harm one must understand what is meant by this 'self'. After all, what would self-harm look like, what would it mean or signify, without this discursive structure of the self? This is not to ask the psychological question of what kind of a self (understood as a particular kind of personality) might practice self-harm or be particularly disposed to it, but rather to ask the historical and sociocultural question of what *sense* or model of self, what idea of selfhood and subjectivity, is implied in the presence of the word 'self' in the term 'self-harm' such that the latter makes sense in the context of the former.

The Modern Self

Our contemporary culture and cosmology of psychology tends to be focused on the figure of the individual as Geertz described it at the beginning of this chapter. But the conceptualisation of this figure seems to have had the effect of overwriting the history of how we came to conceptualise it in the first place. It typically appears to us as the more or less self-evident product of biological evolution, the natural atom of human existence and the obvious site in which we can find both the cause and the explanation of human actions. To us this individual is not a cultural model that we apply like a convenient myth or a useful theory to help us understand the enigma of human experience, rather it is taken by us to simply be the given nature, locus and determinant of this experience (Lukes, 1973; Rose, 1991; Kvale, 1992; Jansz, 2004). Indeed, it is still hard to persuade people that this naturalisation of cultural prejudices is a product of social processes and not simply a fact of science or common sense. But it has its roots in what the great sociologist Emil Durkheim called 'the cult of the individual' (2008 [1912]), through which the old ideologies and cosmologies that had tied people's lives into a deeply connected organism of culture, more an inclusive fabric or continuum of humanity than a collection of disparate individuals, not only disappeared with the emergence of the modern world in the sixteenth-century, but were also replaced by an overwhelming concern with the figure and the idea of the individual subject, which was enthusiastically taken up as the new cosmology, the new order that consequently shaped our sense of ourselves, our lives and our actions (Taylor, 1992; Elias, 2000 [1939]; Seigal, 2005).

Although the transformation of the medieval into the modern world was marked by a number of massive tectonic shifts in the organisation of European society, from the end of the feudal system to the emergence of the nation state, the beginning of modern rational–secular philosophy, the scientific revolution, the emergence of banks and the birth of capitalism, there was also a longer process of 'detraditionalisation' at work (Giddens, 1990, 1991), initiated at this time but still very much at work. This is the process by which the idea of supraindividual authority, whether divine, cultural or monarchical, has been progressively brought into question, and consequently all the old solidities and certainties have, in Marx's famous phrase, come to 'melt into air' (Marx and Engels, 2008 [1888]). It is the process by which the old 'vertical' structure of society, to use the terminology of the legal scholar Lawrence M. Friedman (1999), was replaced with a more 'horizontal' one.

Vertical society positioned each person within a single, integrated, organic and divinely willed whole; a grand hierarchy or 'great chain of being' (Foucault, 2001), which 'trapped the individual in a cage of ascription...fixed human beings in definite social roles, pinned them to a given position in the world, no matter how they might wriggle and fight' (Friedman, 1999: vii–viii). The freedom of the individual was severely delimited but their place in the totality was more or less guaranteed. However, the transformation into a progressively 'horizontal' society, beginning with the birth of modernity, has meant that, increasingly, the role, identity and social position of the subject is no longer thought of as a given of destiny but rather a personal project, a challenge to 'make something of oneself' and the whole point and purpose of life (Bauman, 2000; McGee, 2005). It is the supposedly broad, flat or 'level' playing field of horizontal society that has allowed for the kind of fluid, free and agentive forms of life and relationships that are the ideal of modern and late-modern society. And if the sociologist Philip Rieff is right in claiming that a 'culture in crisis favours the growth of individuality' (1991: 279), then as Durkheim also makes clear, in Western modernity the loss of an ideology centred on the traditional social group has been replaced with an ideology of the individual, which has become the new ideal and cult organising people's desires, bodies, relationships and concerns (Durkheim, 2008 [1912]).

In modernity, the individual self it seemed had been unchained and set free after eons of social and political servitude, free to make something of himself (the male pronoun is used advisedly) and rely on his own individual resources and productivity. But as Friedman warns,

> choice is often an illusion. People are firm believers in free will. But they choose their politics, their dress, their manners, their very identity, from a menu they had no hand in writing. They are constrained by forces they do not understand and are not even conscious of (1999: 240).

The paradox folded into Durkheim's phrase, the *cult* of the *individual*, must be taken seriously then. While the *ideology* of modern individual freedom was and is indeed a social and cultural reality at work in the modern and late-modern worlds, these are nonetheless worlds in which this ideology often covers over the tight social, cultural, ethnic and gendered ordering and regulation of people (Miller, 1993). It was not so much social order then that melted away in the modern period but rather the obvious and overt operation of such an order over people's lives, which is to say the governing effect of social order in its blatantly coercive modality. This was gradually to be replaced by an order based on self-government, self-regulation and the internalisation of social and political power (Jervis, 1998).[8] In other words, individualism didn't so much replace the governing effects of social order as it re-packaged them from one based on the idea and ideal of a society to one based on the idea and ideal of 'the individual'. Individualism simply was the new social order. 'The individual' here of course is not simply a way of referring to one person in the abstract but rather stands as an ideology and a social institution that shapes the organic, experiential and social lives of actual people (Crossley, 2006). Two brilliant accounts of this process are available to the cultural sociologist: Foucault's analysis of 'disciplinary' society (1991 [1975]) and Elias's analysis of the 'civilizing process' and the rise of '*homo clausus*' (2000 [1939]). As I will discuss Foucault's analysis in Chapter 5, I will make use of Elias's here.

In his classic work *The Civilizing Process* (2000 [1939]) the sociologist Norbert Elias tracks the emergence and literal incorporation of new discourses and codes of self-control and bodily self-management. The increasing humanism that flowered in the modern age, and the emphasis on the individual and its agency as the new form of order in a more horizontal world, found its expression through various concerns with how to control, contain, conduct and civilise one's body. As legal scholar William Ian Miller neatly summarises:

> Elias writes the Freudian developmental story of the individual psyche onto a social and historical process in which the childlike exuberance of medieval man is metamorphosed into the decorous repressed style of the contemporary bourgeois adult (1997: 171).

Elias illustrates his argument through the literary genre of etiquette books that became popular at the time and which convey a more general cultural concern that people's bodily fluids, emotions and erratic behaviours should be kept under strict self-control; the strictness of the discipline increasing with the passing of the centuries until, as a child is taught the self-discipline and self-awareness to control and civilise its own bodily functions until it becomes a decent and vigilant adult, a new kind of individual subjectivity emerged—modern subjectivity, a contained, bounded and vigilant subjectivity, or what Elias calls *homo clauses* ('closed man'), described in the eighteenth century by the philosopher John Locke as the man who is 'master of himself, and proprietor of his own person, and the actions or labour of it' (1988 [1764]).

In other words, in the movement from a vertical to a horizontal social order the forces of social control changed from being explicit and external forces of coercion, to being internal and implicit forces of self-control and regulation (Mennell, 1992). And as the analogy with the body training of childhood suggests much of this process of internalisation was based on a cultivated economy of personal guilt and shame (Miller, 1997). In this way, the aggressive force of the individual's agency, which might be a problem in a society without a strong and explicit vertical order, was redirected into the policing force of its own self-control, and the body became the primary site through which agency and the control of aggression was demonstrated as it was the body and the self that was now the subject's primary possession and project. Under such a civilising process the subject became characterised by firmer, more comprehensive and uniform restraint of the affects... together with the increased internal compulsions that, more implacably than before, prevent all spontaneous impulses from manifesting themselves directly... [this is] what is experienced as the capsule, the invisible wall dividing the 'inner world' of the individual from the 'external world' or, in different versions, the subject of cognition from its object, the 'ego' from the 'other', the 'individual' from 'society' (Elias, 2000 [1939]: 211).

Indeed, the sociologist Brian Turner describes this process as the emergence of a 'somatic society' meaning 'a society within which major political and personal problems are both problematised in the body and expressed through it' (2008: 1) or, we might add, on its surfaces. It is with the emergence of *homo clausus* then that we arrive at some significant sense of the self of self-harm. In this description we have the central concern with controlling the raw and unprocessed impulses of the body and the powerful sense of a natural, ontological divide between self and other across which communication must occur. In the very metaphor of a *homo clausus* we have the sense of a container in which the unruly fluids and emotions of the natural body may build up, create pressure and threaten an indecent eruption. And in the concern with conduct and the rational control of the body we have the common psychological concern, expressed by Hollander, with processing feelings into rational thought and language. However, while *homo clausus* helps us to focus in on the self of self-harm the lens is still a little too wide, the focus a little too blurred; we must now look to what transformations this modern self experienced as it approached and traversed the twentieth century.

From *Homo Clausus* to *Homo Psychologicus*

In turning the self into a site of fluidity and doubt, and consequently therefore also one of self-regulation and control, the 'horizontal' ideology of the modern world also framed the self and the psyche as distinct and necessary objects of knowledge. If our lives are not determined by their place in the social or cosmic order and our fate is not simply a product of the will of God but rather of our own will and disciplined action, then it matters vitally what this 'will' is, where this action comes from and what kind of thing this individual self is that now occupies the *axis mundi* of human existence. In other words, as the civilising process, or something very much like it, produced a central 'space of questions' by dividing the inner from the outer, so it also created the need for an effective 'language of interpretation' that could interpret and embody this new-found interiority; a language that could help mediate the redirection of (sometimes aggressive) agency onto the self; that could provide an authorised regime of knowledge about these newly construed 'subjects of inwardness' (Foucault, 1978, 2008) and along with it a whole regime of new disciplines and technologies for helping the self to control itself (Wagner, 1994); and that could balance the subtle paradox implied in a *socially* necessary regime of *self*-control. Of course, this new language of interpretation was, as I have already noted, psychology (Rose, 1985, 1991, 1998; Hook, 2007).

As psychologist Steinar Kvale points out '[p]sychology is a child of modernity' (1992: 39); it was a neologism of the sixteenth century, an intellectual discipline in the eighteenth century and a recognised science in the twentieth century (Danziger, 1997; Jansz and van Drunen, 2004). It was a product of the changing social and political conditions of modernity and, as such, it is configured with the very emergence of 'the individual' itself which

> is the result of... procedures which pin political power on the body. It is because the body has been 'subjectified', that is to say, that the subject function has been fixed on it, because it has been psychologized and normalized, it is because of all this that something like the individual appeared, about which one can speak, hold discourses, and attempt to found sciences (Foucault, 2006: 56).

Applying the power dynamics of internalisation and subjectification was not just a matter of creating a moral economy of guilt and shame centred on bodily displays and performances, and it was not simply a matter of rendering a sociopolitical order into a psychological one, but it also included the minting, the production, of whole new disciplines of knowledge and their concomitant technologies; disciplines that manifested the new order and provided a sociocultural scaffold to Elias' civilising process. A scaffold that would, in effect, take problems of social and political governance and recast them as problems of personal, individual and psychological governance (Dreyfus and Rabinow, 1982; Rose, 1991, 1998; Hook, 2007). The historical formation of *homo clauses*, the bounded individual, necessitated, therefore, the historical formation of the psychological and human sciences; as such, they represent two sociocultural patterns that deeply resonate with one another. Because of this psychology became the principal strategy and modality of *homo clausus* as it progressed though modernity; because of this *homo clausus* became what Foucault (1987) once referred to as *homo psychologicus*; and because of this the historian Ellen Herman can rightly refer to psychology as 'the creed of our times' (1995: 1).

The curious paradox at the heart of psychology is that it is a *social* discipline and a cultural system of knowledge and technology, but one that is designed to help people become more effectively *self*-controlled and *self*-regulating. Arguably, then, it promotes two different values and implicitly carries the potential for tension to emerge between them. On the one hand we have an emphasis on self-regulation but on the other there is a hostility to precisely those 'behaviour patterns that demonstrate self-reliance and self-control' (Furedi, 2004: 34). Or at least the kind of self-reliance that denies conformity to psychological knowledge and technology. The writer Wendy Kaminer (1993), for example, describes this tension as it emerges in the co-dependency movement. She notes that while self-regulation is lauded as an ideal of mental health it is also understood within the discourses of mental health and psychology to be something that is unachievable on one's own; indeed, the very idea is taken to be an indication of 'denial'. Rather, a person is accepted as emotionally mature and literate only if they admit that they are 'sick' and need help. Here the idea of regulation *is* ultimately *self*-regulation but it is not framed as a naturally occurring quality of the psychological system; rather, it is a cultivated quality and a product of the civilising process and as such one must *learn* to be self-regulating and one must *learn* to listen to one's emotions, to recognise and accept them, and to find healthy and effective methods for expressing them. And, of course, it is the psychological, as a complex of power relations and knowledge claims (Foucault, 1991 [1975]), which provides this help and guidance, which takes it upon itself to teach us how to do these things. It need hardly be pointed out that the dependence on psychological knowledge and technologies is underlined at nearly every turn in books and internet sites on self-harm through the ubiquitous advice to 'get help'.

So while the psychological cosmology emphasises an 'asocial self' (Rice, 1996), or *homo clausus*, it also makes the well-being of this individualised self dependent on the help, advice, guidance, knowledge, technology and intervention of psychological experts (Rose, 1985, 1991, 1998; Parker *et al.*, 1995; Hook, 2007). This conflict can be largely modelled through Gergen's (2000) distinction between the romantic and modernist senses of selfhood, or Bellah *et al.*'s (1985) near identical concepts of expressive and utilitarian individualism. The romantic–expressive self can be understood as the embodiment of the very forces and powers of nature and the natural body that the civilising process seeks to manage and control, and, in fact, the Romantic movement of the eighteenth century emerged from a sense that the isolation and rigid self-containment of *homo clausus* had gone too far, creating a machine sterility that cut people off from the inherent vitality of life, of the body and of nature (Day, 1996; Gergen, 2000). Following the dialectical challenge of this romanticism part of the great innovation of psychology and the evolution of *homo clausus* into *homo psychologicus* has been the synthesis of the modernist–utilitarian and romantic–expressive senses of self, the recognition that, in Nietzsche's (1993 [1872]) language, we need both Apollo and Dionysius, both control and vitality. And we see this reflected in today's culture of psychology and therapy in the valuation of the emotions and the honouring of an inner self as a true or authentic self. But crucially, as we have seen, this valuation and validation of the romantic–expressive self is dependent on its being controlled and contained by the modernist–utilitarian self: so while emotions may be considered good they are only good as long as they are rationally managed, regulated and processed. The romantic–expressive self appears almost as a lure then, a way of selling the necessities of the modernist–utilitarian self without overtly referring to them as systems of self-surveillance and control. But if this is a sell then it is the regime of knowledge, the institutional complex and the multiple technologies of psychology that are doing the selling. What their discourses are telling us is that we are romantic selves by nature but modernist selves by cultivation and through the civilising process, and it is this process that requires experts, expert discourses and expert methods.

What we are describing then is a dialectal process that takes us from the emergence of *homo clausus* to its antithesis in the Romantic movement of the eighteenth century, and from there on to the nineteenth- and twentieth-century synthesis of *homo psychologicus* in which, and through which, thanks to the discursive innovations of psychology, the modernist–utilitarian and romantic–expressive selves were brought into a working arrangement, although significantly one in which the romantic–expressive dimension of life may be acknowledged and even celebrated but only as long as the modernist–utilitarian dimension is still in control. And, indeed, it would seem that the more we explicitly celebrate the former the more we implicitly privilege the later: our love of romance, in fact, turning out to be our dependence on regulation and yet another example of how deeply the logic of asymmetric binarism runs in our culture and psychology.

But this is not all we seem to be describing here. It is impossible to think about the asymmetric binary of modernist–utilitarian and romantic–expressive modes of selfhood and individualism without also thinking about the asymmetric binary of gender (Campbell, 1987; McGee, 2005). The modernist–utilitarian self maps unmistakably onto the traditional conventions of masculinity and as such has worked to position men as the ultimate product of civilisation, as inherently rational, self-controlled and self-contained; qualifications that legitimised their access to the public sphere of business and politics. While, of course, the romantic–expressive self maps unmistakably onto the traditional conventions of femininity and has worked to position women as being all too mired in nature, as too emotional, too expressive, too prone to losses of control, too prone to crying, to being overwhelmed by bodily fluids and, of course, too prone to madness (Showalter, 1987; Ussher, 1991; Appignanesi, 2008). Historically, this has meant that women have been effectively disqualified from the public sphere and restricted instead to the private, to home and hearth, and yet even then only under strict male supervision and management (Showalter, 1987; Grosz, 1994; McGee, 2005).

But while early *homo clausus* undeniably represents a male ideal against which the female could always be framed as underdeveloped, child-like and 'other' (Grosz, 1994; Jervis, 1998), we might be forgiven for thinking that following the romantic challenge, the emergence of feminism in the twentieth century, the successes of second-wave feminism in the 70s and 80s, the migration of women into the public sphere and the emergence as a result of what many consider to be a more feminine culture characterised, in particular, by the psychological and therapeutic focus on emotions and emotional literacy, that at least our contemporary, post-70s form of *homo psychologicus* might represent a more gender-enlightened and gender-balanced ideal of the individual subject. But what we have to take note of here, if only as a step along the way to a fuller analysis in Chapter 6 of the gender politics of self-harm, is that just as the lure of the romantic–expressive self is, in fact, a strategy for validating the management role and continued dominance of the modernist–utilitarian self, so too must we recognise in this arrangement a strategy for the continued validation of masculine management and dominance over the feminine. In fact, it could perhaps be argued that the need to integrate the two dimensions of the subject arose throughout the twentieth century as a response to increasingly tense gender politics and the impossibility of continuing with a universal subject that was explicitly, if paradoxically, masculine. It could even perhaps be argued that our contemporary late-modern form of *homo psychologicus* actually emerged as a response to the success of second-wave feminism and that if 'the personal is political' was the great slogan of that movement and its project of female emancipation then 'the political is psychological' has been the implicit logic at work in the years that followed and that has largely reintegrated the feminine under a masculine culture of dominance and control. But we will return to these themes in Chapter 6.

Homo psychologicus, then, represents the evolution of *homo clausus*, Geertz's bounded individual, into a particularly psychological modality; a modality of psychological individualism that contains within it an integration of modernist–utilitarianism and romantic–expressivism but in the form of an asymmetric binary that privileges the former as a necessary system of self-control and management over the later; a system that is not natural to the subject but rather one that must be learnt from the discourses and technologies of psychology; discourses and technologies that help to cultivate us as people, which civilise us within the conventions, norms and values of our culture, and that help us along to the discovery of our true or authentic self. Perhaps no better example of this complex arrangement can be given in connection to self-harm than the psychological technology of 'talk'.

Talk versus Self-harm

As we have already seen, the *depth* of the romantic–expressive self, what we think of as the natural and emotional side of our psychic system, is understood as an agent of truth and authenticity only when it is being processed through the rational language and regulation of the modern–utilitarian self, the self that carries the encoded values of the *homo clausus*. The failure that leads to a build up of unprocessed emotion is therefore characterised by people like Daniel Goleman and Michael Hollander as a lack of 'emotional literacy'. Hollander states that people who self-harm 'often just don't know *what* they are feeling.... [They] can't identify or label their emotions' (2008: 37, original emphasis). Psychotherapist Steven Levenkron (1999) echoes these comments when he describes the person who self-harms as someone who 'has not had the opportunity to acquire the language of emotional expression'. Indeed, in these texts the capacity to 'process' does not seem to be a natural capacity at all, and increasingly it is framed less and less as a capacity that is effectively cultivated through ordinary socialisation. Rather the privileged vocabulary of the emotionally literate is unsurprisingly a psychological vocabulary (Hook, 2001). 'Processing', then, implies using these vocabularies and technologies of emotional expression, as defined by the psychological disciplines, in order to work the raw prelinguistic and precognitive emotions into rational labels and regular forms such that they may be accepted into the psychic system, and subsequently expressed 'in a healthy way', as Darcy Lyness of TeensHealth.com puts it (quoted in Williams, 2008: 23). As Harrison and Sharman advise,

> The important thing is to find ways to start talking to someone you trust.... A professional should have the training to listen to you and help you reach your feelings and manage them in a different way (2007: 9).

What such processing implies then is the smooth functioning of the expressive imperative and the effective management of emotions without problematic repression, and therefore also without the build up of unprocessed and unexpressed affect. Indeed, recall Lupton's description of therapy quoted earlier as 'facilitat[ing] the release of unconscious emotions through *talking* to the therapist, thus *relieving the pressure*' (1998: 94, my emphasis), and psychoanalysis, of course, was baptised by one of its earliest patients as 'the talking cure' (Fine, 1997).

In this way a kind of spectrum is constructed with optimal processing and healthy emotional expression as discovered and taught through the psy-complex at one end, ordinary expression in the middle (which may not be satisfying but which also doesn't lead to serious mental health problems) and self-harm *near* the far end. Self-harm cannot represent the extreme end of the spectrum as the ultimate act of repression and certainly the ultimate act of romantic tragedy is suicide, and as we saw in Chapter 1 self-harm has come to mean, in Menninger's phrase, 'a victory of the life instincts over the death instincts' (1938: 285). As such, self-harm must be thought of as being *on* the spectrum of expression, even if only as a last ditch and emergency mechanism of emotional externalisation. The spectrum is an implicit and active part of almost all representations of self-harm and presents a rough but influential equation: the less healthy talk there is the more self-harm there will be, and the more healthy, psychological and therapeutic talk there is the less self-harm there will be. Levenkron, for example, in telling the story of a therapeutic encounter with someone called Simone, notes that when he told her that they had work to do she replied by asking 'What work is that?' He answers: 'The *talk* between us that helps you stop needing to cut yourself on your arms and legs' (1999: 79, my emphasis). He explains elsewhere that '[l]acking the words with which to express her emotional pain... resorts to a destructive physical dialogue with herself' (1999: 49), while Susan describes her self-harm by noting that 'I couldn't talk to him [her boyfriend at the time] or tell him how I felt, so I cut it into myself' (email). It is, of course, a very widely held piece of contemporary wisdom that, as Dee Pilgrim puts it in her information booklet for teenagers who self-harm '[t]alking to someone is always good' (2007: 30).

The sociologist and psychotherapist Ian Craib has observed this contemporary valuation of psychological 'talk' and argues that people often think that they 'can talk about feelings instead of having them, that talking itself solves emotional conflicts and leaves us at ease and peace with ourselves and others' (1994: 104). Of course, this power that people think inheres in 'talk' and that Craib refers to is not necessarily talk in strictly therapeutic situations, but rather the use of psychotherapeutic models for interpersonal communication and the management of relationships, presented as they are in our society as templates for emulation and as exemplars of best practice in our social lives (Furedi, 2004). Although psychological and therapeutic 'talk' may be framed as an ideal, as a kind of pure and perfect communication, it also seems to carry a normative injunction. It is how we *should* talk, and we will experience suffering in proportion to the degree to which we fail to talk in this way (Coles, 1987; Hook, 2001). Such is part of the justification for the massive expansion of therapeutic services and therapy-related goods into a distinct and lucrative industry, from individual and group sessions, to books, CDs, DVDs, lectures, workshops and confessional television (Simonds, 1992; Kaminer, 1993; Greenburg, 1994; Cushman, 1995; Moskowitz, 2001). In this way, the disciplines, regimes of knowledge, collections of technologies and networks of institutions that make up the psy-complex, therapy culture and the culture of the psychological more generally have positioned psychology not only as a privileged language of interpretation that can render the depths of our inner system intelligible to us, but also as a language of normative transformation; a necessary extension of the civilising process into modern and late-modern forms of life. Here then, importantly, words and worlds cross and become confused, and regimes of knowledge and representation are also regimes of personal management and social regulation.

Summary

Toward the end of her insightful autobiography, Susanna Kaysen simply states that '[o]ne of the great pleasures of mental health (whatever that is) is how much less time I have to spend thinking about myself' (2000: 157), a comment we can, perhaps, match with those made by E.M. Cioran, who notes that '[n]o age has been so self-conscious', we are possessed by a 'psychological sense', which has 'transformed us into spectators of ourselves' (1976: 139), no matter what we do '[a]ll activities lead... [the mind] back to itself' (*ibid*: 141). It will, of course, be a recurring theme throughout this analysis as the point is made again and again that self-harm and our psychological culture are significantly co-patterned and resonate deeply with one another. 'Psychology', it must be remembered, is being referred to here as psychiatrist Robert Coles describes it: as a cultural 'concentration, persistent, if not feverish, upon one's thoughts, feelings, wishes, worries—bordering on, if not embracing, solipsism: the self as the only or main form of (existential) reality' (1987: 189). It is within this general sense of psychology that we can position the actual institutions and activities of the psy-complex without assuming either a paranoiac conspiracy or a particularly dystopian perspective. But it is also within this general culture of the psychological, acting as a late-modern manifestation of the broader historical and social themes of modernity and the rise of *homo psychologicus*, the psychological individual, that we can understand the emphasis that is placed on the expressive imperative, its implied ideal of emotional communication and its increasingly normative role in our society. The next two chapters will help us to flesh out some of the other dimensions and implications of this; however, for the moment, I want to bring us back to the observation made in my field journal at the beginning of this chapter and underline the fact that the ideas and values organised by the ontological axis map onto the historical, social, and cultural pattern of the psychological individual and at the same time describe the way that self-harm also maps onto this pattern as a distinctly modern kind of practice. However, more than this, self-harm emphasises this pattern and its dynamics, draws our attention to it—even to the point of exaggeration—and in this way it crystallises or draws our attention to some of the tensions and conflicts that are implicit within it and that may arise for subjects modelled after the late-modern psychological individual.

4
The Aetiological Axis

Introduction: From the Psychodynamic Self to Estrangement

> It was never entirely certain what everyone else knew and what they weren't admitting to themselves. For instance, there are mentions in my diaries of my mother rowing with my grandfather about 'what he got up to', which I take now to mean that she knew what was going on, but on the other hand we never told her anything, so how could she be certain?... [W]e were completely locked into the silence and secrecy. I do blame my mother for not stopping it and for allowing him unlimited access to us... but I think it was her own gaggedness that stopped her finding out more, just as it was ours that stopped us telling her. I do find it all very sad—it's like that picture by Magritte of a man and a woman with sheets over their heads. Communication is impossible, and therefore how can anyone really be sure what's going on?
>
> (Dawn, email)

In this passage Dawn talks about her early family life, her relationship with her mother, and the sexual abuse that Dawn and her sister were subjected to by their maternal grandfather, an abuse that continued over several years until he violently raped Dawn at Christmas time, when she was 16 years old. Perhaps not surprisingly it is a history, and an event, that has since made up the mostly undisclosed and unspoken background of her self-harm. Since the age of 15 she has cut into her skin with razors and broken glass to purge through blood and pain the memories of those early years, and the confusion of these early experiences. It was a home life she was later to describe as 'a conspiracy of silence'; a place where communication had broken down, emotional expression was repressed and even the most familiar relationships had become infected with a sense of estrangement. On the surface of it, the family continued to live and function as a family: there was work and school and dinner and bedtime and Christmas, but behind each of these there was a seemingly impenetrable barrier that rendered each member of the family as a definite 'other' to Dawn; as something strange, unknown and fundamentally *unknowable*. In this way she was not only estranged from her family relationships, but also from the conventions of communication and emotional self-expression. As she explains:

> We grew up in a house where truths were never stated, where unpalatable facts were glossed over, and where self-expression was frowned upon... by the time I'd grown up I felt incapable of saying anything. I think this is what I'm trying to unlock, and one of the signs of progress will be when I become more articulate and less tongue-tied about things of great emotional importance (diary).

That Dawn's self-harm should be tied into a fundamental breakdown in language and communication should be of little surprise as the discourse of the expressive imperative has already positioned it as a desperate mechanism of expression emerging through just such a breakdown. In her emails to me she describes how she had become estranged from ordinary language ('I felt incapable of saying anything'), from self-expression ('it was as if my lips had been sown up'), and from her ability to express and experience emotions ('[p]erhaps I'd be better at anger now if I'd been allowed to express it as a child—or indeed, any other emotion'). And through these sentiments the expressive imperative seems to appear, in an estranged modality, to provide a kind of self-evident sense to her summation that 'no one was ever allowed to express themselves and nothing was ever said, it's no wonder I turned to self-harm as the only means of expression I could employ'.

For Dawn, the fault line that the ontological axis traces between self and other, and that frames communication and expression as naturally and inherently problematic, has been torn open by circumstance and the events of her childhood. Now more a gaping abyss it completely separates self from other and renders communication not just difficult but 'impossible'. That her sense of estrangement is rooted in the framework of ideas and beliefs about subjectivity, expression and interpersonal communication that we have looked at through the ontological axis seems to be acknowledged by her and is hinted at by her evocation of Magritte's *The Lovers* (1928). This is an unnerving painting, which depicts the ordinary, even banal, act of a couple kissing but which through lighting, the stark arrangement of elements and the fact that both man and woman are completely veiled from one another as well as from the viewer, also manages to evoke a strangely disturbing atmosphere of dread haunting the very banality of the act depicted. In this picture the cloth veils represent the basic framework of the ontological axis, a definite separation that renders attempts at contact and communication strangely impotent. Like Hawthorne's minister, Magritte has, by masking the figures, summoned the *effect* of both a public surface and a private and psychological depth, each constituting the other and evoking a mystery that can never be finally solved: what is *really* under the veil? Or as Dawn puts it: *what's really going on?*

The cosmology of the modern Western subject then, as described by the ontological axis, problematically conjures both the sense of an inexhaustible plenitude of the unknown into the private space of the self, and *at the very same time and because of this* also posits an impassable barrier to expressing and communicating that plenitude; emotions become *too* deep, our private selves *too* private, and consequently communication and expression are set up as impossible burdens and inescapable desires. Indeed, the expressive imperative seems to be predicated on the very idea of its own limitation, we feel the need to express ourselves precisely because we feel cut off, locked up within ourselves, and ultimately bound by the basic impossibility of fully expressing the essence of one person to another. This inner presence, representing truth and emotional depth, is defined by its dichotomy to the outer world, which, by contrast, represents the false and artificial (Guignon, 2004; Lindholm, 2008), and in this way the subject can be positioned and can become trapped within this web of cultural ideas and beliefs *about* being trapped within themselves, within the inner space of the psychological individual; the whole system of background culture and personal experience becoming a self-reinforcing, self-fulfilling prophecy.

But in as much as the privacy of this inner self and the consequent challenges of interpersonal communication are assumed to be universal features of the Western individual, and as much as Dawn acknowledges these basic problems and difficulties as part of human nature, they cannot alone serve to make her self-harm make sense to her or to us, not as a particular practice and sensibility, not without suggesting at the same time that everyone should be self-harming. It is clear then that she also sees these basic ontological issues as being hugely aggravated by the particular conditions of her early home life and the particular events of her personal history. So while the ontological axis may provide us with discourses about the framework and pressure points from which problems *can* emerge, it does not tell us why, in cases like Dawn's, it is thought that problems *do* emerge; and why indeed some people, and only some people, become pathogenic and turn to self-harm.[1]

Magritte also seems to hint at this need for a supplement. Perhaps anyone can relate to the sense of distance and otherness that characterises even the closest relationships, but Magritte suggests more than just a basic and existential separation. He presents claw-like folds in the veil reaching around the back of the woman's head, folds that carry the impression that the man's hand has grasped her there and taken control of her. It is as if the very space of secrets and the failures of communication created by the presence of the veil also produces the space in which acts of violence and relations of subjugation can hide under cover. In *The Lovers* the banal surface and the sinister depth interpenetrate and constitute one another *as* depth and surface, as *effects* of the boundary positioned between them. The effect is an 'uncanny' one of estrangement (Freud, 2003 [1919]), of the familiar turned other and the banal turned threatening. For Dawn, the same logic played out in the brutal domestic compliment of failed expression and violent abuse; the banality of bedtime and Christmas traumatised by sexual violence, and the familiarity of a mother's words made strange and distant by the impossibility of communication.

The ontological axis, then, does not provide a full range of statements about self-harm but must be supplemented by another dimension of ideas and values, a second axis which complements and extends the first and explains *why* common problems connected to the structure and communicative capacity of the subject as psychological individual lead in some cases, and only some cases, to the activation of self-harm as a mechanism of emergency expression. While the first axis supplies an account within this discourse of those structures which are thought to make self-harm *possible*, this second axis must be brought in to explain what makes it *probable*; not an ontological axis then, but rather an *aetiological* one—an axis of ideas about origins. And if it is the experience of estrangement that shows us that we need this supplement then it is also this experience that forms the next key thematic discourse contributing to common representations and understandings of self-harm.

Traumatic Estrangement: The Key Thematic Discourse of the Aetiological Axis

Of course, Dawn's sense of estrangement is not peculiar to her but rather reflects a key theme typical of representations and understandings of self-harm. Every person that I interviewed for this research articulated some sense of personal, emotional, social or existential estrangement; the sense that a wound had opened up between themselves and their experience, between themselves and their world. It was a wound that left them feeling that life, others, language and even their own sense of self had become strange, disordered and disturbing. As Susan describes her past experiences:

> It was like being a leper who has the disease through no fault of his own, and yet is tossed away and banished for his ailment.... *I felt like an alien* (email, my emphasis).

And as Carla reflects on her past:

> I was so, in so much pain, and my head was never right as a teenager, erm... I never felt belonging or value (in person).

In fact, in one form or another this theme of estrangement has been with us for some time. It was evident, for example, in the statement made by Fiona's facial lacerations, in Sian's sense of being trapped within herself, in Richey Edwards' experience of voicelessness, and in the sentiments of horror and social alienation evoked by the 'The Waste Land', echoed in Trent Reznor's description of the world as 'an empire of dirt' and filtered and refracted through the subcultural ethos of punk, goth and emo. Many people who self-harm feel abandoned in a world that does not make much sense *to* them, and which, in turn, seems unable to make much sense *of* them. As Dawn writes in her diary: 'I don't see how I fit into the world. And then I don't see how it matters. Why *should* I be trying to fit in?' (her emphasis). But while pervasive, this theme of estrangement is also by necessity flexible, nebulous and mercurial, and appears in multiple forms across the spectrum of objectivist to subjectivist representations, although always intimately and complexly tied to the central metaphor of *trauma*.

For example, the more subjectivist evocations of estrangement that we have already encountered rely on a metaphorical and by now familiar sense of trauma, representing it as a kind of rupture between self and world; a distressing tear in the fabric of normal life that has separated the two fundamental poles of Western ontology. The result, as we have already noted, is the common contrast drawn between a sense of inner authenticity and truth on the one hand and a general suspicion of the falsity, superficiality and artifice considered characteristic of the social world on the other. A sense perfectly captured by Louise Pembroke when she defiantly says: 'if that's normal then pass the razor blades' (1996: 15). Yet, despite the confidence of Pembroke's words, it is nonetheless precisely in the context of this sense of disconnection and distinction that voicelessness can occur as neither normal language nor the normal world that deals in it are felt to be fit vehicles for the authentic truth and sincerity, the sheer emotional reality, that haunts the inner life of a person who self-harms, who 'feels too much'. And so we have Edwards' comment that 'you almost feel, like, silent, you have no voice, you're mute.... Even if you could express yourself nobody would listen anyway'. It is what Dawn calls 'gaggedness': the sense of being 'locked into... silence and secrecy'. And trapped in this way what else is there to do but 'pass the razor blades'?

Perhaps this connection of trauma and voicelessness shouldn't surprise us. Dawn's silence is rooted in her traumatic childhood experiences and as the psychiatrist Judith Lewis Herman explains, 'traumatic events overwhelm the ordinary systems of care that give people a sense of control, connection, and meaning' (1992: 33). The idea of post-trauma stress, itself an idea with more of a social history than a natural one, and which reflects our psychological cosmology as much as self-harm (Young, 1997; Leys, 2000), implies that disturbing events disconnect us from the reality that we thought we knew, as '[t]he foundations of our world begin to crumble and the ground begins to shake under our feet. We begin to question our own self-worth and value as a human being' (Parkinson, 1993: 14). Like the representation of raw, unprocessed emotions that we encountered along the ontological axis trauma 'overwhelm[s]' us and submerges those systems of representation, thought and language that we use to make sense of the world and understand it as a familiar and predictable place. Indeed, the *Diagnostic and Statistical Manual of Mental Disorders, 5th Edition* (DSM-5) definition of traumatic events are those that do not fit into 'normal' experience and which therefore cannot be 'processed' through a person's standard and normal ways of thinking and talking (Caruth, 1995). In other words, they represent a crisis in representation. Because they cannot be 'processed', they remain with us as a haunting presence of the too literal, the too real and the threateningly immanent; an indissoluble mass of the seemingly nonsymbolic and unsignifiable. And because they cannot be represented, 'processed' or made sense of, so they also cannot be expressed in language, and as we have already seen what cannot be expressed in ordinary language comes instead to be expressed in 'the language of blood and pain' (Hewitt, 1997: 58)

But in talking of post-trauma stress and DSM-5 definitions we have clearly moved from subjectivist representations of estrangement and trauma to more objectivist ones. Here estrangement appears in less metaphorical and more medical fashion as 'dissociation', an experience common to both self-harm and post-trauma stress, and which, as such, illustrates the close connection, even conceptual fusion, of nonsuicidal self-injury and the psychiatric concept of psychic trauma. Symbolically, of course, this makes both perfect sense and a potent image: the image of an inner, invisible and intangible (psychic) wound made visible, made flesh, made to bleed and weep, or, otherwise put, *made real*, through its expression and literal embodiment in an all-too-tangible injury. In this discourse psychological wounds find their expression in acts of self-injury, while these acts, in turn, find their validity and legitimacy in the technical concept of psychic trauma. It is this mirroring, homologous relationship that, for example, is expressed by *Girl, Interrupted* author Susanna Kaysen when she reflects on her habit of banging her wrists and scratching at her face:

> I was trying to explain my situation to myself. My situation was that I was in pain and nobody knew it, even I had trouble knowing it. So I told myself, over and over, You are in pain. It was the only way I could get through to myself.... I was demonstrating, *externally and irrefutably, an inward condition* (2000: 153, my emphasis).

And if the inward condition of psychic trauma is, as Herman points out, one of disconnection from the world we thought we knew, understood and could talk about, then its symptom is 'dissociation' commonly elaborated through words like '[d]epersonalization, derealization, and anesthesia' (Herman, 1992: 109), where 'derealisation', for example, means a sense that 'the world around the individual is... unreal, dream-like, distant, or distorted' (American Psychiatric Association, 2013: 272). At its heart, dissociation describes a tormenting paradox: a sense of numbness that nonetheless leads to 'a feeling of unbearable agitation' (Herman, 1992: 109), a fear that the self may become utterly cut off from reality or even eventually cease to be real, cease to exist altogether. It is a kind of 'annihilation panic' (Adler, 1985), well described by

Eleanor Hill who, like Dawn, was subjected to childhood sexual abuse:

> I am icy cold inside and my surfaces are without integument, as if I am flowing and spilling and not held together any more. Fear grips me and I lose the sensation of being present. I am gone (1985: 229).

Both the fluid metaphor and a concern with the closed and contained subject as described in the ontological axis are clearly at work here, feeding the fear that if the boundaries are not maintained then the unreality of the world will infect the inner self and it will consequently cease to be a unified presence, a true 'I'. As a response to such dissociation self-harm is often represented as providing a means of shocking the system back into reality, dispelling the clouds of estrangement and reaffirming the boundaries between self and world that had become dangerously unstable. This, of course, is the second of the three most common general explanations for the function of self-harm that I mentioned at the end of Chapter 2. As Conterio et al. put it '[for] patients who feel distanced from reality, isolated, or dehumanised, the sight of their own blood can jolt them back to reality. It reassures them that they are alive, intact, and have personal boundaries' (1998: 64). Or as a poem by an unnamed person quoted in Gardner's *Self-harm* (2001: 3) describes it: a feeling of being 'unreal and distant disconnected with life' leads to the inevitable relief brought by a razor blade. 'Not totally aware [she]...cut[s] into the skin' and is '[j]olted back into reality by the act' finding through it that she is 'still alive that I'm still real' and realising that '[f]or a short while I am in control, for a short while I am at peace'.

It is quite impossible to overstate the importance of psychic trauma as a concept operating within our general sense of what self-harm is and what it is all about. As I've already noted, while the subjectivist and objectivist discursive tendencies can be separated out *as paradigms* this requires, for the most part, an artificial act of abstraction or analysis. In practice, they tend to mix and mingle, and the idea of psychic trauma is exactly one of the key conceptual hubs around which such mingling freely occurs. The idea that mental disorder can be a 'sane' reaction to an 'insane' world is, after all, and at the same time, both a romantic idea and one that is psychiatrically framed. So entrenched, so naturalised and so implicit in our psychologised culture is this way of thinking that even strongly subjectivist texts, including the testimony of people who self-harm, have a tendency to work from the social authority and cultural capital that accrues to the concept of psychic trauma, albeit in a somewhat elaborated and personalised style. Nonetheless the basic idea remains the same: that their sense of estrangement is the product of a pathological dissociation, *a psychological state* of mental illness that, although it may include, at the level of personal meaning making, a more romantic rejection of the outside world as superficial and perhaps even unreal, is nonetheless caused by, and is therefore reducible to, the dysfunction of the biopsychological system of the individual. A dysfunction that can typically be located in a past traumatic event that has caused psychic damage to the individual; an inner wound that now echoes down through time in the form of self-inflicted injuries (Miller, 2005).

The theme emerges again and again in representations of self-harm, as witnessed by the titles of books like *Secret Scars* (Turner, 2002), *The Scarred Soul* (Alderman, 1997) and *Healing the Hurt Within* (Sutton, 2005). In Jan Sutton's popular psychology book she talks about people who self-harm as those who carry a 'legacy', a 'past [that] cannot be changed' and that 'bleeds away inside' them leaving them with 'the scars of battle' (2005: xxvii). Of course, here 'scars' stands as a single symbol uniting the wounds that 'bleeds away *inside* you', the psychological wounds left by experience, and the outer self-inflicted wounds that express this trauma and testify to it. The idea is that people who self-harm are people who, as the writer Farar Elliott (2001) puts it, are 'trying to survive the world-rocking aftershocks of rapes and battering and torture' (quoted in Fillmore *et al.*, 2003: 119). As Dawn describes:

> I think I will always bear the scars of my childhood, but I'm hopeful that the pus has gone at last (email).

Again we find that the double meaning of 'scars' and the 'pus' she mentions stands as a potent symbol of all the thoughts, feelings and memories, the raw unprocessed emotions as the ontological axis would have it, that seep through these psychological wounds to infect her consciousness and disturb her well-being. It is a theme then that works to explain why it is that people who self-harm seem to be subject to so much more raw and unprocessed emotion than most: it is because they are the traumatised, it is because they have a 'legacy' that 'bleeds away inside', the invisible 'battle scars' of life left from fighting monsters no one else can see, scars that produce emotional 'pus'. But it is also a theme that can be problematic as it feeds a popular and persistent myth: that self-harm is *always* an echo of past traumas in general and childhood sexual abuse in particular. As Favazza notes:

> On several occasions I have had to rescue patients from therapists who were frustrated at not being able to find the cause of an individual's self-mutilation and therefore assumed that he or she must have been abused (Introduction to Strong, 1998: xiv).

And indeed such was the experience of Deborah, who wrote:

> [T]he counsellor I saw spent a lot of time trying to convince me that my parents abused me when they didn't. She was determined for a long time that there would be a 'root cause' somewhere and looking back she was probably gunning for an abuse story of some sort to emerge (email).

The fact is that many people who self-harm may not be able to point to a particular event or series of events that motivated their self-injury in as narrowly a causal fashion as the concept of psychic trauma suggests. To some extent a focus on studies of clinical samples may have skewed the general research and professional picture of 'the self-harmer' toward those people who self-injure but who do so as part of a range problems and issues that have brought them to a clinic. There must therefore be a question mark over how well such samples generalise to the nonclinical population (Laye-Gindhu and Schonert-Reichl, 2005). However, even working from largely clinical samples Favazza maintains that the number of people who self-harm who have been sexually abused as children is between 50% and 60% (Introduction to Strong, 1998: xiv). It is important to remember that while psychic trauma is a powerfully influential concept that helps shape the way people think and talk about their psychological well-being and self-harm, that does not mean that everyone who is influenced by it or who uses it to help make sense of their lives and their pasts will use it in the same way as a psychiatrist would. And even those who can and do point to traumatic experiences in their pasts are far more ambiguous and equivocal in their assessment of the connection between these experiences and their self-harm, as Carla states in relation to her experience of sexual violence:

> What really gets my goat is that people assume I self-harm because of that, there is a strong link... but as I said to my therapist I was

self-harming for two years before that and that's mine, it's not his, it's mine (in person).

Here Carla explicitly lays claim to her self-harm, it is an *owned* practice, it belongs to her and forms part of their way of life, and suggestions that it is a pathological mechanism or, worse yet, that it has been caused by another person may challenge this perspective. So while biopsychological objectivism positions self-harm as a symptom of trauma, and trauma as a causal aetiology, people who self-harm are themselves more likely to use the idea of 'trauma' as a complex of ideas and values which helps them to make sense of themselves, their lives, their world and, in particular, their sense of estrangement.

Despite this, I think it is safe to say that a psychological or psychiatric case history written for Dawn would position her experience of childhood sexual abuse as the *cause* of trauma and this trauma as the *cause* of her self-harm. Indeed, the clinical and literary form of the case history perfectly manifests the logic of aetiology that we are looking at here, implying more than an exploration of the patient's life world or a mapping of the complex membrane of connections and contingencies that sutures someone into their lives and informs their experience. But rather a reaching back through time in search of specific causal agents and mechanisms, a fixing of narrowly and strongly deterministic origins that subsequently act as agents of destiny buried deeply within, actively at work governing present experiences and actions, whether we realise it or not (Caruth, 1995; Young, 1997; Leys, 2000).

Trauma, Aetiology and Case History

The connections between an objectivist aetiological paradigm, the development of case histories as a distinct form of literature and medical technology, and the concept of psychic trauma run deep. In fact, a key part of the development of psychic trauma as a technical, psychiatric concept can perhaps be traced back to the first psychological case history, or at least that text which transformed the traditional psychiatric case history from a dry organisation of clinical notes into 'a new form of literature... creative narratives that include their own analysis and interpretation' (Marcus, 1990: 90). This is, of course, Freud's *Fragment of an Analysis of a Case of Hysteria* (1953 [1905]), and it is certainly a marvellous piece of writing and a clear example of the literary as much as theoretical revolution that Freud brought to psychiatry and clinical psychology. Despite its age and its curiously unsatisfactory denouement it remains a 'living force' (Masson, 1990: 84) in psychoanalysis and can, with justification, be described as 'possibly the single greatest case history in the literature of psychiatry' (*ibid*: 85). But despite this, and the fact that it runs to some 130 pages in the standard edition, the idea of an aetiological agent of destiny is clearly present here as Freud himself reduces his *Fragment* to this pithy 21-word statement, which, for him, sums up and explains the case of 'Dora':

> It is a hysteria with tussis nervosa and aphonia, which can be traced back to the character of the child's sucking (letter to Wilhelm Fliess quoted in Masson, 1990: 434).

Eighteen-year-old Dora was brought to Freud by her father, 'in spite of her reluctance' (1953 [1905]: 23), to be treated for hysterical and delusional symptoms relating to her belief that a friend of her father's, Herr K., had tried to seduce her, a belief that her father rejected outright. His intention in taking Dora to a psychiatrist seems to have been to force her to accept that she had imagined the whole episode and that hers was a case of neurosis and not victimisation. Dora's sense of frustration and betrayal at these events, which constituted a strong experience of estrangement, a 'corros[ion of] the very basis of her sense of what was real' (Masson, 1990: 89), was exacerbated by her suspicion that her father's wilful dismissal of her claims were based in an arrangement of sexual exchange, as he was having an affair with Herr K.'s wife. But even more than just a convenient, if appalling, solution to an awkward bourgeois love triangle Dora seems to have been systematically used as a pawn in any number of similar games of sexual strategy and manipulation by the various members of her family and household; games which were covered by a conspiracy of silence that, it seemed, she alone wanted to break. Her isolation in this desire helps explain her 'aphonia', her silence. As the writer and philosopher Hélène Cixous explains: 'silence is the mark of hysteria. The great hysterics have lost speech... their tongues are cut off and what talks isn't heard because it's the body that talks' (1981: 49). But Dora's isolation also helps explain her 'tussis nervosa', a kind of hysterical cough or gag, which recalls Dawn's silence (her 'gaggedness') and the manner of her silence. As she explains:

> there's always a point at which I become completely unable to speak past a certain level of personal disclosure... it's like a switch closes in my throat and I can't say anything without stuttering, and certainly nothing of value (email).

Dawn's switch is like Dora's hysterical cough, and both are aspects of silence and the multiple processes of silencing. For Dawn, this gaggedness means keeping the family's dirty secret, while at the same time dissociating from it, keeping it at a distance, as an experience and a memory. For Dora, it also meant being held at the centre of her family's dirty secret and having to do battle with it as a reality, a truth, something which really was happening, even if everyone else denied it. For Dora as for Dawn, the trauma, the disordering rupture, existed in the moral order that sutured her personal experience into the network of relationships that surrounded her. In other words, it was a trauma in how she thought she should have been treated within these relationships. But for Freud, however, while he conceded that there may have been a physical sexual trauma in the form of a failed seduction or possibly even multiple betrayals, this hardly seemed to matter. All that was ultimately real or significant about Dora's condition was the conflicted thoughts and feelings that constituted her traumatised psyche. It is important to appreciate that it is at this precise point, as the comparative literature scholar Jane Gallop remarks, that Freud 'stopped believing in a "real" seduction at the origin of hysteria and realised that the source of neurosis is the child's fantasies' (1985: 213). In other words, it is here, in this case history, that Freud stopped thinking that hysteria and similar neuroses were the direct products of actual 'seductions' or acts of sexual violence and abuse, and began to believe that the stories of seduction he was uncovering in therapy were, in fact, psychological constructs. It is here then that the idea of a fully psychological as opposed to neurological trauma was developed and the central idea of contemporary psychic trauma established. As the psychoanalytic philosopher Renata Salecl notes:

> [T]here is no direct correlation between trauma and event. Many subjects can experience an event, but only some will develop a trauma linked to it; while it is also possible that the 'event' never actually happens, but the trauma is nonetheless formed (2004: 130).

The focus of Freud and the massed ranks of therapists that have followed him was and has been on the psychic process of the patient rather than the veracity of the events that may or may not underpin it. It is a deeply individualising and psychologising strategy and, consequently, Dora's seemingly reasonable complaints are frustratingly rendered by Freud into symptoms of pathology, as he writes:

A string of reproaches against other people leads one to suspect the existence of a string of self-reproaches with the same content. All that need be done is to turn back each particular reproach on to the speaker himself (1953 [1905]: 35)

As we noted in the last chapter, then, in modernity all rivers lead back to the individual and the self, and, as such, the connection between self and world, and between the person and reality, can effectively be recast as a burden, a labour that falls entirely on the shoulders of the psychological individual. But as important and influential a moment in the social history of psychic trauma as this is, it is also, on the face of it, significantly at odds with a great deal of contemporary discourse on, and controversy over, the issue of such trauma. Psychologist Tana Dineen, for example, defines trauma as the idea that

for every here-and-now problem, there must have been a dramatic there-and-then cause; that some event in the past, as far back as infancy, was so disturbing that it continues to affect thoughts, feelings and actions (1999: 57).

The focus of this concept, then, appears to be, contra Freud, on the event itself and the effects of the past on the psychic well-being of the individual in the present. This conception of trauma is a powerful and near pervasive part of the discourse on self-harm evident in much popular psychology and media representation; the idea of the 'self-harmer' as a 'survivor', as someone who has been brutalised by life, by a 'past [that] cannot be changed', as Sutton's poem puts it, but who nonetheless journeys from 'darkness to light' and (as the subtitle of Sutton's book suggests) 'healing' (Salecl, 2004: 119–40). Indeed, it does seem to be important in modern therapy culture that the traumatised have suffered real and actual traumas, and that psychic trauma is not simply a useful idea or metaphor that people employ to make sense of their lives and feelings, but rather a powerful, definite and natural response of our psychic system to real events. In Dusty Miller's important contribution to the genre, *Women Who Hurt Themselves* (2005), trauma is not only stated to be the direct cause of self-harm, an assumption which, as I've noted, she shares with many authors, but is also emphasised as such through her coining of the DSM-sounding 'trauma reenactment syndrome', a concept whose central characteristic is described as 'a pattern of intentionally inflicting harm on one's own body' (2005: 9) as a result of childhood histories of interpersonal or family trauma; [people] reenact the harm that was done to them as children and reinforce their belief that they are incapable of protecting themselves because they were not protected as children (*ibid*: 8).

For Miller, self-harm cannot be fully explained on the basis of the expressive imperative or the need to overcome feelings of estrangement, emptiness or unreality. Rather, 'these functions are only part of the motivation for such behaviour; my book addresses the physical and psychological reenactments of childhood trauma expressed in self-harmful behaviour' (*ibid*: 7), a phrase she expands to include alcoholism, eating disorders, addiction to medication, incessant dieting and numerous other practices that 'intentionally inflict...harm on one's own body'. But behind any apparent contradiction between theories of trauma in which the traumatising event may be a 'fantasy', as Freud came to believe, and those in which the traumatising event itself seems to be the key issue, there is, in fact, a broader, underlying and significant agreement.

The traditional Freudian approach does not explore people's pasts as landscapes of meanings and significance as such but rather targets their fantasies, their hidden desires, as revealed by their pasts. The act of writing a case history then is not one of engaging with the life world of a patient so much as it is a search for diagnostic clues. As Dora discovered, to her consternation, for Freud it really didn't matter what was or was not going on in her life; it was the fact of her psychological trauma and only this that he was concerned with. The events and the entire picture of social circumstances, conditions and multiple contingent factors that led to them all fell away as being of secondary importance compared with the psychological process at hand. Even in the construal of this process patterns of personal meaning were rendered secondary to the imagined fact of a psychic mechanism. The rich pattern of a life and the multiple complexities that knit that life into a world are reduced, at first to a document of a 130 pages and then to a summary of 21 words.

Likewise, the key issue for Miller, despite appearances, is also not the multiple and varied patterns of life and action that are experienced and expressed through states of estrangement or acts of 'self-harming behaviour' as these are only 'reenactments' or replays of a deterministic past. And the past itself is never dealt with, never on its own terms. Rather it is the *memory* of the traumatic event, the *psychological mechanism* of adult remembrances of childhood abuse, which is the central issue. For Miller to track this cause is to track the *thing* that sits behind such behaviour and which explains it, and so again the primary focus is not, in fact, on the event or the circumstances which led to it, but rather the psychological effects of the trauma and the ongoing psychological condition that describes the present experience of trauma. In other words, *it is not the event but the memory of the event that is given precedence* just as surely as Freud said that his patients mostly suffered from 'reminiscences' (1975), and not from strained social conditions and estranging marginalisation.

Our contemporary construction or construal of psychic trauma then is not a contradiction of Freud at all, and the full downstream impact of Freud's innovation has only really become apparent in recent years with a certain relativising tendency in the range and type of events that we think of as potentially traumatic. After all, if it is the effect and not the event itself that matters then there is no objective limit to what kinds of events may be understood or experienced as traumatic. The sociologist Frank Furedi (2004) has recorded this effect of what dissident psychiatrist Thomas Szasz (1974) calls 'semantic inflation', noting that a Factiva search of British newspapers revealed a huge increase in the use of the word 'trauma' between 1994 (when it appeared less than 500 times) and 2000 (when it occurred around 5000 times). He argues that this rise tracks the inflation in what the term is used to refer to from experiences or war and childhood sexual abuse to an increasing number of more typical and ordinary life events from accidents and illnesses to divorce and unemployment so that it now 'means little more than people's responses to an unpleasant situation' (Furedi, 2004: 4; see also Dineen, 1999). But while the event at the root of the trauma has become relativised the psychological condition has not, allowing the psychiatrist Steven Sharfstein to claim that trauma is a massive public health issue and represents 'the largest single preventable cause of mental illness' being to psychiatry '[w]hat cigarette smoking is to the rest of medicine' (2006: 3). While another psychiatrist, Andrew Slaby, who, like Farar Elliott, terms trauma 'aftershock', claims that '[w]e *all* suffer from aftershock, maybe less violently but still at a price we shouldn't have to pay. In fact, aftershock is the disease of today' (1989: 5, my emphasis).

Of course, this semantic inflation of 'trauma' maps onto a more general pattern of increasing medicalisation and psychologisation in the way that our culture frames and deals with its problems and dilemmas, framing them less as fundamental problems of social and political organisation than as technical difficulties occurring within the individual mind and body (Rose, 1998; Moskowitz, 2001; Furedi, 2004). And the apparent empathy with which this psychological culture listens to people's stories of trauma should not lead us to think that this objectivist framing is at least leavened somewhat by a strong subjectivist input of meanings and feelings. After all, here again, and as the asymmetric binary remains a constant companion in our journey through these discourses, the objectivist framing is, in fact, left all the more firmly and deeply entrenched by this empathy, naturalised and implicit as the logical form which organises and governs subjectivist content. And the result is a deeply aetiological logic of finding cause not so much in context, or the meaning-making processes of a present and living person, but rather more fundamentally in the psychic condition of the individual, the essential and inevitable pathology hidden within them since the day of their trauma. It is the mechanics and processes of the individual's psyche after all that provides the active link and common denominator between any past events, real or imaginary, and present behaviour, and so it with the individual psyche that psychotherapists from Freud onward have concerned themselves.

Control: The Discursive Complex of the Aetiological Axis

The key thematic discourse of traumatic estrangement is clearly a central concept active within representations and understandings of self-harm, albeit a somewhat dynamic one reflecting different but related meanings and being subject to more or less objectivist and subjectivist constructions, more or less mechanical or metaphorical models and uses, which themselves may be more or less mixed together. But these different emphases on how we think and talk about self-harm through estrangement and trauma may be understood as so many perspectives, so many variable articulations of a common set of concerns and meanings that come more fully and more clearly into view as we pull back along the aetiological axis from the key thematic discourse to the discursive complex that underpins it and which makes its meanings both possible and relevant. The common discursive complex that is conspicuously active here is that of *control*, which stands as both a significant preoccupation of modernity and a core concern of everyday life.

Traumatic events, the psychic lesions that they inflict and that 'bleed away inside' us, and the raw, dangerous, unprocessed emotions, the blood and 'pus', that seeps through them, all, in Herman's words, 'overwhelm the ordinary systems of care that give people a sense of *control*, connection, and meaning' (1992: 33, my emphasis). According to our key thematic discourse and the discourses of the ontological axis such inner wounds cannot be processed, cannot be healed over by our standard schemas of sense making and morality. And like any wound that will not heal these unthinkable and unspeakable emotions that bleed from an unthinkable and unspeakable trauma torment us; never letting go and never failing to remind us that we categorically do not have the control, the agency and the mastery that we once imagined were ours. And so we feel estranged from who we thought we were, estranged from who we think we ought to be and estranged from a world that no longer makes sense. Under these circumstances '[w]e begin to question our own self-worth and value as a human being' (Parkinson, 1993: 14). But as the dark tide of emotions threatens to rise up and overwhelm the self, self-harm can, as I noted briefly in the last chapter, appear as a 'coping mechanism', something definite to cling to and a way of re-asserting control. As Caroline explains:

> I get very wound up and upset and emotional and I just don't know how to calm myself down... and I, I think the self-harm, it's just a release really... I felt like I was on the edge of just completely, totally losing it altogether and I felt like that [self-harm] was stopping me from going over the edge' (in person).

And as Heather describes her experiences of loss following the end of a relationship:

> I felt like I'd completely lost control of my grief, that I had no other way of getting control again... erm... 'cus I'd been like on the floor, I couldn't walk very well, so I felt like I didn't have a way back as it were... erm, and by cutting then after that I was able to pull myself together (in person).

Heather went on to say that after this episode she made a conscious decision not to 'allow myself to indulge in sadness or anguish', as if these emotions were deep, dark waters hiding a strong tide that had pulled her out without her quite realising it, that had made her feel lost and that had threatened to drown her; her only way back being through the distraction of pain and a physical discipline that would counteract the pull. The sentiment is also one simply but clearly captured by Abigail Robson in her autobiography of self-harm, *Secret Scars*, when she states that 'I'd rather shed blood than tears' (2007: 109). Indeed, there is a strong stoical dimension to much of what people who self-harm have to say about it. For Robson, it is a technique of self-control, not just an emergency externalisation or expression of feeling, but a preferable one to crying as crying is weak and 'an indulgence' (*ibid*). Acts of self-injury then are not just about letting feelings out, they can also be about toughening the outer shell of the body, exerting a form of control over the flesh so as to protect the self within, as Kaysen notes:

> Scar tissue has no character. It's not like skin. It doesn't show age or illness or pallor of tan. It has no pores, no hair, no wrinkles. It's like a slipcover. It shields and disguises what's beneath. That's why we grow it; we have something to hide (2000: 16).

Indeed, many people who self-harm take a certain pride in knowing that they can take pain that others would not tolerate and that they can do something, inflict wounds upon themselves, which many others would not be capable of. In remarking on the importance of control within the matrix of meanings that compose anorexia, Susan Bordo quotes psychiatrist Michael Stacks as saying

> people no longer feel they can control events outside themselves—how well they do in their jobs or in their personal relationships, for example—but they can control the food they eat and how far they can run. Abstinence, tests of endurance, are ways of proving their self-sufficiency (quoted in Bordo, 2003: 153).

As, of course, is self-harm; a technique for asserting the boundaries of the self against the disturbing world beyond. In the next chapter I will further explore how this concern with control is connected with the activity of personal agency exercised in the project of self-making and the cultivation of identity, especially under social conditions of insecurity and precariousness but for the moment it is important to note that this connection between self-harm and control is as ambivalent as it is certain. Self-harm may be framed as an agent of self-control, albeit an extreme and perhaps undesirable one, but it is also commonly framed as a loss of control, a wild eruption, a habit and even an 'addiction' (Turner, 2002). It appears as both a technique of control and a symptom of psychological chaos; a coping mechanism and an illness that compels acts of mutilation. And, in the same way, for many people who self-harm, it can appear as something owned, as something secure and supportive to identify with, as when Carla protested that her self-harm was hers and not a symptom of her sexual assault ('it's not his, it's mine'). But it can also appear as something other, something tormenting and persecuting.

As Dana puts it, 'it used to be mine, something that I owned, but then it became the enemy' (email).

Of course, it could be that self-harm is, in fact, a coping mechanism and that this quality of ambivalence is the product of its being damned by association with the disturbing thoughts and feelings it is used to cope with the way that medical treatment can be confused with disease in the memory of the person suffering so that both are remembered as a single cloud of pain and discomfort. But this dual framing fits into a broader pattern of structural ambivalence that goes well beyond any complaint that self-harm is a 'confused and confusing practice' (Pierce, 1977: 377) and instead suggests that it is, by its nature, flexible, mercurial, overdetermined and deeply contingent. So far we have seen self-harm framed as both a rational mechanism of the psychic system and as a dangerous overwhelming of the psychic system, as both an aspect of the rational control of emotions and an eruption of the irrational, as both impulsive and stoical, both agent of control and addiction, and as both something owned and something other; an extension of selfhood and an enemy of selfhood.

It's true that some of these tensions are mitigated by their typically being articulated from different social sites—self-harm as stoicism being typical of people who self-harm, and self-harm as impulse dyscontrol being more typical of psychiatrists. And it's also true that some of these tensions can be mediated by their being embedded into a broader system of meanings; so that self-harm may be understood to be a mechanism of rational self-control and part of a rationally ordered psychic system precisely because its function is to vent off irrational forces, which means that it can be characterised as a rational process with irrational contents. But nonetheless there is undeniably something here of what the philosopher Jacques Derrida (1981) calls the *pharmakon*, a Greek word that has multiple meanings and that can be translated as either cure or curse, remedy or poison. As Susan explains:

> I saw my self-harm as problem and solution, and it is a double natured thing; I tend to think of it as a faceless person in the dark with a split personality, and they are always fighting with one another.... It is its own demise, and it makes the person their own demise too. It's a problem because of other problems, like a chain reaction of events, one thing leads to another, but the solution isn't found, the 'solution' becomes the problem, even if it is temporary. It's like a coin with the same two sides, regardless of its flipped side, it's always the same. I don't know how to tell you in words about its

double nature, it's a double dealing agent in the mind and neither side can destroy it. The problem is solved by the solution, but then the solution becomes the problem (email).

As *pharmakon*, self-harm can be framed as both a 'remedy' to the problem of frustrated expression, a 'morbid form of self-help', as Favazza puts it (1996), and at the same time a 'poisonous' blockage to the development of healthier and more therapeutic forms of expression. Self-harm as *pharmakon* is at once expression *and* a failure of expression, both good ('a victory of the life instinct', as Menninger described it) *and* bad. It is not ambivalently framed and constructed because it is 'confused and confusing' but rather it is confusing precisely because it is supposed to be: because it deeply encodes ambivalence and ambiguity, because it implies both remedy *and* poison, cure *and* curse. As Derrida explains:

> If the pharmakon is 'ambivalent', it is because it constitutes the medium in which opposites are opposed, the movement and the play that links them among themselves, reverses them or makes one side cross over into the other.... The pharmakon is the movement, the locus, and the play: (the production of) difference.... It holds in reserve, in its undecided shadow and vigil, the opposites and the differends that the process of discrimination will come to carve out (1981: 127).

Self-harm then is less concerned with discriminating between positions of control and dyscontrol than with indicating that this issue of control has become an issue of great concern for many people in contemporary society and that it stands as one of the core dilemmas of our culture. Otherwise put: in its expression of overwhelmed voicelessness self-harm gives voice to the fact that so many people do indeed feel overwhelmed and silenced even as they are urged through the values of the psychological individual to be self-controlled, agentive and expressive. Likewise, self-harm does not so much indicate either a rational psychic system or an irrational eruption of unprocessed emotions, so much as it draws our attention to the whole web of meanings that are concerned with the issues and dynamics of rational representation and the rational regulation of emotions and behaviour, the relationship that is between the modernist–utilitarian self and the romantic–expressive self. Such concerns, issues and dilemmas provide less the narrow functions of self-harm, as if it were some blind and narrow mechanism, than the broad fields of meaning, values and significance that the symbolic idiom of self-harm is abroad in, is put to work in, and within which therefore it lives, moves and has its being.

Controlling the 'Real'

In discussing the emergence of the modern subject Charles Taylor notes that

> What one finds running through all the aspects of this constellation [of modernist sociocultural changes]... is the growing ideal of a human agent who is able to remake himself by methodical and disciplined action. What this calls for is the ability to take an instrumental stance to one's given properties, desires, inclinations, tendencies, habits of thought and feeling, so that they can be *worked on*, doing away with some and strengthening others, until one meets the desired specifications (1992: 159–60, original emphasis).

Of course, this idea of mastery and ideal of agency extended well beyond the confines of the self to constitute a central issue and a core challenge inherent to the modern instrumental genius. New advances in science and technology stood not only as new systems of representation, but also as new opportunities for manipulating and controlling nature. Francis Bacon famously crystallised the *zeitgeist* in his aphorism 'knowledge is power', while Descartes writes that the modernist goal is to 'make ourselves masters and possessors of nature' (1964). In light of the increased precariousness and insecurity experienced by people as a result of the modern shift from a vertical to a horizontal social ideology, and the concomitant shift from belonging to self-making, it is perhaps not surprising that Western civilisation developed a fetish for control. But as Taylor reminds us, the primary site for the articulation and literal embodiment of this concern was the self and its body. And to this degree psychomedical concerns with the aetiological are particularly emblematic.

From Bacon and Descartes onwards there has been a sense that the material is the 'real' because it is definite, definable, explicable, predictable and manipulable. The implicit power and persuasive force of the asymmetric binary is perhaps not that hard to explain on the basis of these concerns for control and the 'real' of biology and matter. More control can be exerted, or at least *the ideal of control is more easily applied*, to those factors like individual biogenetic and biopsychological structures and systems than to the ephemera of the distinctly personal, the social, the historical and cultural. It should be little surprise then that in looking for cause we tend not to look for complex webs of contingency and meaning, or for a person's placement in a network of social relations, but rather reduce these to the individual, and the individual to their natural body and brain—moving ever past the symbolic and toward the 'real'.

I put 'real' in scare quotes for the same reason others capitalise it, or italicise it; to note that by this term I do not mean to refer to any objective reality as such but rather to the cultural meaning and general concept that people draw upon when they talk about reality, when they talk about things 'in reality', or finding out what's 'really' going on, or when they claim to be 'keeping it real', or when something or some person is presented as 'the real thing' (Belsey, 2004). Perhaps paradoxically then, the 'real' does not so much indicate any actual or genuinely objective reality but rather a symbolic representation of what the 'real' has come to mean for us (Belsey, 2004), and indeed it has come to mean a great deal, constituting a central cultural fascination in late-modernity. It carries connotations of the natural, the certain, the unquestionable and the definite (Taylor, 1991; Guignon, 2004; Boyle, 2004), and has already surfaced several times.

In Chapter 1 I noted that people talk about diseases and disorders as 'real' only if they can be framed as biogenetic and physical as opposed to the 'not real' of meaning-based disorders, which are often labelled as imaginary and hysterical, as 'all' or 'just' 'in the head' (Showalter, 1991; Hacking, 1995). In Chapter 3 I noted with Deborah Lupton (1998) that part of our contemporary concern with the emotions is their romantic coding as the natural and hence 'real' products of a true self as contrasted with the falsity and conformity of the civilised self and the well-trained ego. At the beginning of this chapter I noted the ontological separation between self and other conjured into our intersubjective lives by the emergence of the psychological individual and the effect this has on cultivating an isolated sense of self and making it difficult, as Dawn put it, to *'really* be sure what's going on' (my emphasis). Then we saw that Freud and Dora's difference of opinion about what was 'really' going on in her life translated through the twentieth century into the different emphases placed on the reality of actual traumatic events on the one hand and the reality of psychic processes on the other. And, of course, we have seen that estrangement and dissociation are typically described through words like 'derealisation' and the sense that the world has become somehow unreal. We traced this to the way that psychic trauma stands for us as a crisis in representation, a breakdown of our capacity to symbolise and semiotically encode experience, to 'process' traumatic events such that they linger in our psychic system as an indigestible mass of the 'real'.

But as much as the 'real' stands as a central fascination in contemporary culture, like similar fascinations with the emotions and the romantic–expressive self, this interest does not reflect an uncritical approval but rather hides a deeper mediation. In this case through the value of control. As Descartes, Bacon and biomedicine remind us the 'real' is good when it gives us a sense of control and mastery over ourselves and our world. But as psychic trauma reminds us the 'real' can be bad when we seem to be unable to work into our systems of representation, when it stubbornly refuses to made sense of, and, instead, as Herman has pointed out, 'overwhelm[s] the ordinary systems of care that give people a sense of control, connection, and meaning'. And self-harm, of course, understood as an example of *pharmakon*, plays with this ambivalence of the 'real'.

As we have seen, the very idea that self-harm can act as a pressure valve or an emergency act of expression is based on the notion that what is being vented-off and expressed are the raw, unprocessed, all-too-'real' emotions that bleed through inner psychic wounds, which are themselves the stubborn remnants of traumatic impacts with the 'real'. And it is within this complex of meanings that self-harm can appear as a tear, a trauma, in the web of signification and meaning that has otherwise failed to 'process' these feelings; a tear then through which the inexpressible may be expressed and the unspoken may be said, even if in 'the language of blood and pain' (Hewitt, 1997: 58). As the psychotherapists F. Miller and E.A. Bashkin observe of one of their self-harming patients: 'he preserved in the flesh, in a dramatic and conspicuous manner, the history of events he could not integrate into the fabric of his personality' (1974: 647).

The physical trauma of a self-inflicted wound then is not so much thought of as the representation or symbol of an inner, psychological wound as it is understood to be the direct expression of it. Self-harm appears as a peculiarly metonymic kind of disorder. Compare it, for example, to the rich and densely metaphorical symbolism of Freud's cases of hysteria or even to anorexia nervosa, which can be thought of as symbolising the issue of control in as much as it is culturally wrapped up with the social 'tyranny of slenderness' (Chernin, 1985). Against these overtly symbolic idioms self-harm appears to be a curiously literal action. Perhaps this is one of the reasons why we are so predisposed to understanding it as some kind of biological mechanism rather than a symbolic action. And yet if we recall what Susanna Kaysen said, her self-injury was all about 'trying to explain' her inner wound by making it 'real', validating the psychic wound and the emotional pain by making them physical, transforming them into a physical wound and a physical pain and so outwardly 'demonstrating, externally and irrefutably, an inward condition'. For Kaysen, it is the 'real' of the outer wound that testifies to the reality of the inner wound. As Donna puts it:

> If you've got a cut and there's blood you can point at it and it validates the feeling because for me I wasn't having my feelings recognised or validated... if I cut one day I wouldn't need to for a few days because just looking at the cut was enough to calm me down because it was like saying 'yes, it is real' (telephone).

And so we find the ambivalence, and perhaps even the paradox, of self-harm and the 'real'. It appears to represent the point at which the 'real', building up within and overwhelming systems of self-care, bursts through the surfaces of the body to inscribe itself on the flesh. And yet it is the visceral, bloody, tender flesh wound whose reality validates the supposed 'real' of the inner emotions. And it is the symbolic power imbued in this very real flesh wound that grants some sense of control over the all-too 'real' feelings within. It seems then that self-harm *is* a metaphor after all but *a metaphor of the metonymic*, a symbol of the unsymbolic and a performance of the 'real'. It is not an actual and literal break in representation and signification but rather stands as a symbol *that signifies* a break in representation and signification, that seeks to emphasise the essential vitality of an inner state by symbolically expressing the impossibility of expressing it. And it can only do this and it has only become such a significant symbol for us because of the cultural value that we place on the idea of the 'real thing'; the idea that only a physical biopsychological mechanism could be considered 'real', that anything less would be fanciful, hysterical, unreal. And it is only because it encodes this value that self-harm can carry the cultural leave to say what otherwise cannot be said and express what is otherwise felt to be painfully trapped within. Self-harm is a symbol then but one that symbolises the desire to reach beyond metaphors and symbols, beyond language and signification, and to find something 'real', something that, as Brian Patten said, 'by its rawness, that by its bleeding, demands to be called real'. Something *authentic*.

Authenticity: The Order of Discourse for the Aetiological Axis

Just as the thematic discourse of traumatic estrangement only makes sense within the experience of subjects for whom personal agency and control have become sensitised issues, so the discursive complex of control only arises within a 'space of questions' defined by dualism, by the difference felt between self and other. If we did not think of ourselves as being in essence bounded, separate individuals then the question of how much agency we could wield, how much control over the world we could exert, would not assert itself quite as acutely. But as Charles Taylor reminds us modernity is indeed characterised by an obsessive focus on control and this itself is nested within the 'ideal of a human agent who is able to remake himself by methodical and disciplined action'. The body for *homo clausus* is more material, more 'real', than it is essence, than it is self, and, as such, the 'ability to take an instrumental stance to one's given properties, desires, inclinations, tendencies, habits of thought and feeling' implies a paradoxical position. To the extent that we identify our bodies with our sense of self then we consider the properly 'human agent' to be an ideal that we must build up to and cultivate, the 'real' of our bodies being controlled and made into the correct form. And to the extent that we consider our bodies and our 'given properties, desires, inclinations, tendencies, habits of thought and feeling' to be the possessions or garments of an inner essence, a true and vital inner self, we will consider the ideal human agent to be an inner reality that is externalised, embodied and made flesh through the process of cultivation and regimes of 'methodical and disciplined action'. Here the 'real' of our bodies must be controlled in order to reveal the essence within. This paradoxical position, which nonetheless, either way, asserts the idea of an ideal human agent for whom control, self-control and the control of the 'real' of bodies, emotions and events is an issue, this order of discourse, is the idea and the value of *authenticity*.

The authentic is the true, the essential. It is also therefore the certain, and there is an important and obvious sense of control wrapped up with the value of certainty. As an issue it represents a central fascination and source of anxiety for the modern age (Taylor, 1991). According to the literary critic Lionel Trilling (1974), our concern with the authentic developed out of an increasing emphasis on sincerity, which itself began in the sixteenth century with the multiple transformations and social upheavals of that period, and which we noted in the last chapter. As I mentioned there, the beginning of a long process of detraditionalisation and the emergence of a horizontal social ideology undermined the old social order that had 'provided its members with secure positions in a divinely sanctioned hierarchy' (Lindholm, 2008: 3). The result was a kind of 'existential anxiety' (Giddens, 1991), a sense that once one had shaken off what the sociologist Georg Simmel called 'the rusty chains of guild, birth right and church' (quoted in Elliott and Lemert, 2006: 55), one was of course liberated but also no longer guaranteed a place in the world as such a place now had to be earned, and the self, the agent, that would claim such a place had to be actively made through Taylor's methodical and disciplined action. As the historian Perry Anderson notes, the emergence of the modern horizontal order implied a 'tremendous emancipation of the possibility and sensibility of the individual self' but also

> a profound disorientation and insecurity, frustration and despair, concomitant with—indeed inseparable from—the sense of enlargement and exhilaration, the new capacities and feelings, liberated at the same time (1998: 42).

And as Lindholm explains: 'the pleasures and possibilities of social mobility coincided with feelings of alienation and meaninglessness' (2008: 3). This new culture not only expressed itself in greater opportunities, but also in 'greater potential for guile and deceit' (*ibid*). The face-to-face exchanges and community-based business interactions characteristic of the feudal system had been pushed out by the increasing flow and scope of capital, while the increasing movement of populations meant that many people not only lived with strangers, but also did business with them. Under such circumstances trust and sincerity, honesty and integrity took on new and quite practical dimensions. If the spirit of burgeoning capitalism can be tied to the spirit of an emergent Protestantism and puritanism, as Max Weber (2011 [1905]) famously claimed it could, then we should remember that the Protestants valued sincerity and plain style very highly. However, this new sincerity, understood as a symmetry between intent and action, raised issues familiar to us from Hawthorne's minister about how one could know one's own mind and intent, while also introducing a friction between the demands of individual integrity and the obligations of social life. Increasingly, the inner and the outer came to be defined in binary opposition to one another, with the inner understood to be a realm of vital essence and truth, and the outer suspected as a place of 'guile and deceit'. In this way authenticity emerged from sincerity to become a deeply familiar concern in modern culture, and the individual self became enshrined as the source of agency and the one true anchor of identity, the only 'real' sanctuary from the insecurity and precariousness of life.

The cultivation of the *homo clausus* and the separation between the inner and the outer conjured up a particular concern for the issue of one's own inner essence, presence and true self. Accordingly, as the philosopher Charles Guignon explains, since the sixteenth century people have been increasingly

> preoccupied with what is going on inside themselves—their feelings, intentions, desires and motives. And they are able to make a sharp distinction between what is truly them—that is...the seats of their deepest feelings, desires and intentions—and what is only extraneous and transient.... The distinction between true inner self and outward, bodily existence makes it possible to look on one's own body, feelings, and needs as things 'out there', distinct from oneself, to be worked over (2004: 29–30).

Since the emergence of these concerns they have, of course, become increasingly acute, being significantly amplified in late-modernity (Boyle, 2004), and being as Guignon notes 'absolutely central to all the movements that make up the self-improvement culture' (2004: viii). But as the paradoxical position above suggests, there are really two versions of authenticity in contemporary culture. On the one hand there is what the anthropologist Charles Lindholm calls 'genealogical' or 'historical' authenticity, having to do with origins, with how we are 'true to our roots'. And on the other there is what he calls 'identity' or 'correspondence' authenticity that has more to do with content, with whether or not our lives are a 'direct and immediate expression of [our]...essence' (2008: 2). Of course, we have already encountered this ambivalent construal, for example with Deborah Lupton in the last chapter, and it is also evident in Guignon's quote above, the idea on the one hand that the true self is our 'feelings, intentions, desires and motives' in their natural and instinctual forms, something inherent to us, and yet the idea on the other hand that our true self is our 'feelings, intentions, desires and motives' as they have been processed and civilised. The distinction is consequential for how we think about trauma and the 'real' as for the latter, objectivist and modernist, formulation (the true self as civilised), trauma consists of the 'real' of the word overwhelming our systems of representation and signification. While for the former, subjectivist and romantic, formulation (the true self as natural and inherent), trauma consists of a failure in the interpersonal, linguistic and social worlds to handle, to process, the 'real' that is within us, perhaps because, as Richey Edwards evidently felt, these worlds have become too superficial, too unreal, too inauthentic. The excess of uncommunicated and uncommunicable 'real' emotion and sentiment then can only surface, can only be vented off, through a correspondingly 'real' medium: the blood, pain and carved flesh of self-harm.

In practice, as always, any real clash between these two different formulations is kept at arm's length by the action of the asymmetric binary and our tendency to not look too closely at irreconcilable differences such as those between the ethos of a cultivated modernist true self ('become who you truly are'), and a natural and romantic true self ('find your inner self'). Ultimately, however, both constructions feed into and contribute to the broader culture of the psychological. The modernist true self requires the technologies of the psy-complex to achieve fulfilment of its project of self-cultivation (see Chapter 5), while the romantic true self requires the vocabulary and therapeutic techniques of the psy-complex to find, uncover and embrace the authentic self within. The underlying unity, the field on which both conceptions are at play, is the idea of the psychological individual and the paradoxical reliance that this idea, in either formulation, has on its surrounding society and culture.

The Prison House of the Self

Although authenticity and control exist as broad themes of modernist concern, they also make their presence felt directly in the sharp, lived experience of self-harm. To reverse the direction of our movement along the axis for just a moment we can see that in understanding ourselves through the order of meanings and values that we call 'authenticity', in understanding ourselves as an inner essence, we create the challenges and dilemmas of control, whether it is control of the world or the control of the self. And in doing this we also create the possibility of traumatic encounters with the 'real'; aspects of the world that we can, in fact, make sense of but not in our own chosen and privileged terms, not alongside our chosen ideal of authentic human agency, and which lead us therefore to turn to a signifier of the unsignifiable, to the idea of psychic trauma and self-harm, to symbolise and express them, while also keeping them isolated from our standard schemas and systems of representation. And it is in this traumatic encounter that estrangement can occur. And in the face of this estrangement the self, cut off and alienated from its world, clings to itself, to its sense of authenticity and of being a sanctuary, all the more tightly. The problem is that this can lead to further estrangement and the transformation of the sanctuary into a prison. To help us understand this we can once again, return to the case of Dawn:

> I had always felt that there was a glass screen between me and other people; that I could connect with them up until the glass screen but after that there was a place where nobody could touch... I've always had the feeling that I'm two people (email).

Here she describes a sense of withdrawal from the world, a reaction to estrangement that, like the poet Sylvia Plath's more famous glass metaphor of 'the bell jar' (2005), cuts her off from the outside world and traps her inside herself. But, interestingly, this is not where the estrangement and the withdrawal end, rather it seems to seep through the usual barriers of the body and selfhood to infect aspects of the inner world. Dawn's sense of herself begins to split as she makes a distinction between that part of her that is on the public side of the glass screen and that is personable, and that prides itself on its social skills and gregariousness; and that part of her that is on the private side of the screen and that is secret, the Dawn who is safe ('where nobody could touch') but silenced. This kind of splitting is a common tope amongst people who self-harm, Deborah, for example, explains:

> I am cheerful around others even when I'm not that happy inside... I know that my being happy around others contributes to them not knowing if there's something I'm upset about but I'd rather it that way... I think that the only person who can actually help you is yourself so I don't really see the point to inviting half the world to know about your problems, it just makes people end up judging one another *since no one really understands anyone else* (email, my emphasis).

Here we are reminded of Magritte's veil and Dawn's comment that it results in no one knowing 'what's really going on'. Sadie also talks about 'a thick pane of glass between you and the rest of the world', a barrier of truth, value and essence beyond which 'nothing seems very real and it doesn't feel like I'm in control' (email). But as common as this glass metaphor is it is not as common as the image of a prison, and the self as a prison. Carla describes here the feelings that led to her first act of self-harm:

> [talking about what led up to first self-harm] I just felt so much pain in my head and... like um... like being in an emotional prison really, um... I knew I had to kind of, I see it as like you know... when you give something an electric shock and you shock it into change? It felt like that (in person).

She describes her situation as being 'stuck, stuck inside, stuck in my head, stuck in my house', and further explains this prison as

> not being able to... be... sort of... entirely myself because there's stuff in my head all the time, there's like, I call it like white noise in my brain, um... there's all this, like when I was a teenager there was all this stuff going on and I tried to maintain... the essence of Carla I call it [laughs] but it's taken me until about my late 20s to realize what I'm about (in person).

Here the image of a prison connects both to a sense of a withdrawing into and hiding in a sense of essence, of an authentic and true self. It is safe and yet it robs the subject of their connection to the world. The prison then is most often represented through the dual logic of the *pharmakon*, being both curse and cure, both prison and sanctuary. As Allie explains:

> I used to hide myself away, both emotionally and physically—always pretended to be OK when I wasn't, didn't leave the house alone or even open the curtains. Didn't answer the door or phone.... [I]t was a self-imposed imprisonment with the intention of keeping myself safe—definitely more about things out than keeping them in. I hid myself away for my own protection, but in doing so totally deprived myself from life (email).

And this is the end point of estrangement, a point where, whether it is seen as the psychological process of dissociation or else the experience of social alienation, it has seeped through the world, through others and through language to infect the self, which, as it turns out, cannot be so comprehensively cut off and isolated after all. Asking what is authentic or true within the self is a little like asking what the 'I' is; each part of the body and self is turned into an object, into an other, through the very act of considering it. If the true self is the true subject then the more one looks for it as a safe retreat the more of oneself will become object rather than subject, and as such the more of oneself will become infected by the impurity of the false self and the outside world. Authenticity retreats under conscious inspection and so estrangement spreads like a cancer. And it is this pervasive sense of estrangement, the frustration and anger of self-imprisonment and *imprisonment within the self* that describes the lived experience of self-harm. But as the foregoing discussion has hopefully shown it is not an experience that can *simply* be read as a psychological state, let alone a pathological condition, rather it is a pervasive sense of trauma that haunts the person and provides a background of meanings, ideas, values and associations that help make self-harm make sense to the person doing it, and that helps that person to make sense of themselves through their practice of self-harm.

Aetiology and the Haunting Absence of Dora

If a concern with authentic being leads to a concern with issues of agency and control, which in turn leads to an objectifying interest in the matter of life, the body and the 'real', then perhaps it should be little surprise that we tend to root the idea of aetiology, of causes and origins, in the material and the bodily, believing that this gives us more control over it. We seek to exert the truth of our authentic being, the psychological consequence and implication of forming the *homo clausus*, on a world that we feel ought to be malleable, that ought to conform to the shape that we have decreed for it. And perhaps this is why we experience those impediments, those stubborn parts of the 'real' that resist representation and the reshaping calculus of the civilising process, to be so traumatic; to be something that not only threatens us physically, but also existentially. As Salecl notes of contemporary psychological and therapy culture:

> Anything that is perceived as an impediment to the subject, who is supposed to be fully in control of herself, constantly productive and also not disturbing to society at large, is quickly categorized as disorder. While the subject's inner turmoil and dilemmas in regard to social expectations quickly get names as anxieties (2004: 3).

And once they are so named they are objectified and once objectified they become the subject of science, of observation and measurement and of attempted manipulation—or in this case, treatment. What is resisted through the familiar action of the asymmetric binary, what is hidden by this prejudice for objectification, is the more nuanced and challenging idea that our anxieties, our distress and our traumas may be significantly connected to the multiple conditions and contingencies of our lives as they are contextualised in complex networks of relationships and systems of meanings and values. And that the subject may not be as central or as sovereign as we like to think. There is a sense then, that in treating Dawn or Dora simply as the bearers of symptoms emanating from a biopsychological mechanism, that what we lose is the sense of an actual life. A messy, complex, contingent, heterogeneous and thoroughly situated life, but an actual life for all that. Still, as I have tried to argue throughout this book so far, the asymmetric binary is not a conspiracy or a rank discrimination, rather it is a subtle prejudice and a pervasive tendency in our ways of thinking that seeks to balance the multiple ambiguities and ambivalences of our culture and subjectivity as it attempts to acknowledge the romantic while rationalising life to the modern. Aetiology and its literary expression in the case history are crystallisations of this effort and in many ways this is what makes the case history such an interesting and enigmatic kind of a document.

It seems to me that case histories articulate the action of the asymmetric binary so well precisely because they often do, in fact, try to write the person in. Here, at least some of the details of a life *are* gathered, and a narrative *does* to some limited extent fill out the flesh and human face that are otherwise lacking in formulas of diagnosis, treatment and prognosis. However, despite this and at the very heart of their description, exactly where the living reality of an actual person ought to be, there is a kind of erasure and estrangement instead. The central position of the person becomes a void that exists as a curious counterpoint to all the detailed information about genetics, biology, psychology and biography that might be gathered and depicted; a strange, enigmatic and tragic *punctum*, in Barthes' (1993) phrase, that haunts the narrative. It is in this way that such texts not only help report the silence of the hysteric (classical and contemporary), but also reproduce it, making her a strangely voiceless figure even within those texts that are supposed to penetrate the veil of her symptoms and the enigma of her pathology.

Paradoxically, it is for this very reason that despite its impressive length, complexity and sophistication there is an unshakable sense as one reads through the *Fragment* that Freud somehow fundamentally 'missed' Dora; that behind the tapestry of psychological analysis and interpretation there is a void precisely where the living and immanent truth of Dora is supposed to be. Dora appears in these pages as a kind of haunting absence within the story of her own case history, just as she appears to have felt herself to have been something of an absence within the story of her own life. Indeed, the enigma that she has represented for people in the century since the publication of the *Fragment* seems to emerge from within an aura of pervasive and multiple estrangements.

Dora is a deeply estranged figure. From her own point of view she is estranged from all those people who profess to love her and should be close to her but who instead seem intent upon using her as a pawn in a game, or a gift in an exchange; from her father's point of view, that to some extent appears as a proxy for these other people that surround Dora, she has become pathologically estranged from her family and friends and from speech and sanity; and from Freud's point of view she is estranged from her own feelings, her own unconscious desires and wishes. And bookending this list of estrangements there is a sense of a more fundamental alienation from reality itself. At one end there is Dora's experience and version of reality, which seems to be under attack by everyone else; and at the other end there is Freud's calling into question the very nature of trauma itself.

When, finally, Dora has extracted a confession from Herr K. as to the reality of the attempted seduction, and doggedly fought for truth with respect to the other tangled relationships and webs of interests that had sought to use her and then position her as pathological, she presents the facts of her case to Freud who then presents his diagnosis and conclusion as to the psychology of her pathology, and indeed the summation of her case history. As he writes:

> Dora had listened to me without any of her usual contradictions. She seemed to be moved; she said good-bye to me very warmly, with the heartiest wishes for the New Year, and—came no more (1953 [1905]: 108–9).

It is hard not to see and feel behind these words Dora's sigh of resignation and a polite smile as disappointment bites once more. And that despite her bravery and commitment to what she saw as the truth of the matter she had nonetheless once again been misunderstood and perhaps misused. It is little wonder that she did not return. In Dora we find someone whose symptoms of silence express what must have felt almost like a conspiracy to her, one in which the truth was hidden, her closest relationships soured as she found herself used and manipulated instead of loved and understood, and her ability to connect with her friends and family, or with the authorised discourses of her culture, and eventually even with speech itself became deeply estranged and problematic. As Masson puts it:

> [S]he was preoccupied with matters of truth and honesty. She felt conspired against. She was conspired against. She felt lied to. She was lied to. She felt used. She was used. She was beginning to lose her faith in justice, in integrity—in short, in the world (1990: 101).

Both the hysteric and 'the self-harmer', then, appear as people who are strangely absent from the conditions of their own lives and indeed from the very texts that are used to make up and describe that life, and as such they become increasingly withdrawn into themselves as all they have left. It is a withdrawal well expressed in Dawn's description of a 'glass screen' that cuts her off from the outside world and eventually begins to cut off parts of her sense of herself, splitting and becoming 'internally' estranged.

In trauma, the world overwhelms and swallows up the person, and the site of the problem lies with them and their capacity to process (objectivist tendency) 'real' feelings and memories, or else their capacity to deal with the fact their own recognition of the 'real' is trapped within by a world that has become distinctly unreal (subjectivist tendency). But while the subjectivist perspective encodes an implicit critique of the social world in its inauthenticity it still focuses on the individual and their existential dilemma. What must not be lost sight of, however, is that within a culture concerned with control it may be the political systems, the networks of power relations that position and embed the person that are too 'real' and that are ultimately traumatic rendering one socially, as well as psychologically estranged. While Dora understood her problems as an issue of what was really going on in her life and home, Freud saw them as an issue of what was really going on in her psyche, but *both* conceptualisations and patterns of meanings were active, and laboured under different valences, because of the very social conditions and relationships that positioned Freud and Dora. And indeed it is tempting to say that far from Dora's real problem being a failed seduction, or a manipulative father it was her gendered position in *fin de siècle* Europe that constituted the actual basis of her problems.

Summary

The structures of meaning that surround the issue of cause then are complex, subtle and at times convoluted. The strictly aetiological logic of the case history provides one significant dimension of meanings as it locates self-harm in estrangement and estrangement in psychic trauma. By contrast, while more subjectivist representations do rely on the value of the medical conception of trauma in order to validate experience and identity in a medicalised society, the general use of the concept is less literal and more metaphorical. It is used to locate the cause of self-harm less in specific events or psychological mechanisms and in a less narrow and deterministic manner, and more in a general sense of a traumatic rupture with and a general estrangement from the world, language and even the self. Likewise, the apparent literal and metonymic logic of self-harm must be understood as significant symbols in and of themselves; in other words, they are signs that indicate what the literal has come to *mean* for us; namely a 'recourse to the real' (Žižek, 2000), a connection to nature more than culture, to harsh physical truth more than representation, and to pain and blood more than words and language (Hewitt, 1997; Belsey, 2004). And in this recourse to the real there is a bid for control, for authentic self-realisation and for an un-estranged foundation to subjectivity. But for all of these circulating meanings and construals, it is vitally important to understand self-harm in terms of the *pharmakon* as it cannot be seen in any uncomplicated fashion as an agent of the 'real' or an agent of control or indeed anything else specifically, but rather it must be understood to be abroad and active within a culture that is deeply concerned with these issues and that has produced self-harm as a crystallisation of them and an articulation of the tensions, contradictions and problems that can arise from them.

5
The Pathological Axis

Introduction: Stigma and the Dynamics of Being Secret and Being Seen

The celebrated sociologist Erving Goffman reminds us that it was the Greeks who 'originated the term stigma to refer to bodily signs designed to expose something unusual and bad about the moral status of the signifier' (1968: 11), some 'special discrepancy between virtual and actual social identity' (*ibid*: 12–13) that acts as a sign of a 'tainted, discredited' self (*ibid*: 12), the realisation of something 'defiling' within (*ibid*: 18), which leads not only to feelings of 'shame', but also 'self-hatred and self-derogation' (*ibid*). Indeed, it was Goffman who presented us with the classic contemporary analysis of stigma as a social and a psychological process, but it was the Czech novelist Franz Kafka who left us with the most visceral and affecting evocation of stigma in the operation of his combined torture and execution 'apparatus', as described in his short story *In the Penal Colony* (1992 [1919]). In this typically minimalist tale the outer stigma is a 'sentence', both a judicial sentence and a literal sentence of words articulating this judgement, inscribed into the flesh of a prisoner through the slow, excruciating action of a set of glass needles. Strapped to a table and subjected to this mutilation over a period of 12 h as the needles cut deeper and deeper, the sentence becomes a spectacular means of executing criminals, presumably as an example to others, but it is also a means of exposing a truth about the criminal, his sentence, and not just to others but also to himself as he is, in fact, unaware of what his sentence is and must 'decipher it with his wounds' (1992 [1919]: 137).

Kafka's disturbing story is a favourite among writers on body modification and mutilation (Mascia-Lees and Sharpe, 1992; Curtis, 2000), but its interest for us here lies less in the literal carving of flesh and more precisely in the delicate play of forces conjured into the operation of the machine. The outer stigma, at first, has the function of marking the deviant's body as different, marking them out, and sits in line then with various other spectacles of punishment, from putting someone in the village stocks to making children sit and face the wall. But as the needles inscribe their grim message the sentence becomes the visible expression of an authoritative knowledge, passed from an institution with power to be sure, but made flesh within the person of the deviant—*they* 'decipher' their stigma and so learn what kind of deviant they are. That which is thought to hide within then, the substantive essence of their deviance, is positioned as an object of knowledge and made visible both to both the criminal and others through the operation of this knowledge, and the operation of technology, and most of all through the mark of stigma that seals the judgement.

Indeed, these subtle power politics of embodiment and visibility, which have been with us since Chapter 3, when we first discussed *homo clausus* and the civilising process, are deeply significant matters for understanding self-harm. For one thing, Kafka's machine symbolises the complexity of control that we explored at the end of the last chapter and the sense that we may be trapped within a body that has become cut off from the world through its essential traumatic difference or deviance; a body that we own and yet which is subject to the influence of outside forces and as such can also be experienced as 'other', a body whose essential taint is made 'real' by the outer signal of its stigmatic wounds. Indeed, the play of visibilities is intensely ambivalent for people who self-harm for whom their withdrawal is, as we have seen, both a sanctuary and a prison, and whose practice is often highly private and yet codes a basic cry for help. As Susan describes it:

> This is linked to my self-harm; because I couldn't put my feelings into words, I did it in the worst way possible; when people see self harm marks though, it rings alarm bells; it was the only way I could silently say 'please help me'. My cutting was begging for help; I felt like I couldn't physically speak to people when I felt that low and hurt myself, so I did it in the only way someone would see and automatically know it was bad (email).

Here, Susan's practice is predicated on her wounds and scars becoming public and yet like so many other people interviewed for this research her self-harm was kept intensely private. Dawn describes this ambivalence as that between 'the desire for self-effacement and the desire, not to be looked at exactly, but just to be recognised'. The word 'recognition' is particularly important as it carries connotations of acceptance. To be recognised is not simply to cease being invisible but to have one's basic identity and sense of self confirmed by another. Typically, within this common and dynamic tension between being secret and being seen the promise of being seen is articulated through a rescue fantasy and a hope that if she is seen then the person who self-harms will be understood, and if understood then she will be accepted and her inner pain recognised and validated by virtue of the inescapable 'real' of her outer stigma. Allie provides a good example of this desire from her childhood:

> [W]hen I was in primary school I used to stand alone on the edge of the playground and stare at a church in the distance. As well as wishing I was there instead of where I actually was, I always hoped one of the teachers would take the time to come over and ask if I was OK so I could tell them I wasn't (email).

But if self-harm is a message to others then perhaps we should think of it like a letter that has been written but not sent, set aside in a safe place with the possibility that it may be sent in the future and with the hope that by then the recipient will be able to understand it, to recognise the truth that it contains. And in this sense it is both a public act and a private act. The writing of this letter, of inscribing 'please help me' onto the body, would seem in and of itself to often be enough, at least for the immediate psychological needs of the person self-harming. But more than this, remembering what we said about the social origins of the self in Chapter 2, and as Goffman noted in his study of stigma, because we learn to see ourselves by seeing our presence impact upon others our perception of ourselves always carries with it this sense of the other, a kind of 'generalized other' (Mead, 1967) or 'big Other' (Lacan, 2007), where this latter carries not just the sense of the other, but also the moral order, the public norms and values, that come with others. As Roland Littlewood observes with respect to the expressive function of such idioms of distress, 'an individual is frequently their own principle audience' (2002: 164). And if this is the case then it is easy to imagine the fantasy dimension that can be overlaid onto this sense of a generalised other; that in performing an act of self-harm, albeit in private, the person has somehow 'put something out there', has made it 'real', and can now feel some small sense, even momentarily, of the recognition and validation that they would hope to be met with, ideally, if they were to go public. But here we meet a dilemma common to self-harm: the 'real' of a wound is ambivalent as, on the one hand, it validates inner experience by manifesting emotions as blood, pain and scars, while, on the other, it acts as a stigma, as a mark of deviance and shame, as evident of a defiled, tainted and discredited self. And as this chapter will demonstrate feelings of guilt, shame and self-hatred, and representations of self-harm as self-punishment, are very common among the people I have interviewed, as well those who post on the internet or publish their autobiographies.

But with these considerations we seem to have moved on from ideas about the ontological structures of self-harm, and ideas about the aetiological conditions that cause it, and have moved instead into the experience of the person who self-harms and the phenomenology of self-harm as an expression of these ontological structures and aetiological causes. And so we begin our third and final axis. While the ontological axis groups and organises ideas about those ontological structures that facilitate self-harm, that make it a possible and even at times a necessary function for *this* kind of subject, who has *this* kind of body and *this* kind of psyche, the aetiological axis organises ideas about what particular kinds of events can happen within the context of these ontological structures to make self-harm appear in some instances of this kind of subjectivity but not others; the two together only cover those ideas about how someone might come to self-harm in the first place and do not describe what it is like *to be* a 'self-harmer', the *content* of the practice as such. And so it is this area of meanings that we will now add and that the third axis organises and describes. As these effects and experiences describe the common living shape of self-harm for people who use it, how someone with self-harm 'presents', their particular profile of current symptoms as it were, I have called it the *pathological axis*.

Self-Persecution: The Key Thematic Discourse of the Pathological Axis

> I couldn't see myself as a strong, determined and enthusiastic person; I saw myself as a pathetic, snivelling, ugly, crying, cut and bleeding fuck up, to be plain. I had failed myself and my family and I wasn't of any use at all (Dana, email).

Here Dana gives brutal voice to a near pervasive theme in participants' accounts and subjectivist representations of self-harm in general: the theme of self-loathing, self-hatred and self-punishment, which, along with its associated subdiscourses, makes up our next key thematic discourse: *self-persecution*. As Dana explains, '[i]f I failed, failure meant punishment.... I had failed myself and my family and I wasn't of any use at all.... My self-harm was self-punishment, it's the best way I can explain it' (email). These are sentiments echoed throughout the interviews that I conducted and indeed the multiple conflicts and tensions that we have been looking at throughout the previous two chapters have a consistent and crushing tendency to be experienced by people who self-harm through this singular lens of self-punishment. And yet what we are talking about here goes well beyond this, beyond the sense of a situated correction or measured response to a wayward deed, no matter how unjustified the rest of us may feel this judgement is or how inappropriate acts of self-injury are as a form of punishment. What we are talking about here is properly described as self-*persecution* because it connects to a sense of unrelenting and pervasive responsibility, as Alyson explains:

> I always feel the... the depression is my fault... and I feel that I'm useless and pathetic and... it's all my fault and if I was any better then I could get myself out of it and I'm being... you know, awful to my family and friends and I'm a terrible person, so... part of it is self-punishment (telephone).

As the operator of Kafka's apparatus makes clear '[t]he principle on which I base my decisions is this, guilt is always beyond question' (1992 [1919]: 132), and the by now familiar focus on the self, its powers and responsibilities, and its dynamics and limitations ensures that failure and punishment are not understood here as matters for occasional self-management or measured correction but rather represent a more fundamental stigma; an indelible mark demonstrating the deep failure of the self, a judgement inscribed into flesh and delivering the sentence of the self as 'a pathetic, snivelling, ugly, crying, cut and bleeding fuck up'. If, following all that we have discussed in the last two chapters, the limit of your world is the limit of your sense of self, and you judge yourself to be guilty, then your world is not just one of punishment but of unremitting and relentless punishment.

It was when people voiced sentiments like these that, more than at any other time in the interviews that I conducted, I could relate to some of the feelings that clinicians Allen Francis and Fiona Gardner described in the Introduction (p. 2); feelings of being helpless and horrified, frustrated and furious. It was at these times that I often felt as moved to shout at my participants in sheer exasperation as I did to put my arm around them and comfort them, wishing they would escape the prison of self-persecution that they had sentenced themselves to. There is an obvious narcissism in the spectacle of a world shrunk to the size of a self, and when confronted with narcissism, or at least the narcissism of others, we have a tendency to lash out at the reflective surfaces, a desire to burst their bubble. But this is hardly a greedy or selfish narcissism; it is brutal, harsh, relentless and unforgiving (literally). It is a torment and it is hard not to feel moved to empathy when you talk to someone who is trapped within their own emotional world like this, even as you feel vexed and upset.

But despite this, or perhaps because of it, this theme of self-persecution is often strangely underplayed, marginalised or even completely ignored by more objectivist representations and texts. It is often mentioned, although more in passing than in detail, and often appears in lists of the symptomatic and psychological experience of 'the self-harmer', yet it is nonetheless rarely considered as part of the fundamental reason *why* people self-harm. But then perhaps this shouldn't surprise us. If the pathological axis organises ideas about the experience and presentation of self-harm, its emotional and behavioural topography, then these are precisely the kind of idiographic features that the psychiatrist, psychologist or psychotherapist, working from the objectivist stance of what the cultural studies scholar Nikki Sullivan calls the 'dermal diagnostician' (2002), tend to *look past*. The surfaces of experience are taken to be indexical markers directing them toward a deeper, more 'inner' truth. As the counselling psychologist Caroline Sweet articulated the perspective of the dermal diagnostician, 'what we do on the surface nearly always has some deep structure behind it' (quoted in Pitts, 2003: 25). But if it is quite typical of the asymmetric binary to marginalise the features of the pathological axis effectively, then here I want to explore and describe what otherwise seems quite obvious to nonexperts: that the very pattern of meanings and actions that describes self-harm fundamentally codes a tendency to self-punishment, which—as we will see—can ultimately be thought of as a relationship taken by the self *to* itself and characterised by persecution. As a participant in research conducted by social work scholar Helen Spandler put it,

> Self-harm is not a medical issue. It's not about being mentally unstable.... It has to do with hatred for yourself, feeling that you're

not worthy of anybody's love or attention...self-punishment. You deserve this, you deserve to hurt (1996: 68).

Responsibility and Expectation

Julie cut the words 'I hate me' into her arm and in so doing sentenced herself, starkly expressing the sentiments underpinning self-persecution. Julie had grown up in a highly 'punitive' household, which had only become more so after her father's death when she was 14 years old and her mother then looked to Julie for help in raising the younger children and to take responsibility for housework. As Julie describes it: 'I was just constantly being punished for whatever...so it [self-harm] became something that *I* could control' (in person). Julie's intonation emphasised the word 'I', underlying some of the meanings of control explored in the last chapter and also illustrating the sense of subjective internalisation that I discussed in the ontological axis: if punishment was her daily experience then, as she could punish herself, she could also take symbolic control of it, identify in part as the punisher and by so doing experience some control in her own life. Julie's story, and her internalisation, are also characteristic of another common aspect of participant's accounts, including those of Dana and Alyson, that in many cases and from an early age there has been some sort of pressure or expectation placed on them to suddenly become more responsible, more adult—an expectation often connected to looking after younger siblings after the departure of one of the parents or else, as in Dana's case, to look after a sick parent. Dana's story of self-harm begins with her mother's illness and her subsequently becoming her care assistant from a very early age. Here she talks about a moment of sudden realisation regarding the impact this role and its expectations was having on her:

> we were in a tiny space, cornered off by a curtain, and there was a drunk man swearing on the other side at a nurse who was trying to stitch up his hand, when he fell into the curtain and nearly through it. I nearly laughed out loud, you know, you find people falling over funny and stuff like that at a young age, but I knew in a hospital things were very serious and I had to be nice so I didn't laugh, and as a nurse was hooking my Mum up to a machine, she smiled at me and said 'well aren't you a brave little thing? You're very grown up'. I think she was praising me for my behaviour and I felt proud, but then it slowly sank in; I realised I was grown up, too grown up for a five year old. Five year olds shouldn't have to know their parents [sic] medical details off by heart and know CPR and the recovery position. A five year old shouldn't have to stand in a corner hidden

behind a curtain in a strange and scary situation and listen to a drunk man swearing and bellowing at people trying to help. A five year old shouldn't have to look after their parent, it should be the other way around.... I wanted to cry for feeling so different and so 'picked out' for this (email).

The internalisation of an adult role with adult responsibilities implies the internalisation of adult standards of self-control, and helps knit together other themes that we have explored in the other axes, as Dana notes:

> All of this links to my communication difficulties, as a child and as a teenager; because I was so well behaved and up to scratch with Mum's illness, I don't ever remember my grandma, or anyone asking me how I felt about it; the times in hospital, recovery, etc; no one asked me how I felt, and I couldn't put my emotions into words, So I packed them up tightly and buried them away somewhere; I couldn't talk about something that I couldn't give words (email).

In this passage, the pressures and expectations that Dana internalises and identifies with become the basis for her traumatic rupture with the world, her being 'picked out', as she puts it, made different, cut off and estranged from other forms of relationships and communication. The dynamics of Julie's story are similar to Dana's in that after her parents split up she became the 'emotional support' for her mother, as well as taking on more responsibilities for housework and looking after her younger brother. She describes how she effectively switched roles with her mother, becoming responsible for her mother's well-being while, for her part, her mother became increasingly 'emotionally manipulative'. One night she tried to go out with a friend 'just to get away from it all' but as she went to leave the house her mother

> burst into tears... so your choice is you stay and look after her or you're the heartless daughter who abandons your crying mother... you know, it was like 'why should you go out and have a nice time if I'm still miserable getting over your dad'... it was always *your* dad in these situations [laughs]; yeah, it was always on me (telephone).

One of the interesting things that emerged from many of these mother–child relationships was that even where the father appears to have been the more abusive or manipulative parent it is still the mother who is typically held to account for the child's internalisation of responsibility, their failure to learn an adequate emotional vocabulary and therefore also their incapacity to 'process' feelings. Perhaps this is because the mother has traditionally been framed as archetype of the feminine and therefore as the guardian of the heart and the hearth 'whose primary life-giving functions were to comfort, nurture and provide' (Bronfen, 1992: 66). The cultural association of women with the emotions and emotional expression may lead to the expectation that it is the mother's responsibility to teach the child to experience and express emotions in a healthy way (Lupton, 1998). John, for example, the only man who participated in this research, provides a case in point. Although he describes a tense and difficult relationship with both his father and his brothers as they, and he, struggled to reconcile their working class background with his sexual identity as a homosexual man, it is his mother that he blames for his history of self-harm:

> She was there the whole time and if I'd fallen out with my dad then... then I could have handled that if, if she would have talked to me... and let me express myself properly you know? But she didn't want to know and so I've grown up... not knowing how to express myself really, not... not knowing how to be emotional (in person).

John also provides a particularly vivid and visceral example of the theme of self-loathing as his self-harm often symbolically reflected the profound sense of guilt and shame that he felt in connection with his sexuality. On one occasion he used a syringe to gather the liquid dirt from the bottom of an industrial bin, cut deeply into his arm with a razor blade and then injected the dirt directly into the wound, sewing it up afterwards and hoping to get an infection as this inner pollution would be 'what I deserved really you know? That was just how I was feeling on the inside like dirt and shit and so that's just what I thought about myself, so yeah... that's why I did it'. What John's example dramatically illustrates is that this theme of self-persecution operates through a moral economy of guilt and shame, where shame is, as cultural studies scholar Sarah Ahmed describes it, 'an intense and painful sensation that is bound up with how the self feels about itself, a self-feeling that is felt by and on the body' (2004: 103).

Examination, Judgement, Punishment

Abigail Robson, in her autobiographical account of self-harm, *Secret Scars*, writes:

In a way I really don't want any help, in case it lulls me into a false sense of security where I think I might be worth something... I need to suffer—why can no one understand that? I need for people to see that I'm getting what I deserve, to comfort them, just so they know that I am aware of the horrible person that I am (2007: 96).

The shame and guilt so often felt by people who self-harm tends to be connected to personal standards that are incredibly high, even impossible, but standards that are nonetheless taken as *normative*, as measures that the person *should* be able to meet and embody. Dana internalised adult responsibilities and adult standards of self-control from a very early age, and looking back on this process she describes this aspect of her personality as her 'superhuman' persona, suggesting that she now understands these standards to be ideals, although at the time she expected them of herself and took them as normative and binding. Reflecting about this superhuman persona she notes that

In superman, spiderman, batman, green lantern, etc, all comic books; they get the girls, they get the baddies, everything works out fine. If they get hurt it doesn't show, they don't bleed when you cut them, they don't give up when its impossible, but this is all just a very high standard, something beyond being human that we idolize and need in society... in reality... when we need the inspiration and the light, we struggle to find it, and we rarely find the motivation to find it and use it (email).

For Dana it was her superhuman persona and the endeavour to meet 'impossible' standards that became the basis for the kind of splitting in her sense of self that I noted in the last chapter. But it is not just a question of conflict between human limitations and superhuman ideals, but rather of taking these ideals as normative expectations of the human, as *shoulds* and *oughts*. Failure to achieve these expectations then is not understood or felt to be the failure to meet an ideal but rather the failure to meet the basic criteria of personhood, a fundamental failure of human being. Hence, Dana's brutal assessment of herself as 'a pathetic, snivelling, ugly, crying, cut and bleeding fuck up'. Deborah also expresses this deep sense of failure through her description of herself as 'wrong':

As far back as I can remember I have tried to change to fit in, to gain approval and acceptance. Then through school I was still an outsider so I tried to be someone different and I discovered that if I was just who people wanted me to be then they would leave me alone. But for me this resulted in the useless me becoming increasingly unacceptable and shameful and it just wouldn't go away. That part of me is wrong, but it is the real me so hence I am wrong and anything that wrong shouldn't exist... the other me acts as a barrier it keeps me away from the world and the world away from me (email).

It is impossible to miss the intense sense of self-judgement that runs through this and other accounts; of standards which must be met but which are generally failed, and the punishment that inevitably and necessarily follows. But it is also important to note that these standards are connected to the fulfilment of social roles, and the expectations that people like Dana and Deborah internalise are those that they perceive to come from others, they are expectations as responsibilities. Alyson demonstrates this through her internalisation of, and taking responsibility for, the expectations of others, and especially her parents, stemming from her early academic success and the pride this evidently gave her mother and father. She notes the way that her internalisation of other people's judgements of her leads to a strong sense of pressure, which, in turn, arouses anxiety and leads to self-harm. As she explains these pressures:

My self-esteem rests very much on my ability to please others... that's how I have my self-esteem by being good at my role, I don't... I don't believe in my heart of hearts that I'm a good person or intrinsically a good person or intrinsically a loveable person really... I have to be a good wife and a good daughter and good at my studies... I have to be... not for my own sake but for other people's sake (telephone).

It is in this way that the people I interviewed, as well as many who have written about their self-harm in books and on the internet, display a heightened sense of responsibility for the welfare of others and a sense of tremendous pressure that they must not disappoint or let those people down. But as their standards virtually guarantee failure then they are also virtually guaranteed to feel deeply guilty: guilty of failure, guilty of not matching up to expectations, guilt of having let others down, guilt of having let themselves down, guilt of having failed at life and guilt of having failed as human beings. And, as Dana made clear above, this economy of responsibility/expectation and shame/guilt only serves to further direct attention back onto the self, which, and as the last two axes have described, is consequently experienced as isolated, individualised, estranged and ultimately trapped within its self. It is a moral and emotional economy that works through processes of intense self-scrutiny recalling the vigilant regime of self-surveillance, self-control, that describes the *homo clausus*. Indeed, these themes of expectation and failure constitute very strong judgements against the self, which is watched constantly, analysed and evaluated constantly to see if it is matching up to standards and expectations, or whether it is simply and predictably failing again. As Dawn describes this regime:

> I have to do the right thing! It has to be perfect or I will get rejected because I am not good enough. Without approval I am very lost and trying to gain acceptance has been an unobtainable goal. With or without these things being offered I feel the same because on the rare occasions someone does offer their approval or acceptance I reject it as a lie. And know I have never been able to accept or approve of myself because there is nothing in me that deserves it (email).

This constant self-surveillance, examination and judgement describes a regime of reflexivity that can become debilitating, a kind of hyper-reflexivity in which the person's belief that they will always fail leads to their inability to make decisions or take actions. In her autobiographical account of her self-harm, Abigail Robson describes an example of this when one day, as she was driving to work, she simply

> kept driving. I couldn't make a decision to stop, or turn, so I just drove straight until I reached a crossroad. I sat there until someone honked behind me. I looked at the signs and realized that if I turned left I could get onto the London Orbital and keep driving round and round without having to make a decision (2007: 136).

It is the normality of these avoided decisions that is so striking here and in what my participants shared with me. The paralysis of hyper-reflexivity is far more focused on clothes, food and housework, standard aspects of someone's daily role and identity than more major decisions such as whether to submit themselves to hospitalisation, for example. What one is left with is a strong impression of a never ceasing internal monologue of criticism, analysis and anxiety all built up from a platform of unassailable expectations and aspirations. This is often connected with a withdrawal from the world and the idea of a prison house of the self. As a sense of failure deepens it affects even very basic decisions and ordinary life becomes untenable. As Robson tells us: 'the voices dripped constantly in my head like a Chinese water torture, telling me that I wasn't good enough, that I was a fraud and an imposter who didn't deserve to be well' (2007: 103).

Salvation

The failure to meet such high standards, then, is not typically read by people who self-harm, as evidenced that these standards are, in fact, *ideals*, to be aspired to perhaps but ultimately never achieved. Rather, their failures are taken to be an inescapable judgement laid on them by life, by others and eventually even by themselves. A judgement that they are in some deep and essential sense a failure ('a pathetic, snivelling, ugly, crying, cut and bleeding fuck up'). But if this apparent fatalism is both deep and dark it is only apparent nonetheless. In fact, like all economies, the moral and emotional economy of self-persecution works through a dynamic or contradiction between two poles, in this case representing two different ideas of the self. On the one hand, we all too easily and clearly find the self as failure, the self as Dana's 'cut and bleeding fuck up'. But, on the other, we also find, implicit in the theme of self-persecution, the *ideal* of the self who could meet such high standards and who *is* worthy of love, praise and affirmation. So recalling Menninger's definition of nonsuicidal self-mutilation, there does indeed seem to be, if not a victory of the 'life-instinct' then at least a constant sense of, a constant desire and holding out of hope for, a better life and a better, non-stigmatised, self.

Of course the cycle of self-punishment and the moral economy of self-persecution requires that this worthy self be taken not as an ideal at all but rather as a normative aspirational expectation and therefore as an imperative. But the point is that regardless of whether this worthy self is understood as an ideal or an achievable aspiration it exists as part of the moral economy and so represents a vital and active part of the discourse of self-persecution, which works by both carrot and stick; indeed, it is the carrot that makes the stick bearable and even desirable. So despite the seemingly crushing and relentless logic of failure, guilt and punishment typically described by the people that I interviewed there was always also evident, if implicit in what they were saying, a sense of possible salvation, a sense of what it would mean if they ceased to fail and met expectations. Indeed, for many people self-harm is experienced precisely as a technique of moral discipline and as such a true form of self-*punishment*; a means by which the 'fuck up' may work toward, or at least gain the chance to become, the more worthy self through the payment of punishment, discipline and control into the moral economy of examination, judgement and guilt.

And like so much of the meaning caught up in self-harm we are again confronted here by ambivalence. Self-punishment implies corporeal punishment directed against a discredited self and yet it also represents the purging of bad feelings and negative emotions that don't belong to the more idealised and worthy version of the self, the authentic and true-self. If, in our Christian-informed culture, wounds mean suffering (in part shame and stigma, and in part objective validation) then they also mean repentance, forgiveness, purity attained and a return to authenticity (Bradford, 1990). This, of course, is also the same pure and authentic self that lies at the heart of so many texts of therapy culture; recall, for example, from the last chapter the images used by Sutton and Miller of a journey back to 'light' and 'healing'. And so we find stigma in concert with salvation, with the idea that the self could indeed be who it ought to be, if only it could clear itself of the taint of failure and guilt and reveal the happy and mentally healthy self that is firmly felt to be a latent possibility held within.

Within this discourse of self-persecution then we find a problematic conflation between the ideal and the normative, a conflation that describes and interprets an entrapping moral and emotional economy (incorporating a sense of pressure and expectation, of responsibility, of inevitable failure and the hope held out of an eventual salvation), as well as the regime of self-examination, judgement, punishment and rehabilitation that regulates this economy. It is a complex of meanings and values that can help us to understand the ambiguities of the secret/seen dualism. Being seen holds out the hope of short-circuiting the relentless cycle of this punishing economy by offering the possibility, perhaps entertained only in fantasy, of being seen; of being seen deeply, which is to say of being understood deeply, and therefore of being accepted for who the person considers themselves to truly be. It is the possibility that someone will look past the 'pathetic, snivelling, ugly, crying, cut and bleeding fuck up' to see the authentic soul within. But while such a moment offers the possibility of bypassing the hyperjudgemental processes of the self-harm it is also generally regarded as a fantasy. For one thing, most people who self-harm seem to be confirmed cynics when it comes to the possibility of such a perfect interaction with someone else. Beside which, it would mean lumbering that person with their emotional baggage, which would not be an internalisation of responsibility but an externalisation of it—and that is not their way.

Discipline: The Discursive Complex of the Pathological Axis

The key thematic discourse of self-persecution articulates a sense of self that is constantly watchful and vigilant, always examining and assessing itself, and always finding itself falling short of some ideal standard taken as a normative injunction. It should be remembered that such thematic discourses describe the experience of self-harm and, as such, map out the patterns of meaning associated with it. These are the meanings that people really are living with and suffering through; however, they are not determined by neurochemistry, cognitive architecture or psychodynamic metapsychology. Rather, they are the experiential knots tied into the web of significance and signification that is the surrounding culture. The meanings and values that make up our culture are the same meanings and values that we use to make up our sense of selfhood and identity; the same meanings and values that we use to make sense of our lives, our experience and our world. Our psychology, then, is patterned after our culture, although perhaps not determined by it as we use the meanings that we find there according to our particular situation and circumstance, our needs, interests and perspectives as they are formed through personal experience and social interaction. The structures that underpin the knot of psychological and emotional experience described by self-persecution then are not to be found within the knot itself but rather in the web around it, in its shape and organisation, and in the forces, the ecology, that have informed this shape. Of course, in this regard, Elias's analytics of the civilising process and the emergence of *homo clausus* are highly suggestive as they map the emergence of a kind of psychological individual characterised by self-vigilance, self-control and the policing of emotions like shame and guilt. However, the exact features of the discourse of self-persecution suggest more the second of the two analytics of modern *internalising* subjectivity I mentioned in Chapter 3—not Elias's civilising process then but rather Michel Foucault's *disciplinary society* (1991 [1975]).

From Spectacle to Discipline

Foucault's important book *Discipline and Punish* (1991 [1975]) begins with a graphic description of the public torture and execution of Robert Damiens, an attempted regicide, in 1757. He immediately follows this with a description of the mundane details of the daily regime of life in a Parisian house of corrections just 80 years later. The contrast could hardly be more striking, and between the colourful evocation of a truly public spectacle of violence and the flat and frankly boring grind of daily life in prison, Foucault argues that we can locate not just a seismic shift in the general style of social order and the operation of justice, but also a shift in the way that power and violence work within society. Foucault believes that in this shift we witness the emergence of a new strategy of power, which rendered violence both more private and more complete, and which in the process helped to establish a new kind of subject.

The brilliance of Foucault's observation lies in its deconstruction of our common reading of this seismic social shift. If, as Dostoyevsky said, a civilisation can be judged by entering its prisons (1985 [1862]), then of course this shift can be, and often is, read as a key moment in the ongoing liberalisation and democratisation of modern society. However, Elias has already helped us to read more into the word 'civilisation' than Dostoyevsky perhaps intended, and we understand that along with such transformations in social order it also implies the degree to which a society's regimes of power and control have become focused on the figure of the individual subject and the concomitant degree to which systems of self-control have been cultivated and violence internalised (Jervis, 1998).

And indeed Foucault argues that what has actually changed between the public spectacle and the modern prison is not the degree or amount of power and violence exerted but rather its *strategy* of application. The old regime of power works through spectacle and the overt and vulgar public threat of violence. It is brutal but it is also honest: it takes people as they are and simply reminds them in blood, gore and screams what will happen to them if they step out of line. In the modern regime, however, this strategy of visible spectacle has disappeared and instead 'by contrast, power works by making those subject to it visible—by surveillance' (Crossley, 2006: 40). In the new regime prisoners are watched, their behaviour is monitored and their daily schedule and conformity to it maintained. As the operation of power becomes *less* publically visible then, it invests itself instead in the figure of the individual by making them *more* visible, by submitting them to a constant regime of visibility such that, not knowing when they are actively being watched and when not, they internalise the watcher so that 'control [now] operates through internalisation, [and] becomes, to a large extent, self-surveillance' (Wolff, 1990: 125). As Foucault explains:

> he who is subjected to a field of visibility and who knows it, assumes responsibility for the constraints of power; he makes them play spontaneously upon himself; he inscribes in himself the power relation in which he simultaneously plays both roles; he becomes the principle of his own subjection (1991 [1975]: 202–3).

Foucault's seismic shift then is not really, as we might otherwise have it, from punishment to rehabilitation but rather, as the literature and sexualities scholar Lisa Downing puts it, a shift 'from the punishment of the body to the punishment of the soul' (2008: 76).

But the visibility of the prisoner goes well beyond their being watched during their daily routine and has to do with the way that they themselves are construed as subjects for study and objects of knowledge. Along with the tectonic social transformations that forged modern societies came new systems of representation, new ways of thinking and talking about prisoners and people in general. Systems of representation that, in taking the human as a subject of objective and scientific enquiry, created new vocabularies, new explanations and new technologies all focused on opening up the inner-space of the *homo clausus* and rendering visible what, as the mask of Hawthorne's minister suggests, these same tectonic transformations had helped hide away in the first place. Foucault notes that '[a]s well as punishing acts, the penal system becomes a way of naming, judging, isolating, and controlling the "shadows lurking behind the case itself" ' (1991 [1975]: 17). The criminal is watched in prison and known by its appointed experts, the criminologists whose knowledge reveals the 'shadows... behind the case', the inner substantives that dispose the criminal to their crime and render them into a certain kind, a certain category of person. In this new regime of visibilities then, as Foucault notes, systems of knowledge become inextricably caught up with systems of power. As with Kafka's apparatus the emergence of socially authorised knowledge about the subject becomes the very basis upon which the subject themselves discovers the 'truth' about themselves and, as such, is interpellated into a particular identity and subject position. Through this act of interpellation systems of socially authorised knowledge become systems of self-knowledge and the surveillance of the individual subject becomes the subject's own self-surveillance and the very 'principle of his own subjection' (*ibid*: 203). To be known is to be seen and to be seen is to see yourself, albeit through the eyes of another, to come to know yourself as they know you, and to do this is, to some extent, to become identified with and through the category of person that they know you to be.

Having mapped the arteries of knowledge and power as they branch out through the structures and regimes of the prison, Foucault brilliantly shows that this carceral system is, in fact, a model not just for the modern prison, but also for the modern social order in general. Beginning with what Goffman (1991) calls its 'total institutions', its military barracks, schools and psychiatric hospitals but spreading beyond this to the factory floor and the modern workplace, before eventually, through twenty-first-century surveillance and consumer culture, coming to characterise the general organisation and regime of contemporary society, this disciplinary regime, the means by which surveillance becomes self-surveillance and self-control, has come to symbolise the logic of modern Western society. Indeed, as philosopher Sandra Bartky explains, '[i]n the perpetual self-surveillance of the inmate lies the genesis of the celebrated "individualism" and heightened self-consciousness which are hallmarks of modern times' (1990: 65). Hallmarks that we have seen powerfully evident, for example, in Dana's judging her human self by the standards of her superhuman ideal, and in Julie's taking over the role of her own punisher.

Foucault's disciplinary society then is a society in which the regulation of populations through the coercive powers of an overt social order has been replaced by the regulation of populations through a more implicit order of the individual subject; a self-imposed order of the self backed by expert knowledge and moral and institutional technologies. And here we might pick back up on the theme that the emergence of the human sciences and the psy-complex were intimately tied to the emergence of the modern individual, and that as such these new disciplines of knowledge and systems of representation also implied new systems of power and of *subjectification*, which is to say the processes by which people become certain kinds of subjects and find themselves subjected to certain kinds of conditions and relationships (Rose, 1985, 1991, 1998; Hook, 2007). By emphasising the separation of the inner and the outer, and by constituting the realm of the inner as one containing deep, profound and authentic truths about who and what we are at root and in essence, modernity imposed a cultural obligation on us to see and understand ourselves (to become visible to ourselves) as psychological individuals and, as such, this is increasingly how we have come to identify and recognise ourselves in contemporary society. We are interpellated as psychological beings and, as such, we turn to regimes of psychological knowledge, practices, strategies, technologies and relationships to tell us with authority and science what this means and what we are supposed to do about it; what normative standards we are supposed to civilise and discipline ourselves into. As sociologist Stewart Clegg puts it:

> ways of constituting the normal are institutionalised and incorporated into everyday life. Our own reflexive gaze takes over the disciplinary role as we take on the accounts and vocabularies

of meaning which are available to us, while certain other forms of account are marginalized or simply erased out of currency (1989: 156).

In contemporary, late-modern society and culture there can be little doubt that our prevalent 'accounts and vocabularies of meaning' are distinctly psychological and quite often medical in nature. Psychology represents more than just a regime of knowledge but also a whole system of moral technologies through which we define ourselves as normative subjects, and by which we come to examine, judge and discipline ourselves in order to meet these normative standards. As the social critic Ivan Illich observed '[s]o persuasive is the power of the institutions that we have created that they shape not only our preferences, but also our sense of possibilities' (1972: 132). Or, as Ann believes, 'everyone should see a counsellor at some point in their lives, I mean we all have issues we need to work through, I'm sure everyone does' (telephone). The psychological and moral technologies of the individual then are also moral technologies about the individual, and through their application subjects have become more individualised and of course more psychologised. Social psychologist Derek Hook argues that

> the prominence and accelerated growth of [psychology], the very fact that it has not been confined to the narrow parameters of a purely academic exercise, must be seen in the context of a new culture of power that massively prioritizes the docility of the individual subject (2007: 15).

'Docile' here referring to the way bodies are made into modern selves through processes of subjectification. An individual is docile to the extent that she 'may be subjected, used, transformed and improved' (Foucault, 1991 [1975]: 180), all notable late-modern concerns and ones to which we will shortly return. The irony then is that the modern and late-modern fascination with the psychological individual, set as it is within the values of freedom and agency, does not, in fact, work to liberate the individual from the shackles of society at all but rather breaks the chains only so that it may be subjected to an even more incisive form of power.

A Post-disciplinary Society?

While Elias and Foucault offer different, although somewhat complementary, accounts of the civilising process and the emergence of a disciplinary society, there has been some debate in recent years on the relevance of these arguments outside of the specific historical and social conditions that were drawn on to formulate them. In particular, some people have started to talk about a 'decivilizing process' (Mennell, 1990), focusing on the perceived increase of violence *within* societies, which, it is argued, runs counter to Elias' model of suppressed and internalised intrasocial aggression; and the emergence of an 'informalization process' (Crossley, 2006), through which there has been a general relaxation of manners, etiquette and the old public values of starch-collared reserve and decorum. These twin debates have connected with a related critique of Foucault, namely that our culture has become less disciplined, even since the 1960s when Foucault began formulating his arguments, and that the subject in his disciplinary society is more a two-dimensional cipher for social control and an example of what some have dismissively called a 'cultural dope' (Bordo, 1997), rather than the independent, agentive, rich and complex person that most of us take ourselves to be.

Indeed, at first glance it might seem difficult to maintain Elias' arguments about the strict control of bodily displays and privacy in the face of a hypersexualised media and a society that is increasingly tolerant of casual clothes, relaxed manners and taboo language. Nonetheless, Elias and his defenders (Elias, 1996; Mennel, 1990; Wouters, 2004), while acknowledging the social and cultural trends described by the 'informalisation process', and explaining these through the breakdown of the old regimes and the rituals of power that have traditionally described the relationships of men to women and adults to children, notes that this process of breakdown has created whole new populations (women and children, for example) that used to be more coercively controlled but who are now more subject to the processes of internalisation and subjectification, as described by Foucault and himself. An example of this might be noted as a qualification to my comment about hypersexualised media. Although it is certainly true that over the last several decades there has been an increasing informalisation in the standards of what can be shown, and increasingly graphic displays of flesh used in advertisements, television, magazines and music videos, it is also nonetheless the case that these bodies do not represent raw or natural bodies but, on the contrary, highly disciplined and controlled bodies (Winkler and Cole, 1994; Bartky, 1997; Bordo, 1997, 2003). Of course, on the other side of the lingerie billboard, those who witness these increasingly graphic displays are not only expected to take on some of the same values and ideals of discipline and control that are on display, but are also expected to control any sexual or bodily reactions to such displays, which, of course, are no more acceptable to us now than they were in Victorian times.

A problem with a lot of these arguments for 'informalisation' or the end of a disciplinary society is that they tend to focus on the content of the normative rather than the *strategy* by which the normative (of any given time) is being enforced, although it is precisely the strategy that Elias and Foucault are identifying. The sociologist Nick Crossley, for example, argues that '[i]f aerobics is body-power then body-power is nothing to worry about' (2006: 50), neatly ignoring a society in which ideals of the body beautiful have been taken to such extremes, and taken to be so bindingly *normative*, that we have whole idioms of distress like anorexia that reflect our cultural fixation with diet and exercise (Bordo, 2003). The key dynamic in a disciplinary society is that ideals, justified through systems of expert knowledge, are taken as norms and experienced as moral imperatives. We all know that we are supposed to be 'fit and healthy' but what does this mean, what is 'fitness'? It is not just a question of who defines the standards (the experts) but rather who understands the knowledge generated in this way as authoritative, as normal, natural and simply the way things are, such that they pursue it and may identify and define themselves in the context of this pursuit (essentially all of us). Indeed, in our culture the ideal of 'fitness' seems bound to a standard that always recedes from us, as the sociologist Zygmunt Bauman notes '[t]he pursuit of fitness is the state of perpetual self-scrutiny, self-reproach and self-deception, and so also of continuous anxiety' (2000: 78). By contrast, Crossley seems to imagine that a subject can simply step out of their culture to view its norms with a kind of independent choice and agency. For example, he argues that informalisation is

> creating social spaces wherein choices rather than norms steer behaviour. Choice will be shaped by many factors, of course, but in the absence of norms and sanctions actors may opt in or out of them (2006: 38).

Of course, it is hard to see how choice would be possible at all without the value systems provided by public norms to get one started, but, more than this, as I shall argue in the next section, the provision of choice itself can be understood as a disciplinary means of making the subject police their own subjectivity, their own choices and decisions. Bauman notes that 'everything in a consumer society is a matter of choice, except the compulsion to choose—the compulsion which grows into an addiction and is no longer perceived as compulsion' (2000: 73). So a range of contents may nonetheless mask a monopoly of strategy, a strategy that sensitises the issue of what we do but only in as much as it can address the issue of who we are. As sociologist Liz Frost argues:

> The media circulate a limited set of highly normative and very seductive meanings connected to consumer capitalism. The desires they create are not just about wanting *to own* but also about wanting *to become* (2001: 196, original emphasis).

We may in some abstract or legalistic sense have the choice of whether or not to go on a diet, but the ideal of the healthy and beautiful body, policed by the reactions and opinions of others, as well as our own internalised versions of their opinions, means that such choices are not value or norm free, and, in practice, the choice is not whether to go on a diet or not, or at least whether to think and feel that we ought to go on a diet, but rather which diet, which exercise programme and which keep-fit fad. This apparent range of choices then is not without its underpinning and sharply disciplinary dimension. As Bartky argues:

> Dieting disciplines the body's hunger: appetite must be monitored at all times and governed by an iron will. Since the innocent need of the organism for food will not be denied, the body becomes one's enemy, an alien being intent on thwarting the disciplinary project (1990: 66).

The surface details of an apparently de-disciplinary and informalised society, then, must be taken along with the continuing, and if anything savagely intensifying, efforts and self-scrutiny that many people subject themselves to in the name of becoming beautiful, or successful, or popular or finding their true-self, or perhaps more deeply if prosaically, in the hope of finding satisfaction, happiness, fulfilment, recognition and validation. The result is what we might describe as a kind of 'ascetic hedonism' (Žižek, 2007) which restates the modernist logic of the disciplinary society in the context of late-modern consumer culture. Under conditions of ascetic hedonism it is our very commitment to choice, to pleasure and to 'living life large' in all the many ways that we imagine the Victorians didn't that provides all the normative impetus and sanctions for us to work ourselves through stringent, sometimes brutal, but always hypervigilant regimes of self-discipline (Winkler and Cole, 1994).

'Talk' and the Disciplinary

A key element in the technology of disciplinary power as described by Foucault is 'the examination', meaning everything from a medical examination, to a psychiatric evaluation to a school exam (Foucault, 1991 [1975]; Downing, 2008). What ties these different senses of examination together is that they are all in one way or another tools of the visible in that they externalise, make known and visible that which might otherwise be hidden within the body or mind. Frequently, such examinations involve the measurement of these externalisations and on the basis of such measurements we can be compared to others, ranked and placed on a chart of idealised normativity, and designated as deviant or diseased should we be placed as outliers. Examination applies a 'normalising gaze' which, as Foucault explains, 'establishes over individuals a visibility through which one differentiates them and judges them' (1991 [1975]: 184). Of course, such measures have become endemic in late-modern societies and are clearly evident in the meanings and values that characterise the self-persecutory theme in self-harm discourse as people constantly examine and judge themselves against social standards that are not taken as ideals, but which carry the power of the normative. And, as I pointed out in Chapter 3, one normative ideal at work within the complex of meanings that make up self-harm is that of psychological and therapeutic 'talk'.

For Foucault, 'confession' (1978, 2003b), from its religious to its psychodynamic embodiments, is as much a technology of the visible, despite its literally being verbal, as those explored through the prison and, as psychologist Alexander Butchart (1997) reminds us, confession is a form of examination, whether it is of sin or psychopathology. He notes that confession is a strategy 'through which the most confidential ideas and private secrets...are amplified to audability and lifted into socio-medical spaces as devices of disciplinary subjectification' (1997: 107). Through the 'talk' of psychological confession one is not only positioned within a psychological culture and the social network of the psy-complex, but one is also subjectified in a distinctly psychological fashion. Hook (2001, 2007) has researched the effects of therapeutic 'talk' in psychotherapeutic contexts, noting that, on the one hand, '[t]he performance of therapeutic listening functioned as a form of inspection, a means of observing, *assessing, monitoring*; an *auditory surveillance*' (2007: 20, original emphasis), while, on the other, the 'inactive intervention' of the therapist encourages the patient to attend to themselves 'such that the therapeutic narrative came very close to resembling the therapeutic *monologue* of a self-monitoring patient' (*ibid*, original emphasis). He goes on to summarise his findings and argues that patients in such therapy demonstrated '*a powerful impetus to normative self-evaluations*' and that the '*process of locating self relative to social norms quickly became an automatic and self-implemented task for patients*' (*ibid*: 25, original emphasis).

But while the actual therapeutic encounter is quite easily modelled as an examination and as a disciplinary process, the effects that Hook has noted seem to have become general norms and values within the lives of the people that I interviewed and quoted earlier in this chapter. Of course, in this connection we can remind ourselves of the spectrum of expression common to self-harm literature and generalised throughout many texts of the psy-complex and therapy culture. Here it was not just actual psychotherapeutic exchange but the ideal of psychological and therapeutic 'talk' that had become idealised as the best possible way to express oneself, communicate with others and so avoid mental health problems. My point here is that in late-modern culture it would seem that this ideal has become more of a pervasive normative injunction, as indicated, for example, by Anne's belief that everyone needs to see a counsellor, and as such more ordinary norms of communication and expression have been pushed *relatively* further down the scale. Virtually all of my participants described themselves as having some considerable difficulties expressing themselves and communicating with others, believing that they are worse in this regard than most people; however, by and large, I found them to be highly articulate people who could very well communicate to me and express complex thoughts, feelings, experiences and concepts. Although, for all sorts of reasons, we can't take this as too significant an observation, it does seem to generally indicate something quite important: that people's felt difficulties with communication were *felt* to be difficulties in comparison with some ideal of self-expression defined by its capacity to communicate the very essence of the person, reveal them and make them visible in such a way that they would be guaranteed to be recognised and accepted by others.

Here then the ideal of psychological 'talk' connects with the idea of the authentic or true-self and its need for validation from others, linking the disciplinary regime it is a part of to the value of, and felt need for, salvation. Indeed, Foucault notes that the imperative to confess and express, whether religious or psychological, articulates ideals of salvation, liberation and mental health (Foucault, 1987). And even the idea of the 'examination' more generally defined encodes more than an assessment of the present and a tracing of the past but also a sense of 'potentiality', of 'future capability' (Hook, 2007). Although at one time this may have implied the sense in which, for example, anthropometric examination was thought to be able to predict criminality, in contemporary psychological and psychotherapeutic discourse it has taken on a much broader significance. With the advent of 'positive psychology' and the shift in psychotherapeutic goals from a resumption of common unhappiness, compared with pathological misery (Freud and Breuer, 2004 [1895]), to a quest for an optimal state of mental health, psychological authenticity, self-actualisation, maximised potential and even 'happiness' (Moskowitz, 2001; McGee, 2005; Bruckner, 2010), the processes of examination, both clinical and personal, have become a powerful way to produce desire around the figure of the individual self and their future potential. As such, the twin ideals of psychological 'talk' and authentic selfhood not only create a desire to realise these ideals, but also help circulate a disciplinary moral economy through which they are taken less as ideals than as normative standards for psychological functioning. Failure to achieve these standards then is implicitly framed as a failure to be fully or properly human, a failure to be a normal person, and this is the pervasive stress that in some becomes an acute distress and finds expression through the articulation of stigma.

Project: The Order of Discourse for the Pathological Axis

The ideal of psychological 'talk' requires and articulates the concomitant ideal of the authentic self. The fantasy of expressing one's essence perfectly and being completely understood and accepted by those around you implies an 'essence' to be expressed, while the ideal of the authentic self is itself, as Lionel Trilling made clear (1974), a product of the division of the inner and the outer and the emergence of the modern psychological individual as a monad closed off from others except through lines of expression and communication. But the essence of one's self and identity is itself a question and a problem for the modern subject as in the sweep of social history she now finds herself independent and responsible for her own fate, and she must work on herself so as to 'make something of herself' and so exploit the conditions of a horizontal social order. What we find with the emergence of this modern subject then is a concern with agency, with reflexivity and what we can call *project* by which I mean precisely this injunction to *make* something of oneself, to treat one's life, one's body and one's self as a project to be worked on and worked over (Taylor, 1992; Jervis, 1998; Bauman, 2000).

Sociologist Craig Calhoun notes that 'identity is always project, not settled accomplishment' (1994: 27), although Bauman argues that whatever existential basis there may be for this statement is greatly amplified by the social conditions and culture of modernity, which for him means 'having an identity which can only exist as an unfulfilled project' (2000: 29). It is within this idea of project then, this broad and organising order of discourse, that the cult of the individual is matched to the modernist obsession with control, mastery and progress, and that the idea of the disciplinary regime, and by extension the discourse of self-persecution, come to be both possible and meaningful. Self-persecution is the experience of the self trying to work on itself through the values of expectation and responsibility and the technologies of self-examination, judgement and punishment. While the disciplinary regime describes these very technologies and demands that work *on* the self must also be work *for* the self. And beyond this the organising idea of project represents the moral imperative that the self is not only something that *can* be worked on, but also something that *must* be worked on and worked-up to meet some kind of goal or ideal (Jervis, 1998; Bauman, 2000).

Reflexivity

'[T]he curse of the modern self', notes sociologist John Jervis, '[is] that it cannot, must not, 'forget' itself—it is condemned to reflexivity' (1998: 69). Meanwhile, Zygmunt Bauman observes that under such conditions we have become increasingly reflexive beings 'who look closely at every move we take, who are seldom satisfied with its results and always eager to correct them' (2000: 23). As Victoria Leatham writes in her memoir of self-harm, *Bloodletting*:

> Everyone, it seemed was thriving. I felt a sense of frustration. Why couldn't I thrive? What kept me from engaging with life? (2006: 185).

That this self-regarding emphasis is tied into the social and historical development of modern psychological individualism is confirmed by the literary historian Stephen Greenblatt when he notes that the early modern period became highly sensitised to these issues and that it was during this period that there was 'an increased self-consciousness about the fashioning of human identity as a manipulable, artful process' (2005: 2). No other text from this period better illustrates this social and psychological transformation, embodying the contemplation of this new subjectivity with all its concomitant concerns for agency and reflexivity, and the doubts and anxieties which are associated with the combination of these, than Shakespeare's *Hamlet* (1992 [1603]).

Hamlet brilliantly explores the vagaries of agency; the capacity of the self to live up to its burden of self-directed action and personal control in the fulfilment of its projects, and, in particular, it depicts the potentially paralysing effect that reflexivity may have on this burden. Throughout the play the old vertical order of family and moral duty exerts its pressure on Hamlet calling on him to exact revenge on his uncle for the death of his father. However, instead of acting directly, knowing with certainty what the right course of action is and following it as such, Hamlet falters, wavers and vacillates; wondering instead whether or not his father's ghost tells the truth, wondering what he should do and wondering whether he should simply escape this terrible burden of decision and agency by taking his own life. In other words, Hamlet is paralysed by his own inner and highly individual depth. And even when he finally acts to avenge his father it is not by decision but by impulse and the liberating expectation of his own impending death. What *Hamlet* reveals is that within this complex of control, reflexivity and project there are no easy answers but rather much anxiety and paralysis of action. It is a play that, through its depiction of the tortured ambivalence of its hero, puts the lie to the tritely modern advice Polonius gives to his son: '[t]his above all else: to thine own self be true'.

Hamlet, then, seems to represent an early clash of Gergen's modernist and romantic selves: on the one hand, the power of reason and thought, and, on the other, the power of doubt, passion and isolation to undermine thought and turn it into a force that actually debilitates action. Hamlet might stand a chance of being true to his own self if, in fact, he knew who or what his own true self was, but the essential character of his psychology is self-doubt, overanalysis and a self-inflicted impotence. And in this Hamlet's experience of self and subjectivity resembles nothing more strongly than the experience of self and subjectivity characteristic of people who self-harm. It is a connection that has not been lost in popular culture, especially as 'the self-harmer' is stereotypically represented by the figure of the 'emo'. Enter the words 'Hamlet' and 'emo' into a search engine (as an exercise in cultural free association) and see what happens: my own returned over a million matches. While this may not be significant in substance it does testify to Hamlet's ongoing translation by a contemporary audience and in light of precisely those structures of modern subjectivity that are felt to be both emphasised in late-modern culture, and in cultures of self-harm like emo. In this connection it is also interesting to note that the chapters of Ben Myers'

(2011) fictionalised biography of Richey Edwards are all introduced by epigraphs taken from *Hamlet*.

But as highly reflexive as the modern subject may have been, in late-modernity this process has only become even more amplified, exaggerated and universal. The sociologist Anthony Giddens notes that now '[t]he self is for everyone a reflexive project—a more or less continuous interrogation of past, present and future' (1992: 30), albeit one that perhaps somewhat ironically proceeds not purely from within this self but rather through 'a profusion of reflexive resources: therapy and self-help manuals of all kinds, television programmes and magazine articles' (*ibid*). Giddens himself is largely sanguine about this combination of inner demand and outer supply and the impact and influence that such resources may have on our lives but other commentators have sounded a more sharply critical tone. For example, the sociologist Nikolas Rose argues that

> there are certain costs to the obligation to assemble one's own identity as a matter of freedom. And the exercise of choice may be parodic and playful, but it seldom remains so for long. For in the choices one makes, and in the obligation to render ones everyday existence meaningful as an outcome of choices made, one's relation with oneself is tied ever more firmly to the ethics of individual autonomy and personal authenticity (1991: 272).

So, as I noted in the section on the disciplinary society, while the content of our choices might at first reflect some kind of freedom of choice this apparent variety masks a deeper unifying order; the order of 'the ethics of individual autonomy and personal authenticity' and the constant reflection of self mirrored in all things.

From the Narcissistic Self to the Belaboured Self

It was reflecting on these developments and dynamics that led historian and social critic Christopher Lasch to formulate his theory that American society, and perhaps late-modern Western culture more generally, articulates a fundamental and narcissistic personality disorder. In our efforts to fulfil our projects and assemble our identities and sense of self, we have become possessed by a kind of 'narcissistic self', by which he means a self in search of validation for whom 'the world is a mirror' (1979: 10). Otherwise put, and to recall the words of Robert Coles in Chapter 3, our contemporary culture describes a 'concentration, persistent, if not feverish, upon one's thoughts, feelings, wishes, worries—bordering on, if not embracing, solipsism: the self as the only or main form of (existential) reality' (1987: 189). In the 1960s and 70s, when Lasch was making his observations and formulating his theory, he saw evidence of this narcissism all around him in post-war America from the counter-culture to west-coast spirituality, although he singled out therapy culture and the ethics of the personal growth and self-awareness movements as emblematic, their spread being symptomatic of the broader cultural malaise. For Lasch, a growing dependence on a more tightly woven fabric of state, bureaucratic and corporate structures had left the individual with little actual autonomy and little personal responsibility. Paradoxically then, this oversocial condition created an undersocialised subject, self-centred and grandiose, and yet desperately needing the approval and validation of others. For Lasch, this is quite literally an infantilised subject, pathologically trapped by the prevailing social conditions in an early stage of psychological development.

Of course, Lasch was a polemicist and a provocateur, although several of his favourite themes resonate strongly with what we have been discussing; the cult of the individual and a strong fixation on the self, a condition of 'inner suffering' cultivated through this fixation (1979: 43), and what we can describe as a kind of basic double bind—the compulsion to fixate on the power of the self but to so utterly crave at the same time the recognition and validation of others. And while it is true that Lasch uses the term 'narcissistic' to refer to a general personality structure defined by psychodynamic psychology and not overtly as a pejorative dismissal of the contemporary subject, it is at the end of the day quite hard, especially given the polemical nature of his work, not to read it in this fashion. Susanna Kaysen's reflection that '[o]ne of the great pleasures of mental health (whatever that is) is how much less time I have to spend thinking about myself' (2000: 157) might help us to soften the sharp edges of Lasch's critique of our contemporary focus on the self with its suggestion that our 'narcissism' is no simple love of self but rather a labour to be borne by us, a cross to bear and one forced onto us by the social ideology of project; by the pervasive compulsion to self-creation and the unforgiving imperative for intense self-reflexivity, examination, judgement and discipline. But even with all that said and done, Lasch still provides condemnation more than empathy and there seems to be little to gain by describing people who self-harm as 'narcissists'.

An alternative formulation of these issues, and perhaps a more appropriate and useful characterisation of the late-modern subject, has been provided by the sociologist Micki McGee (2005) when she suggests that we consider that the contemporary self is not so much 'narcissistic' as 'belaboured'. A term that, on the one hand, refers to that highest obligation of individualised life spent in a 'horizontal' society; the moral injunction and social imperative to make something of yourself, to cultivate a self, an identity and a place in the world through 'methodical and disciplined action', as Charles Taylor (1991) put it. The duty, in other words, of self-mastery. While, on the other hand, suggesting that, as McGee puts it, this very imperative toward '[s]elf invention, once the imagined path to boundless opportunity, has become a burden' (2005: 13). The self, now understood and experienced not just as a subject, but also as an object of concern, an object of expertise and the object worked over by the disciplinary regime of self-control and self-improvement, has become, both literally and figuratively, overworked. '[T]he self under advanced capitalism', McGee tells us, 'is nothing if not belaboured...a site of effort and exertion, of evaluation and management, of invention and reinvention' (*ibid*: 15–16). As the sociologists Anthony Elliott and Charles Lemert observe:

> Living in an age of individualism requires individuals capable of designing and directing their own biographies, of defining identities in terms of self-actualization and of deploying social goods and cultural symbols to represent individual expression and personality (2006: 53).

It is a requirement that connects with the cultural value of authenticity and that emphasises the powers of the subject; powers of agency and reflexive self-mastery. And yet alongside this order of values and expectations there is an experience common to most if not all people that reveals the self as simply not that powerful, as something which, in fact, does not have the capacity to completely direct its own fate. Of course, as I argued in Chapter 2, selfhood is inherently social and specular, we recognise our self in the process of having this sense of self reflected back to us through our interactions with others. And identity is also social, something that must be validated in the recognition and acceptance of others. But in the last decades of the twentieth-century and the first decades of the twenty-first the relative impotence of the self has become more obvious and more acutely felt.

In the carcass of post-war Fordist certainties, the assurance, for example, of a job for life and a marriage for life, and a relatively stable and settled pattern of existence, a new experience has arisen characterised by short-termism, insecurity and precariousness. The rise of neoliberalism is the 1980s brought with it the so-called 'flexibilisation' of employment and a transformation to increasingly unstable, unpredictable and irregular work patterns (Beck, 1997; Bauman, 2000; Sennett, 2006). The taming of the unions, the gradual dismantling of the welfare state and disappearing access to benefits, the wide-scale transformation of full-time to part-time employment, the surge in temporary contracts, the threats of outsourcing and unemployment, and the expectation that people should expect to change career paths several times during their working life and go wherever the jobs are regardless of other family, community or personal concerns have all worked to produce what the sociologist Richard Sennett calls the 'spectre of uselessness' (2006). And haunted by this spectre those that do find work are all the more ready to accept regimes of constant monitoring and surveillance in the workplace, tough audits, strict targets and regular performance appraisals.

The belaboured self then is not only responsible for making something of itself, but is also responsible for shouldering the weight of anxiety produced by the fact that there are many social, economic and political factors that impact on our personal trajectory and success, over which we have no control. Under these circumstances the typical reaction has not been one of widespread social, economic and political activism but rather an even more committed turn into individualism. As McGee observes:

> The figure of the self-made man—and more recently that of the self-made woman—comforts and consoles us, suggesting that vast material, social, and personal success are available anyone who is willing to work long and hard enough. The fantasy has maintained considerable appeal, despite its troubling corollary: if success is solely the result of one's own efforts, then the responsibility for any failure must necessarily be individual shortcomings or weakness (2005: 13).

The individualised reaction to those shortcomings brought to light by an increasingly unstable and volatile market has been a tendency for people to become entrepreneurs of the self. Self-marketing, as well as self-mastering, and always willing to change their brand and their product if that is what the market demands. As Elliott and Lemert remark it is no longer

> the particular individuality of an individual that is most important. What's increasingly significant is *how* individuals create identities,

the cultural forms through which people symbolize individual expression and desire, and perhaps above all the *speed* with which identities can be reinvented and instantly transformed (2006: 53, my emphases).

Just as we have individualised our lives so we have individualised our responsibility and the imperative we feel in the face of such insecurity is, as the social critic Isabell Lorey points out, to 'shape one's 'own' body, life and self, and thus also one's 'own' precariousness' (2015: 26). We are encouraged to own oneself and so we are encouraged to own the precariousness that comes along with life, to frame and deal with it as an individual problem in need of individual solutions. Indeed, from the beginnings of *homo clausus* the discourse of self-mastery included the fantasy of self-sufficiency, of 'mastering one's own precariousness' (*ibid*), while, in turn, it is the individualised burden of precariousness itself that fuels the desire for self-mastery.

Of course, the task of owning oneself and one's precariousness, the capacity to reinvent one's self and re-launch brand 'me' is facilitated by precisely those disciplines and regimes of expertise and technology that purport to have a 'special competence in the administration of persons and interpersonal relations' (Rose, 1998: 11), which is to say the psy-complex. And so, like Lasch, McGee ties the emergence of the belaboured self to the rise of therapy culture, the personal growth movement and self-improvement literature, although unlike Lasch she does not reduce this relationship to one of naive determinism, seeing instead a pattern of resonances vibrating between culture, subjectivity and selfhood all within the social, political and economic context of late-modernity. Ultimately, what she finds in this literature is the hope of discovering or cultivating an authentic 'unique, and stable self that might function—even thrive—unaffected by the vagaries of the labour market' (2005: 16). And, as such, the belaboured self describes a self that is having to work harder, under more demanding market conditions, while always predicating the success or failure of this venture on the self's ability to invent, reinvent and market itself.

The belaboured self, as described by McGee then, perfectly reflects the disciplinary processes observed by Foucault and provides a model of subjectivity that is subject to the implicit moral imperative of ascetic hedonism but, crucially, without requiring us to further psychologise the self as Lasch does, or forgetting that the 'psychological individual', the 'psychodynamic self', the 'ascetic hedonist' and, indeed, the 'belaboured self' are not actual empirical selves as such but rather cultural patterns of meaning at work informing and shaping people's experiences and identities through the multiple processes of the disciplinary regime. More than anything they work by organising power and by placing the self of each actual empirical person at the centre of a web of power, situating this self as the primary site of social control and therefore also as the primary site of conflict.

That it is the *self* that is being identified here as the primary site of control and conflict is important as several highly valuable Foucaultian and feminist-inspired analyses of idioms of distress, such as anorexia and self-harm (Bartky, 1990; Frost, 2001, Inckle, 2007), have focused on precisely these dynamics but as they relate particularly on the body, for example through female beauty regimes and the kind of daily labour that women invest in maintenance and appearance of their bodies (Bordo, 2003; Jeffreys, 2005). But while the body is obviously something that bears a close relationship to the self it is nonetheless quite specifically *the self* as a constellation of bodily and psychological elements that has emerged at the sharp edge of the disciplinary processes explored here and the not the body as such. As we saw in the discourse of self-persecution it is the *self* as an objectified essence that is the subject of guilt and hatred, more so than the body. And the concerns and anxieties that reflect the perceived failures of people who self-harm circulate issues of moral behaviour, fulfilling social and familial roles, communicating effectively and generally fitting in. And, to take another example, while the desire for an authentic self may be symbolised by a trim, fit and beautiful body, it nonetheless focuses more on the ideal of a psychologically healthy and functional person who fulfils their roles, meets their duties and obligations, communicates effectively with others, can express themselves and their emotions and who does not hate themselves. From this we might argue that the carrot of desire that keeps the belaboured self labouring is the idea that it can, indeed must, complete and perfect its project, and that it can produce or become a self for whom life and selfhood are no labour at all. This is what 'salvation' means here.

In late-modern disciplinary society then, we are stigmatised by the expectation to be perfect and caught within the double bind of an overwhelming sense of responsibility on the one hand and an actual experience of relative impotence on the other, a double bind that guarantees our failure and our resubmission of self to the disciplinary cycle. The self today must make itself, improve itself and master itself, yet also subject itself to social conditions beyond its power. The self must recognise and, in fact, market its own sense of power, agency and authenticity, and yet remain flexible to market demands and seek recognition, validation and legitimacy from others, even as their criteria for judgement changes as swiftly as the market itself. In short, it is a self under strain, it is a self belaboured with the business of being a self and bound to blame itself should this labour fail as it almost inevitably must. This blame expresses a sense of failure or of being a discredited self, a sense that may result in a stigma standing as an outward sign of an inward taint; a stigma that may take the form for some of acts of self-harm. Of course the broader culture, especially as it represents a consumer culture, has its part to play in this belabouring process. Consumer capitalism subjects us to a daily pedagogy of insufficiency, inadequacy and self-dissatisfaction, carving out the gap or lack in our lives that we will fill with goods and services, seeking to fulfil a desire for authentic selfhood and legitimate identity as much as for any specific commodity. Working as a disciplinary regime such values are normalised and become woven into the very fabric of late-modern subjectivity, but this is the issue that we will turn to in the next and final chapter.

Summary

The moral regime of the disciplinary, emerging from the modernist obsession with project and progress, and reflected through its late-modern modalities in psychology, therapy culture and consumer culture, describes a social and cultural pattern of subjectivity that is particularly concerned with processes of self-making and self-fulfilment, and that works from idealised standards taken as normative expectations. Arguably then, the sentence that is inscribed through self-inflicted injuries is a moral and judicial sentence precisely in the same sense as Kafka's apparatus: a stigma marking the failure of the self to succeed at this process of self-making, a failure that is perceived by the person who carries it as a judgement on their very essence as a person.

In the opening line of Kafka's short story, the operator of the disciplining machine proudly declares that '[i]t's a remarkable piece of apparatus'. And so it is, clever and insidious in its logic, but what is really remarkable about the apparatus of disciplinary society is that it is a regime of order written into the subject by the subject themselves and, in this way, between them, Kafka and Foucault offer us a useful model of 'the self-harmer': she is someone who is both the operator of the apparatus and its condemned. As I will explore and argue more fully in the next chapter, self-harm appears within our culture and society as a meaningful idiom, a meaningful way to experience and express distress and estrangement, because it articulates, in a symbolic and exaggerated fashion, these tensions and conflicts, which are, in fact, characteristic of the culture as a whole. It is in this way that self-harm is, in Bordo's term, a 'crystallisation', a symbol of its time and place and an enactment of its principle dilemmas. And so it is with the dynamic of the secret and the seen. Self-harm is less a mechanism that mediates people's complex and ambivalent feelings about keeping secret or being seen than it is a symbolic evocation of this dilemma and the dynamic tension between keeping secret and being seen that is acutely felt by the late-modern subject. Self-harm points us toward the sensitisation of visibility and the technologies of visibility in our society. A sensitisation to what is known about the self and what may be known if it allows itself to be revealed to others, if it opens up and bears all. And such a sensitisation can only really make sense within the context of a disciplinary society in which the subject relates to itself as both an object of knowledge and a project of self-making.

6
The Belaboured Economy of Desire

Introduction: A Pathogenic Society

On Friday 17 April 2015 a letter appeared in the *Guardian* newspaper signed by 442 psychotherapists, counsellors and academics, addressed to the major political parties of the UK who were at that time preparing to fight a general election.[1] The letter condemned the austerity policies of the Conservative-led coalition government and damningly described the 'profoundly disturbing psychological and quality-of-life implications' of a 'society thrown completely off balance by the emotional toxicity of neoliberal thinking'. As those that found themselves working at 'the coalface in responding to the effects of austerity politics on the emotional state of the nation', the cosignatories explicitly drew a link, despite the somewhat pervasive biopsychological reductionism of the psy-complex and the dominance of the medical model of mental disorder, between arrangements of social order and organisation on the one hand, and the development, impact and prevalence of mental disorder on the other. Society, it seems, can be pathogenic. To be fair the typical effect of the asymmetric binary had never suggested otherwise but rather tends to filter the impacts of social organisation through the central concept of 'stress', which is regarded as one of the main, proximate causes of mental disorder, albeit conditioned by genetic, temperamental factors. Social and other environmental factors may then be tied to mental disorder but largely through the ways in which they contribute to the levels of stress experienced by an individual and the degree to which that individual is biologically and psychologically equipped to deal with such stress.

However, from the beginning of this book it has been my contention that patterns of mental disorder, and not just their prevalence, are fundamentally related to, and shaped by, the social order in which we live. This social order is mediated through the symbolic order, through cultural systems of meanings and values, so as to shape our experiences and expressions of personal distress and social estrangement, while 'at the same time declaring our public values' (Littlewood, 2002: xi). Symbolic idioms of distress and disorder like self-harm then appear as the product of 'conceptual categories which encode aspects of our social order' (*ibid*: 58), and which shape and mould our culturally situated psychology and subjectivity, albeit as exaggerated expressions of this order and not just the mirror of it. It is in this way that self-harm can be, as Bordo reminds us, characteristic of its culture and a crystallisation of its tensions and discourses. Or as the anthropologist Jules Henry has it: '[p]sychopathology is the final outcome of all that is wrong with a culture' (quoted in Bordo, 2003: 130).

As such, self-harm has become one of *the* paradigmatic expressions of mental disorder characteristic of the late twentieth and the early twenty-first centuries not just because, as the cosignatories to the *Guardian* letter suggest, these have been particularly tough times, but because self-harm, as we have seen over the last three chapters, helps to symbolise and support a particular theory of mind, a particular culture of values, and a particular set of social, economic and political arrangements, as well as the experience of selfhood and subjectivity that emerges from these, even as this pattern of subjectivity itself, and in turn, symbolises and supports this social order. But perhaps self-harm's paradigmatic status also rests, somewhat like alcoholism, poor diet, chronic debt and excessive drug use, as one of those patterns of life and action that stands ambiguously between the outright disordered and 'ill', and so indicates a general cultural condition and awareness that, as the *Guardian* letter suggests, our lifestyles and our social arrangements are making distress and illness more or less normative.

The idea, that there is something deeply and abidingly wrong with late-modern consumer capitalist societies, especially in their neoliberal modality, and that they are responsible for producing disturbingly high levels of addiction, illness, mental disorder and suicide, is one that is both familiar from the middle of the twentieth century at least, and one that seems to be increasingly finding its time. From psychoanalyst Eric Fromm's concerns over the 'marketing character' (2003) to Lasch's critique of the narcissistic society, which in the age of the selfie has continued to be updated for the twenty-first century (Twenge, 2006; Twenge and Campbell, 2010) to more recent arguments about 'affluenza' and the semiotically infectious disease of materialism and the 'selfish capitalist' (de Graaf *et al.*, 2005; James, 2007, 2008), there have been any number of attempts to ground the prevalence of late-modern Western distress and disorders in the prevailing social order. Nor are such concerns without a solid empirical base as a series of now famous studies carried out by the World Health Organization (1973, 1979; Jablensky *et al.*, 1992) and a more recent series of large-scale epidemiological studies have demonstrated (Wilkinson, 2005; Wilkinson and Pickett, 2010).

But as much the prevalence of late-modern distress has been tracked, mapped and argued over, there has been relatively little effort to map the pattern of disorders, their idiomatic and symbolic function, onto consumer culture and neoliberal capitalist society, although there have been some notable exceptions (Warner, 1985; Frost, 2001; Bordo, 2003). Despite this, it seems to me, as we saw to some degree in the last chapter, that self-harm can help us to understand this general sense of social unease by signalling to us that the self has become a site of acute pressure and tension. That it has become acutely belaboured and is, to all intents and purposes, a battleground; torn within the disciplinary logic of the double bind, the destructive co-dependent relationship between an inflated and overly individualised sense of agency and empowerment on the one hand and the sense of failure, insufficiency and impotence endemic to late-modern society on the other. With this in mind, in this last chapter, I want to briefly reverse the flow of our analysis, turning from using culture to interpret self-harm to using self-harm to critically interpret late-modern culture and society, and by so doing discover exactly what it is that is so 'wrong with [our] culture', as Henry puts it, that self-harm is not only a meaningful way to experience and express distress and estrangement, but also an increasingly prevalent one. And along the way I also want to return to an issue explicitly raised in the Introduction and only partially and implicitly present in the chapters that have followed: namely the issue of gender and the cultural coding of self-harm as a particularly feminine practice.

The Economy of Desire

As we have seen, the self of self-harm is a fundamentally belaboured self. A self that is urged to cultivate or discover an authentic self-mastery over itself as a self-contained (*homo clausus*) psychological individual. But a self that is also deeply frustrated, in part because of the basic need for selfhood to be validated by others no matter how self-creating we may be, but more specifically and acutely because of the requirement that one re-create and reinvent oneself in line with the shifting demands and requirements of an all-too-capricious marketplace, while all the time assuming a deep and persecutory sense of personal responsibility for the conditions, circumstances and outcomes of its life. But, as I briefly mentioned at the end of the last chapter, the belaboured self is also the self of late-modern consumer capitalist society and culture. And the disciplinary logic of self-surveillance, examination and regulation is by no means unique to the psychology of 'the self-harmer' but rather represents a general strategy for the 'conduct of conduct' (Rose, 1991), a strategy that only finds a crystallisation of itself in the desperate and exaggerated symbolism of self-harm.

To say this is not to say that patterns of distress like self-harm are a result of too much shopping, or too much avarice or even too much materialism as such. Rather, we must understand 'consumer culture' in a much broader sense as a whole system of representation, of ideas, meanings, images and values assembled around large parts of the fundamental organisational and institutional infrastructure of society, which themselves are assembled around the basic economic paradigm characteristic of late-modern 'Western' life, namely consumerism. And we must understand the 'self', at least as I am using the term here, to mean less a psychological entity than a cultural pattern that encodes normative ideas about who and what we are, that guides our attempts at self-making and self-understanding and that therefore also helps shape our experience of selfhood.

These clarifications and caveats are important if we are to avoid the perhaps naive idea of docile, 'cultural dope'-type subjects being pressed into existence through a uniform cookie-cutter process directed from above by political and economic elites (Giddens, 1976; Bordo, 2003). Rather, what is particularly important about Foucault's mapping of the disciplinary regime is that it describes how the multiple and heterogeneous yet systematic processes of government are not, in fact, focused purely in a centralised apparatus of power, in a parliament or president's palace, but rather are diffuse and widely distributed, and describe the various ways in which human life is organised, ordered and governed, from the management of the individual body and mind to the management of whole populations. This 'governmentality' (Foucault, 2010), far from describing the cookie-cutter image of social determinism, describes the disciplining and regulative effect of power acting 'from below', of power applying a normative yet negotiated pressure on the subject to think, speak and act as 'one' is supposed to think, speak and act. And to want what one is supposed to want. In fact, it is arguably the case that every disciplinary regime is mirrored by its complementary economy of desire, by which I mean a pedagogy of wants and associated values that dynamically motivates a person's engagement with their particular environment and that explains why, far from being 'cultural dopes', we, as subjects, actually buy into the conditions of our own subjectification, regulation and 'government', and keenly pursue them. As Bordo puts it, 'socialization is not done behind people's backs, but involves their active participation' (2003: 304).

The disciplinary regime as it is acutely experienced by people who self-harm may represent something of a juridical stick by which we discipline ourselves toward some desired goal but the regime itself works less through coercion than through aspiration and inspiration, through cherished values, internalised normative standards and a whole structure of wants, wishes, cravings and longings. It is this latter, and its interactions with the world, that I mean by 'economy of desire', and it is more carrot than stick. Of course, the carrot of desire in late-modernity circulates through a consumer culture and economy that, as we have seen through the belaboured self, and as Liz Frost points out, focuses less on 'wanting *to own*' things than 'wanting *to become*' a particular kind of authentic, self-sufficient and satisfied person (2001: 196, original emphasis). Indeed, 'consumerism', as John Jervis has noted, 'entails a market-oriented quest to articulate and satisfy desires, and desires are as much to do with identity as with material goods' (1998: 93). Consider, for example, the ways that commodities are marketed and bought as more than just goods and services but rather as keys to a better life, as signs and symbols of a particular kind of lifestyle and a particular kind of identity. Consider the sheer amount of commodities that are based on the display of status, personal style and the presentation of self; on the assumption that people will pursue 'self-construction through the consumption of goods' (Lindholm, 2008: 54). And consider how much money, time and energy we typically pour into the maintenance and performance of brand 'me'.

But, of course, the elusive ingredient X of authenticity is added more in the process of marketing than production, and each purchase keeps us unfulfilled, unsatisfied and yet still yearning for more (Bordo, 1997; de Graaf *et al*, 2005; McGee, 2005). The consumer-led quest for the realisation of a satisfied self leads only to an inexhaustible source of desires since, as sociologist Craig Calhoun argues, '[o]ur identities are always rooted in part in ideals and moral aspirations that we cannot realise fully. There is therefore a tension within us' (1994: 29). And if the belaboured self is founded on an intractable double bind, here we have the expression of that productive yet immiserating ambivalence in the common economy of desire of late-modernity. It is, like capitalism itself, an economy that is debt-funded, based in a fundamental lack and the ongoing, cyclic drive to pay back or fill in this lack. It is based on a constant pedagogy of invalidation and dissatisfaction which only serves to feed our longing for authenticity, the real, enlightenment, fulfilment, optimisation, actualisation, legitimacy and an end to insufficiency (Taylor, 1991; Boyle, 2004; Furedi, 2004). As Bordo points out:

> the very essence of advertising and the fuel of consumer capitalism [is that it] cannot allow equilibrium or stasis in human desire. Thus, we are not permitted to feel satisfied with ourselves and we are 'empowered' only and always through fantasies of what we *could* be (1997: 51, her emphasis).

While the economist Michael Perelman flatly states 'disappointment is endemic to a consumer society' as '[c]onsumption by definition is never fulfilling. Envy and the desire to distinguish oneself at the expense of others are what drive consumption' (2005: xi). And, as he notes, a consumer society and culture can only lead to what the economist Tibor Scitovsky (1976) calls 'the joyless economy'. But again the issue is less a purely psychological one. 'Envy' is an ugly emotion and is as limited a way to describe people who self-harm as Lasch's 'narcissism'. The point has to be that under conditions of consumer capitalism we are all subjected to, and subjectified through, a pressure of competition and comparison that we saw in the last chapter and that drives both our search for satisfaction and our tendency to engage with commodities marketed as a means to achieve this satisfaction. There is a sense, then, that far from accusing people who self-harm of 'envy' we should perhaps rather see them as the canaries in the coalmine, calling out to us that this pervasive modality of the disciplinary regime and its concomitant economy of desire are exerting a pathogenic pressure on the self, belabouring it and bringing it to breaking point.

That constant comparison to others under the condition of an assumed competition is not exactly conducive to happiness and satisfaction, is not a new observation and can, in fact, be traced back to our old friend, the horizontal ideology. In fact, the man who first coined the term 'individualism', the French lawyer and historian Alexis de Tocqueville, noticed, while travelling around nineteenth-century America, an air of social isolation and status anxiety. In a chapter of his *Democracy in America* (2003 [1835]) entitled 'Why the Americans are Often so Restless in the Midst of Their Prosperity' he notes that

> When all the prerogatives of birth and fortune have been abolished, when every profession is open to everyone, an ambitious man may think it is easy to launch himself on a great career and feel that he has been called to no common destiny. But this is a delusion which experience quickly corrects. When inequality is the general rule in society, the greatest inequalities attract no attention. But when everything is more or less level, the slightest variation is noticed.... That is the reason for the strange melancholy often haunting the inhabitants of democracies in the midst of abundance and for that disgust with life sometimes gripping them even in calm and easy circumstances (2003 [1835]: 622).

Of course, as we have noted, in such 'horizontal' societies everything is not 'more or less level' it is just that we are encouraged to think that it is. A level playing field means that we compare ourselves not so much to those who are closest to us but to everyone, even those that have, in fact, enjoyed much greater access to opportunities and resources than ourselves, and to those ideals of success, achievement and fulfilment that are now held up as normative standards. The result is a crushing sense of status anxiety, of feeling that we have not done enough, achieved enough, become enough to satisfy the ever-moving goalposts of our expectations. Following the passage above, de Tocqueville adds ominously that '[i]n America... I am told that madness is commoner than anywhere else'.

But as pathogenic as the issue may have been in nineteenth-century America, and as much as this matrix of stress and pressures may help us to understand some of the earliest cases of self-harm that would follow on shortly after, it does not immediately help us to understand why it is the late-modern self that is so belaboured, or why it is this self that has turned so prevalently to self-harm. Consumerism, of course, is a modern phenomenon, despite a certain tendency amongst each generation to think that, like sex, they invented it, it is 'bound up with the idea of modernity, of modern experience and of modern social subjects' (Slater, 1997: 9). And from the beginning it has implied an emphasis on the private sphere, on the ideology of personal choice the moral obligation and existential imperative of self-making. But despite this late-modern consumer culture does represent a particular development and form of consumerism. From the middle of the twentieth century, concomitant with the emergence of ego psychology and positive psychology, success was no longer judged purely in terms of professional status and career advancement, or in material wealth and power, but by values of 'self-actualisation' and a realisation of personal potential and happiness or well-being. As sociologist Micki McGee explains:

> While the self-made man of nineteenth and early twentieth centuries aimed to achieve success in terms that were largely external and measurable—for example, accumulation of wealth, status, or power—late-twentieth-century self-making involves the pursuit of the rather more elusive and variable state of self-fulfilment (2005: 19).

And, of course, '[w]ith the emergence of an emphasis on self-fulfilment, one finds there is no end-point for self-making: individuals can continuously pursue shifting and subjective criteria for success' (*ibid*). And in as much as authentic selfhood is constituted as a bottomless well of potential then a sense of failure and the feeling that we are living unfulfilled and insufficient lives is inevitable. Alexis de Tocqueville's young Americans may well have been modern and may well have been consumers but they were not consumers of the authenticity industry. An industry that goes well beyond the marketing of the authentic as an elusive ingredient X in consumer goods and services, and which instead focuses on the direct sale of authentic selfhood through the empowering and therapeutic technologies of psychology (Herman, 1995; Dineen, 1999; Moskowitz, 2001; Furedi, 2004; Bruckner, 2010; Moloney, 2013). Authenticity is the ultimate consumer good since, as Patrick Hutton points out,

> The quest for self-understanding is a journey without end. Even in the deepest recesses of our psyches there are no experiences which, if evoked, will reveal our true identities... we are condemned to a quest for meaning whose meaning is that our human nature is continually being reconstituted by the forms that we create along the way (1988: 140).

Or, as psychologist Louis Sass describes what he calls the 'paradox of the reflexive', that it is precisely our 'desperate attempts to constitute the self [which are] precisely what tears the self apart' (1987: 144). In this way, as McGee observes, the late-modern 'contagion of insufficiency constitutes the self-improvement industry as both self-perpetuating and self-serving' (2005: 18) as its very own 'retinue of self-improvement experts, motivational speakers, and self-help gurus' are in no small part responsible for 'conjur[ing] the image of endless insufficiency' (*ibid*: 17) into the lives of late-modern subjects. In truth, the desire to find authenticity is likely to lead less to self-fulfilment than to an 'elevated concern with the self [which] is underpinned by anxiety and apprehension' (Furedi, 2004: 21), which Jervis observes 'brings costs in the vulnerability of this self to the world [that] it purports to control' (1998: 38), as well as creating a market for therapeutic services, insisting 'that the management of life requires the continuous intervention of therapeutic expertise' (Furedi, 2004: 21).

These observations, in a way, bring us full circle. If, as I argued in Chapter 3, psychology emerged as a privileged language of interpretation for the subject now that it had been, like Hawthorne's minister, rendered an object of interest and suspicion through the civilising process, and therefore also rendered as an object of study and expertise. And if, as I argued in the last and the present chapter, psychology has helped to form the individualised subject of consumer capitalism. Then the emergence from the 1970s onward of a powerful and lucrative psychological and therapeutic industry in which not only psychological expertise and technologies are offered as services, but psychological states and skills are also offered as goods, represents the logical outcome of the overlapping and intermingling contributions that psychology, consumerism and late-modern consumer capitalism, especially, as the cosignatories to the *Guardian* letter make clear, neoliberal capitalism, to a single, complex, heterogeneous and dynamic social ecology.

None of which, it must be emphasised, is to suggest some kind of grand conspiracy dreamt up by a cabal of psychologists and advertising executives. Rather, it is to map the social ecology of late-modern culture and society through those forces of resonance, co-patterning, co-structuring and symbiosis that make an ecosystem, even a social ecosystem, an effective and functioning ecosystem. If there is a conspiracy at its centre it is a conspiracy of contingencies and belongs to the system itself rather than to any individuals or groups within it. However, that does not mean that the conspiracy cannot have an organising point or a direction, even if it is unintended or unconscious. And if this conspiracy does have a point then it seems to be the centripetal, individualistic logic that keeps us focused on the self (whether through consumerism, popular culture, psychology or therapy) as our core and central concern, causing the social processes that developed, supported and maintained this 'cult of the individual' to be effectively effaced and rendered invisible, and allowing the public sphere to fade into the background of the social consciousness, pushed-out by the overwhelming focus on the private, and rendering it all the more available and vulnerable to neoliberal deregulation. The letter to the *Guardian* should leave us in little doubt about the 'profoundly disturbing' effects and 'damage that neoliberalism' inflicts on mental disorder, although it is now time to examine why one demographic in particular seems to be peculiarly effected by the inflation of the private sphere and the pathogenic effects of modern and late-modern society.

The Economy of 'Female Perversions'

While it is true that the best demographic research, taken as a whole, tends to suggest that a significant number of people who self-harm are male, perhaps anywhere between a third and a half, it also true that the weight of available research does nonetheless tend to support the contention that most people who self-harm are female. And besides which, self-harm is clearly coded at the cultural level as a feminine practice, and thought of as a particularly female way of experiencing and expressing distress and estrangement. It is a commonly held idea, for example, that men turn their anger and frustration outward while women turn it inward toward themselves. In as much as such claims are presented as assertions about essential sex differences rooted in genetics, biology and the fundamental architecture of the brain I tend to be quite sceptical (Fine, 2010). But in as much as such claims represent cultural patterns of meanings and values then it is possible to isolate the discourse and leave open the issue of its particular impact on actual people, regardless of their reproductive differences, an impact that is best assessed on a case-by-case basis. I take gender, then, to be a patterning force that exerts a normative pressure on differently sexed bodies and minds. A force which, as such, works as much from below as from above, and which provides a repertoire of strategies for acting and being feminine or for acting and being masculine. The feminine and the masculine being, as Valerie Walkerdine puts it, 'fictions linked to fantasies deeply embedded in the social world which can take on the status of fact when inscribed with the powerful practices...through which we are regulated' (1990: xiii).

And understood in this way, as 'fictions linked to fantasies' and the 'practices' governed by those fantasies, it is undeniable that gender runs deeply within and through all of the discourses that we have dealt with so far, constituting, in fact, a final *order of discourse* that modifies and transforms the previous three that we have examined. For example, in axis one we saw that framing self-harm as a problem generally means framing it as a problem for someone who is too emotional, too impulsive, too irrational and too inarticulate, someone who lacks the ability to process their emotions into rational language and thought. In axis two we saw that this framing of 'the self-harmer' presents them as someone who suffers from being too vulnerable, too sensitive, too natural, too 'real' and too literal, which again brings us back to the issue of 'processing'. And in axis three we saw that such people are also thought of as being too private, too secretive, too narcissistic and too self-punishing, always turning aggression in on themselves and not projecting it out into the world where change may at least be effected. The gender dimensions of these characterisations are unmistakable (Ussher, 1991; Grosz, 1994; Jervis, 1999). Each represents a cluster of gender stereotypes, 'fictions linked to fantasies', but structures of gender nonetheless, even if they are structures that have for far too long been written primarily by men or at least written to the benefit of the masculine. Otherwise put, and to be clear: the gender dimensions evident in the axes of continuity relate more to social and cultural stereotypes of the feminine than to the character traits of actual women.

Women, Modernity and Demons

If modernity produced the *homo clausus* as the prototype subject, the model to be aspired to, then as several commentators have made clear, it is a distinctly gendered prototype, which reads the subject as inherently masculine (Grosz, 1994). As philosopher Moira Gatens points out, while the male subject is

> constructed as self-contained and as an owner of his person and his capacities, one who relates to other men as free competitors with whom he shares certain politico-economic rights.... The female subject is constructed as prone to disorder and passion, as economically and politically dependent on men... justified by reference to women's nature. She 'makes no sense by herself' and her subjectivity assumes a lack which males complete (1991: 5).

And remembering the emergence of the psychological individual from *homo clausus* the health psychologist Jane Ussher argues that 'psychology has developed as a singularly male enterprise, with men studying men and applying the findings to all of humanity' (1991: 9). The consequence of this has been that the binary of the subject and it's other has been used to map the binary of male and female so that, while men have been traditionally positioned as the ideal products of rational and civilised cultivation, women have been simultaneously held to a male standard, while being excluded from it and, along with children, have consistently been cast as having one foot in civilisation and the other irredeemably mired in nature (Showalter, 1987; Ussher, 1991; Grosz, 1994; Lupton, 1998). So while men, as true *homo clausus*, are understood to be able, by virtue of their gender, to fully symbolise and hence rationally 'process' their natures, women and children are understood to be subject to problematic, or at least distasteful, eruptions of nature, eruptions of the 'real'. And it is in this sense that women have often been tied to madness in a way that men, as a gender, simply have not. As literary critic Phillip Martin observes:

> Women and madness share the same territory... they may be said to enter a concentric relationship around a central point occupied by a fundamentally male normality. Like some insidious virus, insanity therefore invades the mythology of woman, finding therein a semiotic fluid that it may use for the purposes of self-definition (1987: 42).

If women are both subject and its other then there is, within our culture, an implicit fear that, at times, this 'other' might yet overtake her and cause a dark and dangerous trauma in the fabric of the symbolic order. The text that neatly wraps this eruption of the other into the figure of the female, the figure of the child and also that of the self-mutilator, is William Friedkin's 1973 film *The Exorcist*. This classic horror tells the story of an adolescent girl on the very edge of womanhood, Regan, who becomes possessed by a demon and must subsequently be exorcised by Catholic priests. *The Exorcist*, perhaps inspired by Mark's gospel account of the demoniac Garesene, contained one of the first movie representations of a kind of self-mutilation that was close enough in its associated pattern of meaning to count, at least symbolically, as self-harm. Mark Kermode's 1998 documentary *The Fear of God: 25 Years of The Exorcist* reports, through interviews with Friedkin, that this was originally a simple answer to a basic problem: how to make the demonically possessed Regan look less like an apple-cheeked all-American adolescent and more like she was inhabited by an evil spirit. A number of 'monster make ups' were tried but all gave the impression of a fantastical physical change that suited typical horror special effects but not the semi-documentary realism favoured by Friedkin. Some believable way had to be found to alter Regan's appearance without diminishing the shock value of the transformation, or the audience's belief that this transformation could only have occurred through demonic possession. The solution was to create the effect of multiple lesions on Regan's face, supposedly the result of violent scratching at her own flesh.

The implication of self-harm successfully carried the capacity to shock and disturb. But as Friedkin revealed to Kermode it was further able to convey the drama of an inner battle for control of Regan's body and possession of her soul, her true self. In one scene, Regan's nanny and the priest, Father Karras, enter Regan's bedroom while she is asleep and the nanny pulls up Regan's nightgown to reveal the words 'help me', which seem to have spontaneously appeared on her belly, raised up from her skin like scars. This message, which many of the people I interviewed, like Susan, for example, maintained is the underlying message of their self-harm, appears from what is effectively the unconscious of Regan's psyche where presumably she has been repressed by the invading consciousness of the demon. It is a message that is spoken through her body and represents a literal return of the repressed as Regan seeks to say through her body that which she can no longer communicate directly because she has lost control of herself. This message then, and the intended implications of her self-harm, seems to signify an inner battle tearing through to the surface of Regan's body; the desperate inscription of psychic pain onto skin made by a person in deep conflict.

It is, of course, significant that Regan is an adolescent going through the changes of puberty and transforming from a girl into a woman. Perhaps the dark 'real' that possesses Regan is really her romantic–expressive self insufficiently processed by the modernist–utilitarian self because she is both child and female, and fighting for control of Regan before her entry into full womanhood initiates her into a fully gendered subject position; one defined by its opposition to the male subject and yet simultaneously subject to a normative pressure to conform to this masculine ideal—a double bind and logical precursor to the belaboured self—which would deny her 'nature'. As Kim Chernin points out, women may feel a 'terror of female development' (1985: 21); as such, it is hard not to read *The Exorcist* as being at least a little subversive, despite its denouement, as it has to be admitted that the 'real' of the demon is both more intelligent and more interesting than Regan, who conforms completely with her role as a young and civilised woman. Perhaps then the romantic–expressive self is just a cipher for the feminine and the battle to exorcise Regan is really the battle to inscribe her into the symbolic order of patriarchal society, represented here by the two priests. Certainly, this framing of womanhood untamed as a wild and demonic force appears not only in various readings of the medieval and early modern 'witch craze' (Ussher, 1991; Jervis, 1999), but also in feminist readings of female madness as resistant eruptions or prepolitical protests against the symbolic order of a male-dominated and essentially misogynist society (Ussher, 1991). Interestingly enough, the character of Father Karras, who is eventually able to exorcise Regan, is not only a Catholic priest, but also a psychiatrist.

Women, Late-modernity and Female Perversions

While *The Exorcist* does help us to reveal the recognition and inscription of tensions and conflicts inherent in the modernist construction and positioning of the feminine, it does lack something of an analysis of specifically late-modern translations and transformations of these dynamics and tensions. The same, however, cannot be said for another significant filmic text in the history of self-harm's emergence into public awareness: Susan Streitfeld's 1996 film *Female Perversions*, a narrative exploration of psychologist Louise Kaplan's (1993) nonfiction book of the same name. Kaplan's interest in her book is in uncovering the 'perversions' common to women, which is to say those psychological strategies by which women divert their desires away from the basic trauma imposed by their gender position, and express them instead in ways that not only allow this trauma to be lived with but, in classic disciplinary logic, also keep them re-inscribed into the very gender positions that created the trauma in the first place and which prevent a deeper reconciliation with life and the world. Streifield's deeply interesting, if at times a little heavy handed, narrative representation of this basic idea centres on the figure of the symbolically named 'Eve', a successful and aggressive lawyer who is soon to be promoted to the position of judge. Despite this success Eve is wracked with insecurities, neuroses and anxiety, which she manages through the common repertoire of 'female perversions' such as beauty regimes, seduction and consumerism; methods for maintaining a sense of identity and self-worth while avoiding any of the deeper traumas that underpin the contradictory character of her subjectivity, or the way that these perverse strategies are the very means by which she is continuously subjectified as a woman.

Despite being a driven and professional woman, and a powerful senior agent of the law, she is rendered utterly powerless again and again through this primary subjectification as a woman. She may be a lawyer, wealthy, middle class and soon to be a judge but first and foremost she is positioned by herself and others as a woman. For example, in one scene she is rendered passive, flustered and threatened by a male

African-American beggar and windscreen washer. He is nonviolent and relatively polite but, significantly, he hails Eve as a woman from his position as a man, rather than hailing her as a powerful and wealthy (white) subject from his position as a desperate and penniless (black) one. Of course, what is particularly important is that Eve answers this hail, she recognises herself in it and so allows herself to be constructed as a woman first and only as a powerful member of society second.

The main thrust of the film is to show that 'female perversions' are the very moulding of desires along gendered lines so that the assumption of a normal female identity in a patriarchal society is the very suturing of the individual and their motivations into their own oppression and domination. Indeed, to be 'normal' in this sense is also to be 'perverted'. As Jervis explains it is 'the language of inarticulate desire [that] is expressed through the very body that has to be the source of its [own] repression' (1998: 104), and so Eve's desires become the primary disciplinary means by which she is kept in her place, subsumed to the masculine order and the male gaze. Her inner tension comes from the belaboured contradiction articulated by her desire for power and her sense of responsibility on the one hand, and her inherent powerlessness on the other. Part of this complex of desire and aspiration is Eve's need to impress and please her emotionally distant father and, in the film's non-too-subtle symbolism, to be a man *and* to be a woman. So the inner tension and pressure that eventually results in a scene in which she cuts her breast with a razor blade comes from the struggle to affirm an identity that in its gendered forms, and its economy of desire, is always already self-defeating and self-destructive.

Eve's story is a long-playing one out of the classic feminist maxim that 'the personal is political' albeit here in a largely (but not wholly) non-domestic context. As such, we see that her inner turmoil and eventual self-harm are related to her disciplinary internalisation of, and taking personal responsibility for, a number of social and political forces that threaten to destabilise her psychologically. Her desires are not 'true' to her (within the logic of the film) but are socially constructed, and taking responsibility for them internalises and psychologises what is otherwise a social and political structure of gendered subjectification, a force of external oppression. Internalising the tension that is the inevitable result is to take on one's own shoulders what is otherwise a social struggle. This is the key to understanding Eve's self-harm. When she hurts herself it is a moment of psychological and emotional impasse created by the realisation that her identity and life encode an unworkable and belaboured contradiction, a realisation that is nevertheless still trapped in the false frame of a sense of psychological ownership and responsibility, and hence one that is experienced as an unrelievable pressure and an inexpressible burden.

In *Female Perversions* self-harm takes on the position of *the* key perversion, the pinnacle coping mechanism that Eve is pushed to when all else fails, and yet also the most fundamental, the most basic or 'natural' perversion. A fact symbolised by its association with the only other explicitly self-harming character in the movie: a teenage tomboy called 'Ed' (a suitably gender-neutral name). Ed is a girl that hasn't learnt to be a girl yet let alone a woman, but also perhaps one that would like to be a boy, or at the very least one who knows that she doesn't want to be a woman. She has yet to suffer the trauma of her inscription into female identity but she knows it is coming, and that is difficult enough, as demonstrated by her tragic yet oddly playful explorations of female gender norms as she plays 'dress-up'. No greater evidence that Ed's womanhood is inevitable is provided by her beginning her menstruation, which is here referred to as the 'curse'. The two acts of significance that Ed (who has little screen time) conducts in the film are an episode of self-harm and a strange ritualistic burying of her menstrual fluids ('burying my baby' as she puts it). It is perhaps not too much of an interpretative leap then to see these two bloody acts as symbolically connected in the signifying logic of the film: the only 'real' thing that a woman can do is bleed. But in bleeding she also marks herself as a woman. As Ussher remarks: '[o]ur blood marks us as Other—as we bleed we fail, we fall' (1991: 22).

The final frame of the movie is the *ouroboros* moment between Eve and Ed where the older woman reaches some understanding of her younger self and her subsequent life, and the younger woman perhaps reaches some connection with a more understanding older female, the very figure of her fear. In this scene the two characters are recognised as psychological fragments of a greater feminine consciousness that pervades the movie. Self-harm represents the essential logic (perhaps taken to an extreme) behind all the perversions that are on display in this film: they are all self-destructive, psychologically isolating and *individualising* strategies for warding off anxiety and the realisation of powerlessness and estrangement. Indeed, self-harm's status as a perversion is somewhat clearly illustrated by Ed's final act of cutting in which she has inscribed the word 'love' into her thigh. When asked why she has done this Ed replies that she had wanted to write 'hate'. Through this act the female mode of perversion is revealed as the social and psychic strategy through which female anger and resentment at being oppressed is miraculously transformed into the typically 'feminine' psychological position of wanting love and emotional support, of being the fairer and more emotional sex, and the very process through which 'hate' is transmuted into 'love'. For Ed, this act is the beginning of her taking on desires that are culturally coded as female and that will structure her subjectivity but that will also keep her at war with herself and other women; riven with insecurities, neuroses and anxiety.

But with that said, self-harm is also seemingly presented here as a kind of transcendence of female perversions. It short circuits the masculine disciplinary order coded into the other perversions and appears to be an attempt to hit on something basic, something female yet not 'feminine', something that hides beneath the other perversions as the primal 'real' of the female body before it is gendered into its feminine subjectivity. This authentic womanhood of the body, the body as a zero point of authentic being is symbolised by a large, naked, earth mother character who appears dreamlike in a cave and covered in clay. In this way self-harm links Ed and Eve: the novice and as yet ungendered pervert, and the fully gendered pervert. And, as such, it takes its place as a short circuit between the two, a re-set button on female perversion. It is presented as the cutting through of a feminine artifice to a truth beneath, a testimony of inner authenticity against the unreality of the outer world. And again, through the logic of the *pharmakon*, these tensions, even contradictions, in this symbolic circuit need not be problematic as it is a general indication of key tensions that matters here: the authentic versus the inauthentic, the 'real' versus the unreal, the need for agency to complete the project of selfhood versus a subjectification that renders that agency seemingly impotent and the responsibility that agency implies versus the failure that we feel when we struggle to live up to such responsibilities. *Female Perversions* takes the inner conflict positioned within the heart of feminine subjectivity and which is described by *The Exorcist* and demonstrates that it is a conflict between a subject who is both 'subject' (*homo clausus*) and 'other' (woman), and that the process of keeping her in this conflict ridden double bind are the very 'perversions' through which she works on herself in order to meet these contradictory expectations and roles. In the *The Exorcist* Regan is subject to powerful forces ranged around her, heaven and hell, the demon and the exorcists, but in *Female Perversion* all of these forces of subjectification, surveillance, regulation and control are presented, although significantly supported by culture and society, as nonetheless folded into the very pattern of late-modern feminine subjectivity. Eve is both the demon and the exorcist and together they describe her sense of selfhood and though seeming opposites they mutually reinforce each other as a disciplinary logic, and ensure that Eve's subjectivity and body will always be a war zone.

Pulling it All Together

These filmic texts of self-harm and feminine subjectivity help feel out the intersections between the three axes that we have explored, of psychological individualism with its inner dynamism and constant reference to selfhood, of the ideal of authentic selfhood and its paradoxical guarantee of traumatic estrangement, and of the disciplinary force of project and regimes of self-making. And here also is the dynamic between therapy culture and consumer culture through which the quest for self-making is tied to an ideal of authentic (and, in the case of *Female Perversions*, feminine) selfhood and the never-ending marketised search for perfect mental health, self-expression, self-possession and a balancing of the romantic–expressive and modernist–utilitarian dimensions of the self. What ties these two 'cultures' together is their common disciplinary logic, as the historian Rosalind Williams notes, the 'unprecedented expansion' of goods is not in itself necessarily problematic but 'it has also brought a weight of remorse and guilt, craving and envy, anxiety, and, above all, uneasy conscience, as we sense that we have too much, yet keep wanting more' (1982: 4); while Nikolas Rose compliments this account of the economy of desire by noting that '[s]elves who find...their identity constantly fading under inner and outer fragmentation are to be restored, through therapy, to unity and personal purpose' (1991: 228). Presumably the 'personal purpose' is, in fact, the search for psychic unity and so the cycle of consumption can begin again.

So systems of representation provide moral technologies that allow us to pursue our projects of self-making, and do so through the production of project-oriented desires, which we mostly follow through the acquisition and consumption of commodities, goods and services, and which we hope in some sense will bring us the satisfaction, stability, happiness and recognition from others that we know we need and deserve because our culture tells us that we do (Lears, 1983). Our 'perversions' are so many attempts, doomed to failure, to find this satisfaction and fulfilment, but in its absence we continue to recognise the inherent lack within us, the failure of our subjectivity, and therefore produce the desire to carry on with the project. To repeat: the argument is not, and cannot be, that self-harmers are driven 'mad' by the vicissitudes of consumerism but rather that self-harm, consumer culture and therapy culture resonate with the same core concerns and conflicts, and these reflect the fundamental structure of the subject in modernity, although through distinctly late-modern modalities. It is not consumerism or psychotherapy, or psychology more generally, that I wish to implicate here but rather the kind of self that emerges as a common concern of all three and the tensions and double binds that it is subject to, especially in its feminine form, and the disciplinary logic that is both the process and the product of these binds.

While actual people may articulate the patterns of meaning that make up the double bind in various ways and for various locally complex reasons, my argument here is that the double bind reflects the disciplinary hook upon which the sociocultural pattern of the late-modern psychological individual is stuck. It is this pattern and its inherent tensions, ambivalences and conflicts that self-harm gives expression to and draws attention to. Of course, the double bind can be identified most readily in female subjectivity in the trap between the subject and it's other. Susanna Kaysen, for example, found that her gender represented a radical and tragic circumscription of who and what she wanted to be as a person, her ideals inspired by the advances of feminism, even as her situation was limited by the pace of its advance. During the 50s and 60s gender roles were changing but not at an even pace, and women coming into womanhood at that time were given distinctly mixed signals, as famously represented, for example, by presidential candidate Adlai Stevenson's famous advice to Sylvia Plath's graduating class to write laundry lists instead of poetry (Showalter, 1987; Appignanesi, 2008). It is, of course, telling and tragic that Plath's means and method of dealing with this fundamental conflict was not political but rather quite personal, turning the tensions and turmoil of her situation back onto herself in numerous forms of self-destruction. But what about Eve?

Eve represents a distinctly post-80s femininity; a woman reaping the benefits of second-wave feminism, and aggressively and successfully pursuing a career in the public arena, which had traditionally been the preserve of men. It might seem, then, that the subject position of the feminine should be well past the kind of double bind described by Kaysen and Plath but, as numerous feminist commentators on anorexia have remarked (Bartky, 1990, 1997; Bordo, 1997, 2003; MacSween, 1993; Frost, 2001), if anything, the double bind has simply become that more insidious and that more *disciplinary* in nature. Women today are expected to be 'superwomen' (Bordo, 1997, 2003), a language echoed in Dana's description of her own impossibly high standards, capable of being both the perfect traditional woman *and* the perfect man—both subject *and* its compliment—competing successfully against him in the public arena but maintaining her femininity at home. This double bind seems to impact particularly hard on young women, who find themselves at a point in their lives where they are beginning to take up the expectations and projects of self-making typical of mature women, and so who typically find themselves caught between ambivalent injunctions to be perfect girls—empathic, good at relationships, nurturing, helpful, obedient, polite, nice, emotional, beautiful, sexually muted—while, at the same time, cultivating those qualities that allow them to compete with the boys—aggression, competitiveness and ambition, and being driven, marketable and reason-centred (Bordo, 2003; Frost, 2001).

The choices that characterise Eve's gender position in contrast to Plath's and Kaysen's seem considerable and empowering until you realise that many young women feel that they have to cultivate and embody *all* of these qualities irrespective of the intense tension and conflict between them. She should be marketable yet authentic, flexible yet unique, adaptable and successful yet somehow effortless and natural in the sense of the often repeated advice to 'just be yourself'. The ideals coded into contemporary feminine subjectivity then are both contradictory, describing a double bind, and, as the last chapter demonstrated, not coded as *ideals* at all but rather as normative standards by which one can judge the suitability or failure of the self. Indeed, this tension between ideals and norms is itself a kind of meta double bind as subjects, particularly women, take on ideals that describe authentic selfhood as normative standards, while the ideal of these ideals, authentic selfhood itself, always retreats as it cannot be achieved through the normal, only through the exceptional.

The work that the late-modern female subject must do then can perhaps best be summarised through the concepts of the modernist–utilitarian and romantic–expressive selves. Traditionally in modernity the romantic–expressive self was under the strict control of the modernist–utilitarian self, although this division also inscribed an inherent gender distinction as women were seen as being innately more romantic than men and so less able to cultivate a thoroughly modernist self. But in late-modernity the romantic–expressive self has been effectively marketised. This has happened partly through the ideal of authentic selfhood as it is understood to be achievable through psychological and psychotherapeutic technologies, which themselves have helped create a consumer psychology or therapy culture. It has partly happened through the production of desires based in ideals of authenticity and projects of self-making, as reflected in lifestyle-based advertising so that one is no longer just buying a commodity but a whole identity. And, finally, the romantic–expressive self has also been marketised through the belabouring of the self as an emphasis on the romantic self has promoted a more implicit disciplinary emphasis on the mechanisms and technologies of the modernist–utilitarian self, enabling it to control the raw, emotional nature of the romantic–expressive self and make it available for processes of self-making—these technologies, of course, being provided by the psy-complex and therapy culture. And it is through this inherent tension between these two dimensions of selfhood, refracted as it is through the multiple dynamics of authenticity and 'reality', reason and emotion, expression and repression, control and chaos, and self-making and self-failing, that the late-modern, and especially female, subject has been increasingly individualised and psychologised, and has increasingly seen the political re-inscribed as the private (indeed, there is a sense that, following second-wave feminism, women gained access to the public sphere only to see it transformed into the private). It is this inherent tension that describes Eve's predicament and the key double bind that runs through representations and understandings of self-harm: *to feel powerless and yet responsible*, an agent yet a failure, a true-self and yet one who has lost her authenticity.

None of which, it must be emphasised, is to suggest that self-harm is specifically a woman's problem, although it may be a feminist issue nonetheless. For me, the figure of Richey Edwards comes back into view at this point; the male self-harmer, strongly connected to music, and characterised by his emo style. Most images of people who self-harm are of women with the singular exception of the music industry where the (slim) majority of songs about self-harm are written and performed by men. These are, as I noted in Chapter 2, songs that focus on emotions, and inner turmoil, and that represent a fetish for the romantic–expressive self. Perhaps the emo style brings young men into a similar gender predicament to that of the feminine: namely the double bind of having to represent both genders, and both romantic–expressive and modernist–utilitarian selves, so that there is a key ambivalence inscribed in the heart of the subject. Both Eve and Richey dramatically enact this deep tension and the painful conflicts that it produces, regardless of their biological sex.

Conclusion
Making Sense of Self-harm

> I think it's...I mean...it's a whole big tangle of just, erm...something [laughs].
>
> Donna (telephone)

Donna's confusion in trying to sum up what self-harm is and what it means to her is perhaps understandable. After an effort to make sense of it that has lasted (to date) ten years and that has taken me constantly back and forth between considering the immanent moment when a razor blade cuts through skin and the broadest and seemingly most abstract discursive structures of modern and late-modern culture and society, I now feel that I understand it a lot better than I did when I first sat down opposite Fiona in a small office on her prison wing. And yet I still find it enigmatic, mercurial and difficult to pin down. Perhaps one reason for this is its typical character, emphasised throughout this book, of ambivalence. Perhaps part of the answer to grasping self-harm is to not grasp it too tightly. Its meanings are at play within certain fairly consistent fields of issues and concerns, described here as axes of continuity, and it reproduces these fields, articulates them, but also disturbs, confuses and questions them at the same time. Or, in other words, self-harm simply wouldn't mean what self-harm means, and needs to mean, if its meanings were made clearer and less confused. In his *Critical Essays*, Roland Barthes (1972) argues that the role of literature is not to express the inexpressible but rather to make the reading difficult, to problematise the flow of assumed meaning, to make a 'strange verse', in Dante's phrase, and to 'un-express the expressible'. I think we shall not go far wrong if we try to understand self-harm in the same way. It is, of course, as I noted in Chapter 3, often framed as an expression or the inexpressible, and this is certainly part of its constellation of meanings but, as

I argued in Chapter 4, this does not mean that it actually expresses the inexpressible. Rather it symbolises and acts for the idea of the inexpressible, the idea of a fuller, rawer and more 'real' communication than ordinary language can handle; 'something that by its rawness, that by its bleeding, demands to be called real'.

Self-harm as an idiom, as a prepackaged pattern of meanings and actions tied together by enough of a family resemblance that it can be described *as* a family and be given a family name, sits at, and emerges from, the intersection of the three axes of continuity that we have explored, while the whole structure is itself patterned by the ubiquitous structure of gendered subjectification. Indeed, without the distinction between an inner and an outer, and the emergence of modern individual subjectivity; without the emphasis on emotions and the psychodynamic self; without the idea of psyche as a system and the necessity of expression; without a cultural distinction between the symbolic and the 'real', and a coterminous concern with the dynamics of the 'real' and the authentic; without the associations that connect pain and blood and wounds to the 'real'; without a central concern for agency and control; without the psychomedical conception of trauma; without the internalisation of responsibility, the process of examination and the logic of self-punishment coded into a culture characterised by a disciplinary regime; without an emphasis on reflexivity and the self as project; without the double binds of ideals passed off as norms and emphasis on a romantic–expressive self that must nonetheless be controlled and 'processed' by a modernist–utilitarian self; without the key double bind of feeling powerless yet responsible—without all of these, and all of their many and complex interactions, self-harm would simply not make sense.

Self-harm sits at this intersection as a product of the conflicts that emerge from the meeting of so many complex and rich patterns of meaning, and it brings attention to this intersection and its character of conflict, through an exaggerated performance of these very conflicts. Personally, then, it may be a way, made meaningful within such a social ecology of discourse, to negotiate the tensions and dilemmas that become centred on the self as the primary site of conflict, and it may be a way to move toward expressing this conflicted state to others and begin the negotiation of social restitution. Although, of course, as I have argued throughout, we must understand that if self-harm performs these functions for people then it does so on the basis of its cultural meanings and their social contexts. Indeed, the dimension of personal experience has been central to this analysis, although I have not taken a distinctly person-based methodology. For me, much of the personal fascination of self-harm as a subject of study lies in all the people that I have met over the last ten years of working with self-harm, all the faces and bodies, names and stories, lives and experiences. But the fascination that I have with it as a cultural sociologist lays in the fact that behind closed doors, in a seemingly utterly private and personal moment, just as a person who is caught in the power of their own thoughts and feelings draws a razor blade across their skin and blood weeps from the cut, folded into that highly individual and immanent moment, there is a whole tradition and a whole culture that is implicitly present, yet not overtly so and indeed largely unacknowledged. This culture is the same culture as that conjured and shored up by 'The Waste Land'; Freud's *Fragment*, *Female Perversions*; Marilyn Manson; *Hamlet*; *Bodies Under Siege*; Magritte's *The Lovers*; Kafka's *Penal Colony*; Christ's passion; *Girl, Interrupted*; Princess Diana; Hawthorne's minister; Courtney Love; and Richey Edwards.

And it is the same culture that informs, in the most literal sense, every text and every person that I have referred to in this book, and, of course, the practice and meaning of self-harm. Moments of speech and the structures of language cannot be separated except in the imagination of linguists, and on the ground there is only living language. Likewise, the semiotics that spin the weave and web of self-harm are simultaneously personal and social, individual and cultural. Susan Bordo, writing about cultural criticism, argues that it 'isn't about lacking sympathy for people's personal choices...it's about perceiving consciousness of the larger contexts in which our choices occur' (1997: 16). Likewise, I am not interested in morally judging or medically diagnosing people who self-harm, I am not interested in defining it as an illness, a coping mechanism, an addiction, or a tool, even if by 'tool' we take it to mean something free of values and a simple extension of individual agency.

My point here has been to attempt that 'consciousness of the larger context' and so to place self-harm in its sociocultural position as it draws on, condenses, transforms and exaggerates the key concerns and conflicts of late-modern culture and subjectivity. And if there is a single conclusion to be drawn about these concerns and conflicts it is that the economy of desire promoted by late-modern consumer capitalism is a centripetal economy focused on the longing for a stable, satisfied and self-sufficient, authentic self. But it is also one that, by virtue of this focus, more or less guarantees a consistent and pervasive experience of insufficiency and discontent. In drawing our attention to the battleground that is the belaboured self, self-harm draws our attention to a central pressure point in late-modern subjectivity, the site upon which the tensions, conflicts and dilemmas of our society are focused. If self-harm is telling us something then it is telling us that the belaboured self is not just another construction of subjectivity but rather one that is in crisis, one that has become too belaboured and that is ready to crack.

I have tried to make self-harm make some kind of sense, and one of the key understandings that I have been trying to articulate is that part of the meaning of self-harm is precisely its capacity and function to disrupt meanings, to 'unexpress the expressable', as Barthes has it. But this raises an interesting problem for us. If self-harm is *supposed* to be confusing, ambivalent and disturbing *because* it expresses confusion, ambivalence and disturbance, then the very attempt to make it make sense would seem to work against it. Perhaps such idioms of personal distress and emotional dysphoria should be left open, as traumatic wounds in the normative weave and web of our culture. But then even to say *this* is to make sense of them as just such wounds and the problem is replicated. In the end I think it is important to remember that while social and political implications can be drawn from practices like self-harm they are not in themselves forms of political resistance except in as much as they do resist the completion of normative subjectivity and hence appear as a refusal to be a healthy and normal member of society. The self-harming person and their actions are located within the force fields of discourse, and the matrix of such forces, as they make up patterns and processes of history, culture, society and politics, but we must also remember that the self-harming person is also someone who is usually confused and disturbed, in pain and *in need of understanding*.

Notes

Introduction: The Signifying Wound

1. See http://www.bbc.co.uk/news/special/politics97/diana/panorama.html (accessed 5 November 2012); see also Morton (1998).
2. See http://www.theguardian.com/society/2014/may/21/shock-figures-self-harm-england-teenagers (accessed 15 September 2014).
3. In this book the term 'Western,' following a well-established if somewhat general and inaccurate academic tradition, is used to denote both the sociohistorical complexes of late-modernity and the hegemonic discourses that characterise these complexes, principally 'the largely middle-class, North American/Northern European discourse of public and professional life' (Strathern, 1996: 38). I use the term 'late-modern' in preference to 'post'-modern and in order to indicate the social structures of contemporary capitalist society.
4. A notable exception is in the music industry but I will return to this in Chapter 6.

1 What is Self-harm?

1. To clarify, I take 'culture' to signify semiotic and discursive systems of meanings and values that represent the shared means of making sense common to a given community of people (Geertz, 2000; Inglis, 2004), and 'society' to signify the patterns and processes of relationships and interactions that structure such communities (Elias, 1978). I take these two concepts to be utterly interconnected and interdependent, and yet to possess some degree of relative autonomy with respect to one another (Alexander, 2003).
2. It is worth noting in passing that the anthropologist Serena Heckler, when attempting to explain 'self-harm' to members of the Shuar community of the Ecuadorian Amazon, was only able to gain expressions of puzzlement as to why anyone would intentionally hurt themselves in this way. Self-harm would appear to be an alien concept to her informants who nonetheless have traditionally practised physical ordeal and self-mutilation as part of their shamanic rituals (personal communication).
3. Arguably, by invoking intention, Favazza's definition goes beyond the strict limits of a thin description but such an invocation amounts to little more here than identifying that the act is a self-inflicted act rather than an accident, or that it is carried out with the approval of the person to be mutilated, and that it does not amount to a suicide attempt. Nothing of the meaning or purpose of the act itself is implied in this definition and so it is reasonable to count it as a thin description.
4. The hope is that research following the *Diagnostic and Statistical Manual of Mental Disorders, 5th Edition* (DSM-5) will be more synchronised in

terminology and definition, and many of these problems will clear as new data come in.

2 The Problem of Good Understanding

1. Quoted in 'Mental Health and Creative People: Self-Injury', available at: http://blogs.psychcentral.com/creative-mind/2011/10/mental-health-day-self-injury/ (accessed 29 January 2015).
2. Quoted in 'Famous Self-harmers', available at: https://self-injury.net/media/famous-self-injurers#courtney-love (accessed 23 January 2015).
3. Available at: http://www.bbc.co.uk/news/special/politics97/diana/panorama.html (downloaded 5 November 2012).
4. Available at: www.bbfc.co.uk/what-classification/guidelines/main-issues (accessed 8 June 2015).
5. Villa 65 is a Dutch radio station, and this is an excerpt from an interview conducted by them and downloaded from http://articles.richeyedwards.net/dutchradionov94.html on 21 April 2010.
6. 'McKenna: The Cost of Sanity is Alienation', available at: https://www.youtube.com/watch?v=ufHyOQPWkIA (accessed 20 February 2015).
7. My *use* of the word may be, but the word itself is not.

3 The Ontological Axis

1. The identities of the participants in this research have been protected and their data anonymised, with the single exception of Allie, who requested that her actual name be used.
2. Quotes from participants will be followed by a note about the type of interview that was conducted (i.e. in person, by telephone or by email).
3. From www.bbc.co.uk/health/emotional_health/mental_health/emotion_self harm.shtml (accessed 10 June 2012).
4. A Kleenex advertisement used this message through a featured song entitled 'Let it Out' by Starrfadu.
5. 'Talking About Your Feelings', available at: www.kidshealth.org/kid/feeling/thought/talk_feelings.html (downloaded 10 June 2012).
6. 'Talk About Your Feelings', available at: www.mentalhealth.org.uk/help-information/10-ways-to-look-after-your-mental-health/talk-about-your-feelings/ (downloaded 10 June 2012).
7. 'Mental Health: Keeping Your Emotional Health', available at: www.familydoctor.org/familydoctor/en/prevention-wellness/emotional-wellbeing/mental-health/mental-health-keeping-your-emotional-health.html (downloaded 12 June 2012).
8. 'Internalisation' is a term that will be used several times in this study, especially in connection with the work of Norbert Elias and Michel Foucault; however, it is used here descriptively and in no way presumes, contra Wittgenstein, the existence of an actual 'inner' space. 'Internalisation' here refers more to the disciplining of the body and the cultivation of self-reflective psychological attitudes that promote self-surveillance and self-discipline: it is

about the *patterning of the self* rather than the actual installation of something within the self.

4 The Aetiological Axis

1. Again, it is important to remember that such *ideas* and popular explanations of cause and effect are being described here as a cosmology or metaphysics of subjectivity and distress, as a powerful informing, shaping and moulding influence on those patterns of experience that describe our psychological lives. This does not mean, however, that such ideas are simply and ontologically correct but rather that they are powerfully persuasive and may have something of the character of a self-fulfilling prophecy about them.

6 The Belaboured Economy of Desire

1. 'Austerity and a Malign Benefits Regime are Profoundly Damaging Mental Health', available at: http://www.theguardian.com/society/2015/apr/17/austerity-and-a-malign-benefits-regime-are-profoundly-damaging-mental-health (accessed 10 June 2015).

References

Adler, G. (1985) *Borderline Psychopathology and its Treatment* (Ann Arbor: University of Michigan Press).
Adler, P.A. and Adler, P. (2008) 'The cyber worlds of self-injurers: Deviant communities, relationships, and selves', *Symbolic Interaction* 31: 33–56.
Adler, P.A. and Adler, P. (2011) *The Tender Cut* (New York: New York University Press).
Ahmed, S. (2004) *The Cultural Politics of Emotions* (Edinburgh: Edinburgh University Press).
Alderman, T. (1997) *The Scarred Soul* (Oakland, CA: New Harbinger).
Alexander, J.C. (2003) *The Meanings of Social Life* (Oxford: Oxford University Press).
Alexander, J.C. and Smith, P. (2001) 'The strong program in cultural theory: Elements of a structural hermeneutics', in J.H. Turner (ed.) *Handbook of Sociological Theory*, pp. 135–50 (New York: Kluwer Academic/Plenum Publisher).
Alleyne, R. (2008) 'Popular schoolgirl dies in "emo suicide cult"', available at: http://www.telegraph.co.uk/news/uknews/1935735/Popular-schoolgirl-dies-in-emo-sucide-cult.html (accessed 1 June 2015).
Althusser, L. (1971) *Lenin and Philosophy and Other Essays* (New York: Monthly Review Press).
American Psychiatric Association (2013) *Diagnostic and Statistical Manual of Mental Disorders, 5th Edition: DSM-5* (Washington, DC: American Psychiatric Association).
Anderson, P. (1998) *The Origins of Postmodernity* (New York: Verso).
Appignanesi, L. (2008) *Mad, Bad and Sad* (London: Virago).
Auden, W.H. (2004) *Collected Poems* (E. Mendelson, ed.) (London: Faber and Faber).
Babiker, G. and Arnold, L. (1997) *The Language of Injury* (Leicester: The British Psychological Society).
Bachy-Y-Rita, G. (1974) 'Habitual violence and self-mutilation', *American Journal of Psychiatry* 131: 1018–20.
Ballinger, B.R. (1971) 'Minor self-injury', *British Journal of Psychiatry* 118: 535–8.
Barrett, M. (1991) *The Politics of Truth: From Marx to Foucault* (Stanford, CA: Stanford University Press).
Barthes, R. (1972) *Critical Essays* (R. Howard, transl.) (Evanston, IL: Northwestern University Press).
Barthes, R. (1993) *Camera Lucida* (R. Howard, transl.) (London: Vintage Classics).
Bartky, S.L. (1990) *Femininity and Domination* (London: Routledge).
Bartky, S.L. (1997) 'Foucault, femininity, and the modernization of patriarchal power', in K. Conboy, N. Medina and S. Stanbury (eds) *Writing on the Body: Female Embodiment and Feminist Theory*, pp. 129–54 (New York: Columbia University Press).
Bauman, Z. (2000) *Liquid Modernity* (Cambridge: Polity).
Beck, U. (1997) *The Reinvention of Politics* (Cambridge: Polity).

Becker, H.S. (1997) *Outsiders* (New York: Simon and Schuster).
Bellah, R., Sullivan, W.M., Swidler, A. and S.M. Titpon (1985) *Habits of the Heart* (Berkley, CA: University of California Press).
Belsey, C. (2004) *Culture and the Real* (London: Routledge).
Bollas, C. (1999) *Hysteria* (London: Routledge).
Bordo, S. (1997) *Twilight Zones* (Berkeley, CA: University of California Press).
Bordo, S. (2003) *Unbearable Weight*, 2nd ed. (Berkeley, CA: University of California Press).
Boyle, D. (2004) *Authenticity: Brands, Fakes, Spin and the Lust for Real Life* (London: Harper Perennial).
Bradford, D. (1990) 'Early Christian martyrdom and the psychology of depression, suicide, and bodily mutilation', *Psychotherapy: Theory, Research, Practice, Training* 27: 30–41.
Breggin, P. (1993) *Toxic Psychiatry* (London: Fontana).
Bronfen, E. (1992) *Over Her Dead Body* (Manchester: Manchester University Press).
Brophy, M. (2006) *The Truth Hurts* (London: Mental Health Foundation).
Bruckner, P. (2010) *Perpetual Euphoria* (Princeton, NJ: Princeton University Press).
Bruner, J. (1990) *Acts of Meaning* (Cambridge, MA: Harvard University Press).
Burke, K. (1989) *On Symbols and Society* (J.R. Gusfield, ed.) (Chicago, IL: University of Chicago Press).
Butchart, A. (1997) 'Objects without origins: Foucault in South African socio-medical science', *South African Journal of Psychology* 27: 101–10.
Butler, J. (1993) *Bodies That Matter* (New York: Routledge).
Calhoun, C. (1994) 'Social theory and the politics of identity', in C. Calhoun (ed.) *Social Theory and the Politics of Identity*, pp. 9–36 (Cambridge, MA: Blackwell).
Callero, P. L. (2009) *The Myth of Individualism* (Lanham, MD: Rowman & Littlefield).
Cameron, D., and Frazer, E. (1987) *The Lust to Kill* (Cambridge: Polity).
Campbell, C. (1987) *The Romantic Ethic and the Spirit of Modern Consumerism* (Cambridge: Blackwell).
Carroll, L. (2013) *Alice's Adventures in Wonderland & Through the Looking Glass* (New York: Barnes & Noble).
Caruth, C. (ed.) (1995) *Trauma: Explorations in Memory* (Baltimore, MD: Johns Hopkins University Press).
Chandler, A., Myers, A. and S. Platt (2011) 'The construction of self-injury in the clinical literature: A sociological exploration', *Suicide and Life-threatening Behaviour* 41: 98–109.
Changing, W. (1878) 'Case of Helen Miller', *The American Journal of Insanity*: 369–78, available at: https://archive.org/stream/americanjournalo3418amer/americanjournalo3418amer_djvu.txt (accessed 10 October 14).
Chernin, K. (1985) *The Hungry Self* (New York: HarperCollins).
Cioran, E.M. (1976) *The Temptation to Exist* (New York: Quadrangle/The New York Times Book Co.).
Cixous, H. (1981) 'Castration or decapitation?', *Signs* 7: 41–55.
Claes, L. and Vandereycken, W. (2007) 'Self-injurious behaviour: differential diagnosis and functional differentiation', *Comprehensive Psychology* 48: 137–44.
Clark, J. and Henslin, E. (2007) *Inside a Cutter's Mind* (Colorado Springs, CO: Think).
Clegg, S.R. (1989) *Frameworks of Power* London: Sage

Clendenin, W.W. and Murphy, G.E. (1971) 'New epidemiological findings', *Archives of General Psychiatry* 25: 465–9.
Cohen, J. (2005) *How to Read Freud* (London: Granta).
Cohen, S. (1972) *Folk Devils and Moral Panics* (London: MacGibbon and Kee).
Coles, R. (1987) 'Civility and psychology', in R.N. Bellah, R. Madison, W.M. Sullivan, A. Swidler and S.M. Tipton (eds) *Individualism and Commitment in American Life: Readings on the Themes of Habits of the Heart* (New York: Harper and Row).
Conrad, P. and Schneider, W. (1992) *Deviance and Medicalization*, 2nd ed. (Philadelphia, PA: Temple).
Conterio, K., Lader, W. and Bloom, J.K. (1998) *Bodily Harm* (New York: Hyperion).
Cousins, M. and Hussain, A. (1984) *Michel Foucault* (Basingstoke: Macmillan).
Craib, I. (1994) *The Importance of Disappointment* (London: Routledge).
Crossley, N. (1996) *Intersubjectivity* (London: Sage).
Crossley, N. (2006) *Reflexive Embodiment in Contemporary Society* (Maidenhead: Open University Press).
Crouch, W. and Wright, J. (2004) 'Deliberate self-harm at an adolescent unit: A qualitative investigation', *Clinical Child Psychology and Psychiatry* 9: 185–204.
Curtis, N. (2000) 'The body as outlaw: Lyotard, Kafka and the Visible Human Project', in M. Featherstone (ed.) *Body Modification*, pp. 249–66 (London: Sage).
Cushman, P. (1995) *Constructing the Self, Constructing America* (Reading, MA: Addison-Wesley).
Dabrowski, C (1937) 'Psychological bases of self-mutilation' (W. Thau, transl.), *Genetic Psychology Monographs* 19: 1–104.
Dante (1961 [1320]) *The Divine Comedy Volume 1: Inferno* (J.D. Sinclair, transl.) (New York: Oxford University Press).
Danziger, K. (1997) *Naming the Mind* (London: Sage).
Day, A. (1996) *Romanticism* (London: Routledge).
de Graaf, J., Wann, D. and Naylor, T.H. (2005) *Affluenza* (San Francisco: Berrett-Koehler).
Derrida, J. (1976) *Of Grammatology* (G.C. Spivak, transl.) (Baltimore, MD: Johns Hopkins University Press).
Derrida, J. (1981) *Dissemination* (B. Johnson, transl.) (Chicago, IL: University of Chicago Press).
Derrida, J. (1991) *The Derrida Reader* (P. Kamuf, ed.) (New York: Columbia University Press).
Descartes, R, (1964) *Philosophical Essays* (L.J. Lafleur, transl.) (Indianapolis, IN: Bobbs-Merrill).
de Tocqueville, A. (2003 [1835]) *Democracy in America: And Two Essays on America* (London: Penguin).
De Vries, M.W., Berg, R.L. and M. Lipkin Jr. (eds) (1983) *The Use and Abuse of Medicine* (New York: Praeger Publishers).
Dineen, T. (1999) *Manufacturing Victims* (London: Constable).
Dostoyevsky, F. (1985 [1862]) *House of the Dead* (D. McDuff, transl.) (London: Penguin).
Douglas, M. (1973) *Natural Symbols* (New York: Vintage Books).
Downing, L. (2008) *The Cambridge Introduction to Michel Foucault* (Cambridge: Cambridge University Press).

Dreyfus, H. and Rabinow, P. (1982) *Michel Foucault: Beyond Structuralism and Hermeneutics* (Chicago, IL: University of Chicago Press).
Durkheim, E. (2008 [1912]) *Elementary Forms of Religious Life* (Oxford: Oxford University Press).
Eisenkraft, M. (2006) 'Self-injury: Is it a syndrome?', *The New School Psychology Bulletin* 4: 115–26.
Elias, N. (1978) *What is Sociology?* (London: Hutchinson).
Elias, N. (1996) *The Germans* (London: Polity).
Elias, N. (2000 [1939]) *The Civilizing Process* (Oxford: Blackwell).
Eliot, T.S. (2009 [1922]) *Selected Poems of T.S. Eliot* (London: Faber & Faber).
Elliott, A. and Lemert, C. (2006) *The New Individualism* (London: Routledge).
Emirbayer, M., and Goodwin, J. (1996) 'Symbols, positions, objects: Toward a new theory of revolutions and collective action', *History and Theory* 35: 358–74.
Farber, S.K. (2002) *When The Body is the Target* (London: Jason Aronson).
Farberow, N. (1980) *The Many Faces of Suicide Indirect Self-destructive Behaviour* (New York: McGraw-Hill).
Favazza, A. (1996) *Bodies Under Siege: Self-mutilation and Body Modification in Culture and Psychiatry*, 2nd ed. (Baltimore, MD: John Hopkins University Press).
Favazza, A. (1998) 'The coming of age of self-mutilation', *Journal of Mental and Nervous Disease* 186: 259–68.
Fillmore, C., Dell, A.D. and Fry, E. (2003) 'Domestic abuse can trigger self-mutilation', in M.E. Williams (ed.) *Self-Mutilation: Opposing Viewpoints* (New York: Greenhaven Press).
Fine, C. (2010) *Delusions of Gender* (London: Icon).
Fine, R. (1997) *History of Psychoanalysis* (London: Continuum).
Foucault, M. (1978) *The History of Sexuality: The Will to Knowledge* (London: Penguin).
Foucault, M. (1987) *Mental Illness and Psychology* (Berkeley, CA: University of California).
Foucault, M. (1991 [1975]) *Discipline and Punish: The Birth of the Prison* (London, Penguin).
Foucault, M. (1998) *The Essential Works of Michel Foucault Volume II – Aesthetics: Method and Epistemology* (J. Faubion, ed.) (New York: New Press).
Foucault, M. (2001) *The Order of Things* (London: Routledge).
Foucault, M. (2002) *The Archaeology of Knowledge* (London: Routledge).
Foucault, M. (2003a) *The Birth of the Clinic* (London: Routledge).
Foucault, M. (2003b) *Abnormal: Lectures at the College de France 1974–1975* (V. Marchetti and A. Salomoni, eds) (London: Verso)
Foucault, M. (2006) *History of Madness* (J. Khalfa, transl.) (London: Routledge).
Foucault, M. (2010) *The Government of Self and Others: Lectures at the College de France 1982–1983* (G. Burchell, transl.) (London: Palgrave Macmillan).
Freud, S. (1953 [1905]) *Standard Edition Volume 7* (London: Hogarth).
Freud, S. (1975) *Standard Edition Volume 11: Five Lectures on Psychoanalysis, Leonardo da Vinci and Other Works* (J. Strachey, transl.) (London: Vintage Classics).
Freud, S. (2003 [1919]) *The Uncanny* (D. McLintock, transl.) (London: Routledge).
Freud, S. and Breuer, J. (2004 [1895]) *Studies in Hysteria* (London: Penguin).

Freund, P.E.S. and McGuire, M.B. (1999) *Health, Illness, and the Social Body* (New York: Prentice-Hall Gale).
Friedman, L. (1999) *The Horizontal Society* (New Haven, CT: Yale University Press).
Fromm, E. (2003) *Man For Himself* (London: Routledge).
Frost, L. (2001) *Young Women and the Body* (Basingstoke: Palgrave).
Furedi, F. (2004) *Therapy Culture* (London: Routledge).
Gadamer, H-G. (1989) *Truth and Method*, 2nd ed. (J. Weinsheimer and D.G. Marshal, transl.) (London: Sheed and Ward).
Gaines, A.D. (ed.) (1992) *Ethnopsychiatry* (Albany, NY: SUNY Press).
Gallop, J. (1985) 'Keys to Dora', in C. Bernheimer and C. Kahane (eds) *In Dora's Case: Freud–Hysteria–Feminism*, pp. 200–20 (Chichester: Columbia University Press).
Gardner, A.R. and Gardner, A.J. (1975) 'Self-mutilation, obsessionality, narcissism', *British Journal of Psychiatry* 127: 127–32.
Gardner, F. (2001) *Self-harm: A Psychotherapeutic Approach* (London: Routledge).
Gatens, M. (1991) *Feminism and Philosophy* (Cambridge: Polity).
Geertz, C. (1973) *The Interpretation of Cultures* (New York: Basic Books).
Geertz, C. (1980) *Nagara* (Princeton, NJ: Princeton University Press).
Geertz, C. (1983) *Local Knowledge* (New York: Basic Books).
Geertz, C. (2000) *Available Light* (Princeton, NJ: Princeton University Press).
Gellner, E. (1985) *The Psychoanalytic Movement* (London: Paladin).
Gergen, K.J. (2000) *The Saturated Self* (New York: Basic Books).
Giddens, A. (1976) *New Rules of Sociological Method* (London: Hutchinson).
Giddens, A. (1990) *The Consequences of Modernity* (Stanford, CA: Stanford University Press).
Giddens, A. (1991) *Modernity and Self-identity* (Cambridge: Polity).
Giddens, A. (1992) *Transformations of Intimacy* (Cambridge: Polity).
Goffman, E. (1968) *Stigma* (London: Harmondsworth Penguin).
Goffman, E. (1991) *Asylums* (London: Penguin).
Goffman, E. (1997) *The Goffman Reader* (C. Lemert and A. Branaman, eds) (Oxford: Blackwell).
Goleman, D. (1996) *Emotional Intelligence: Why it can Matter More Than IQ* (London: Bloomsbury).
Goudriaan, A., Grekin, E.R. and Sher, K.J. (2007) 'Decision making and binge drinking: a longitudinal study', *Alcoholism: Clinical and Experimental Research* 31: 928–38.
Gould, G.M. and Pyle, W.L. (2003 [1901]) *Anomalies and Curiosities of Medicine Volume 2* (Whitefish, MT: Kessinger).
Graff, H. and Mallin, R. (1967) 'The syndrome of the wrist cutter', *American Journal of Psychiatry* 124: 36–42.
Gramsci, A. (1992) *Prison Notebooks Volume 1* (New York: Columbia University Press).
Gratz, K.L. (2001) 'Measurement of deliberate self-harm: Preliminary data on the deliberate self-harm inventory', *Journal of Psychopathology and Behavioural Assessment* 23: 253–63.
Greenblatt, S. (2005) *Renaissance Self-Fashioning* (Chicago, IL: University of Chicago Press).
Greenburg, G. (1994) *The Self on the Shelf* (Albany, NY: State University of New York Press).

Greenwald, A. (2003) *Nothing Feels Good* (New York: St. Martin's Press).
Grosz, E. (1994) *Volatile Bodies: Toward a Corporeal Feminism* (Bloomington, IN: Indiana University Press).
Grunebaum, H.V. and Klerman, G.L. (1967) 'Wrist slashing', *American Journal of Psychiatry* 124: 527–34.
Guignon, C. (2004) *On Being Authentic* (London: Routledge).
Hacking, I. (1986) 'The archaeology of Foucault', in D.C. Hoy (ed.) *Foucault: A Critical Reader*, pp. 27–40 (Oxford: Blackwell).
Hacking, I. (1995) *Rewriting the Soul* (Princeton, NJ: Princeton University Press).
Hacking, I. (2002) *Mad Travellers* (Cambridge, MA: Harvard University Press).
Hahn, R. and Kleinman, A. (1983) 'Belief as pathogen, belief as medicine', *Medical Anthropology Quarterly* 14: 16–19.
Haines, J., Williams, C.L., Brain, K.L. and Wilson, G.V. (1995) 'The psychophysiology of self-mutilation', *Journal of Abnormal Psychology* 104: 474–89.
Hall, S. (1992) 'The west and the rest', in S. Hall and B. Gieben (eds) *Formations of Modernity*, pp. 275–332 (Cambridge: Polity/The Open University).
Harré, R. and Tissaw, M. (2005) *Wittgenstein and Psychology* (Aldershot: Ashgate).
Harrison, D. and Sharman, J. (2007) *Understanding Self-harm* (London: MIND).
Harrison, T. (2006) *Diana* (London: Hodder and Stoughton).
Hass, B. and Popp, F. (2006) 'Why do people injure themselves', *Psychopathology* 39: 10–18.
Hawthorne, N. (1986) *Nathaniel Hawthorne: Tales* (London: Norton).
Hendin, H. (1950) 'Attempted suicide: A psychiatric and statistical study', *Psychiatric Quarterly* 24: 34–46.
Herman, E. (1995) *The Romance of American Psychology: Political Culture in the Age of Experts* (Berkeley, CA: University of California Press).
Herman, J.L. (1992) *Trauma and Recovery* (London: Pandora).
Hewitt, K. (1997) *Mutilating the Body* (Bowling Green, OH: Bowling Green University Popular Press).
Heywood, L. (1996) *Dedication to Hunger* (Berkeley, CA: University of California Press).
Hill, E. (1985) *The Family Secret* (Santa Barbara, CA: Capra Press).
Hollander, M. (2008) *Helping Teens Who Cut: Understanding and Ending Self-injury* (New York: The Guilford Press).
Hook, D. (2001) 'Therapeutic discourse, co-construction, interpellation, role-induction: psychotherapy as iatrogenic treatment modality?', *The International Journal of Psychotherapy* 6: 47–66.
Hook, D. (2007) *Foucault, Psychology, and the Analytics of Power* (Basingstoke: Palgrave Macmillan).
Horne, O. and Csipke, E. (2009) 'From feeling too little and too much, to feeling more and less? A nonparadoxical theory of the functions of self-harm', *Qualitative Health Research* 19: 655–67.
Horwitz, A.V. (2003) *Creating Mental Illness* (Chicago, IL: University of Chicago).
Husserl, E. (1970 [1901]) *Logical Investigations: Investigations Vol. 1* (J.N. Findlay, transl.) (London: Routledge & Kegan Paul).
Hutton, P. (1988) 'Foucualt, Freud and the technologies of the self', in (L. Martin, H. Gutman and P. Hutton, eds) *M. Foucault Technologies of the Self* (Amherst, MA: University of Massachusetts Press).
Illich, I. (1972) *Deschooling Society* (Harmondsworth: Penguin).

Inckle, K. (2007) *Writing on the Body?* (Cambridge: Cambridge Scholars Publishing).
Ingleby, D. (1985) 'Professionals as socialisers: the "psy complex"', in A. Scull and S. Spitzer (eds) *Research in Law, Deviance and Social Control* (New York: Jai Press).
Inglis, F. (2000) *Clifford Geertz* (Cambridge: Polity).
Inglis, F. (2004) *Culture* (Cambridge: Polity).
Jablensky, A., Sartorius, N., Ernberg, G., Anker, M., Korten, A., Cooper, J.E., *et al.* (1992) 'Schizophrenia: manifestations, incidence and course in different cultures: A World Health Organization ten-country study', *Psychological Medicine* 20(Suppl.): 1–97.
Jacobs, R. (1996) 'Civil society and crisis: Culture, discourse and the Rodney King beating', *American Journal of Sociology* 101: 1238–72.
Jacobs, M. (2003) *The Presenting Past* (Milton Keynes: Open University Press).
James, O. (2007) *Affluenza* (Reading: Vermillion).
James, O. (2008) *The Selfish Capitalist* (Reading: Vermillion).
Jamison, L. (2014) *The Empathy Exams* (London: Granta).
Jansz, J. (2004) 'Psychology and society: An overview', in J. Jansz and P. Van Drunen (eds) *A Social History of Psychology*, pp. 12–44 (Oxford: Blackwell).
Jansz, J., and Drunen, P. Van. (eds) (2004) *A Social History of Psychology* (Oxford: Blackwell).
Jeffreys, S. (2005) *Beauty and Misogyny* (London: Routledge).
Jervis, J. (1998) *Exploring the Modern* (Oxford: Blackwell).
Jervis, J. (1999) *Transgressing the Modern* (Oxford: Blackwell).
Johnstone, L. (2000) *Users and Abusers of Psychiatry*, 2nd ed. (London: Routledge).
Jones, I.H., Congiv, L., Stevenson, J. and B. Frei (1979) 'A biological approach to two forms of human self-injury', *Journal of Nervous and Mental Disease* 167: 74–8.
Jovanovic, R. (2010) *A Version of Reason: In Search of Richey Edwards* (London: Orion).
Kafka, F. (1992 [1919]) *In The Metamorphosis, The Penal Colony, and Other Stories* (New York: Shocken).
Kafka, F. (1994) *The Collected Aphorisms* (M. Pasley, transl.) (London: Syrens).
Kaminer, W. (1993) *I'm Dysfunctional, You're Dysfunctional* (Reading, MA: Addison-Wesley).
Kaplan, L. (1993) *Female Perversions* (London: Penguin).
Kaysen, S. (2000) *Girl, Interrupted* (London: Virago).
Kenny, M.G. (1978) 'Latah: the symbolism of a putative mental disorder', *Culture, Medicine, Psychiatry* 2: 209–31.
Kilby, J. (2001) 'Carved in skin: bearing witness to self-harm', in S. Ahmed and J. Stacy (eds) *Thinking Through the Skin*, pp. 124–42 (London: Routledge).
King, R.A., Leckman, J.F., Scahill, L. and Cohen, D.J. (1999) 'Obsessive-compulsive disorder, anxiety and depression', in J.F. Leckman and D.J. Cohen (eds) *Tourette's Syndrome: Tics, Obsessions, Compulsions*, pp. 43–62 (New York: John Wiley).
Kleinman, A. (1991) *Rethinking Psychiatry* (New York: The Free Press).
Kleinot, P. (2009) 'Speaking with the body', in A. Motz (ed.) *Managing Self-harm: Psychological Perspectives*, pp. 119–41 (London: Routledge).
Klonsky, D.E. (2007) 'The functions of deliberate self-injury: a review of the evidence', *Clinical Psychology Review* 27: 226–39.

Klonsky, D.E. and Muehlenkamp, J.L. (2007) 'Self-injury: A research review for the practitioner', *Journal of Clinical Psychology: In session* 63: 1045–56.

Knock, M.K. and Favazza, A. (2009) 'Nonsuicidal self-injury: definition and classification', in M.K. Knock (ed.) *Understanding Nonsuicidal Self-Injury: Origins, Assessment, and Treatment*, pp. 9–18 (Washington, DC: American Psychological Association).

Kohen, D. (ed) (2000) *Women and Mental Health* (London: Routledge).

Kvale, S. (1992) 'Postmodern psychology: A contradiction in terms?', in S. Kvale (ed.) *Psychology and Postmodernism* (London: Sage).

Lacan, J. (2007) *Ecrits* (London: W.W. Norton).

Lack, T. (1995) 'Consumer society and authenticity: The (il)logic of punk practices' *Undercurrent* 3: October. The Library of Nothingness Collection, available at: http://library.nothingness.org/articles/SI/en/display/86 (accessed 14 June 2015).

Laclau, E. and Mouffe, C. (1990) 'Post-Marxism without apologies', in E. Laclau (ed.) *New Reflections on the Revolution of our Time* (London: Verso).

Lamacq, S. (2000) *Going Deaf for a Living* (London: BBC Books).

Lasch, C. (1979) *The Culture of Narcissism* (London: Abacus).

Laye-Gindhu, A. and Schonert-Reichl, A. (2005) 'Nonsuicidal self-harm among community adolescents: Understanding the "whats" and "whys" of self-harm', *Journal of Youth and Adolescents* 34: 447–57.

Lears, T.J.J. (1983) 'From salvation to self-realization: Advertising and the therapeutic roots of the consumer culture, 1880–1930', in R.F. Fox and T.J.J. Lears (eds) *The Culture of Consumption* (London: Pantheon).

Leatham, V. (2006) *Bloodletting: A True Story of Self-harm and Survival* (London: Allison & Busby).

Lemert, C. (2008) *Social Things*, 4th ed. (Lanham, MD: Rowman & Littlefield).

Levenkron, S. (1999) *Cutting: Understanding and Overcoming Self-mutilation* (London: Norton).

Leys, R. (2000) *Trauma: A Genealogy* (Chicago, IL: University of Chicago Press).

Lindholm, C. (2008) *Culture and Authenticity* (Oxford: Blackwell Publishing).

Littlewood, R. (2002) *Pathologies of the West* (Ithaca, NY: Cornell University Press).

Locke, J. (1988 [1764]) *Two Treatises of Government* (P. Laslett, ed.) (Cambridge: Cambridge University Press).

Lorey, I. (2015) *State of Insecurity* (London: Verso).

Luhrmann, T.M. (2001) *Of Two Minds* (New York: Vintage Books).

Lukes, S. (1973) *Individualism* (Oxford: Blackwell).

Lupton, D. (1998) *The Emotional Self* (London: Sage).

Lupton, D. (2003) *Medicine as Culture*, 2nd ed. (London: Sage).

Lutz, C. (1985) 'Depression and the translation of emotional worlds', in A. Kleinman and B. Good (eds) *Culture and Depression* (Berkeley, CA: University of California Press).

Lutz, C. (1986) 'Emotion, thought, and estrangement: emotion as a cultural category', *Cultural Anthropology* 1: 287–309.

McGee, M. (2005) *Self-help, Inc* (Oxford: Oxford University Press).

McLuhan, M. (1964) *Understanding Media* (London: Routledge and Kegan Paul).

McShane, T. (2012) *Blades, Blood and Bandages: The Experiences of People Who Self-injure* (Basingstoke: Palgrave Macmillan).

MacSween, M. (1993) *Anorexic Bodies* (London: Routledge).

Manson, M. (1998) *The Long Hard Road Out of Hell* (London: Plexus).
Marcus, S. (1990) 'Freud and Dora: Story, history, case history', in C. Bernheimer and C. Kahane (eds) *In Dora's Case: Freud–Hysteria–Feminism* (Chichester: Columbia University Press).
Martin, E. (2004) 'Talking back to neuro-reductionism', in H. Thomas and J. Ahmed (eds) *Cultural Bodies: Ethnography and Theory*, pp. 190–212 (Blackwell: Oxford).
Martin, P. (1987) *Mad Women in Romantic Writing* (Hassocks: Harvester).
Marx, K. and Engels, F. (2008 [1888]) *The Communist Manifesto* (London: Pluto Books).
Mascia-Lees, F.E. and Sharpe, P. (1992) 'The marked and the un(re)marked: tattoo and gender in theory and narrative', in F.E. Marcia-Lees and P. Sharpe (eds) *Tattoo, Torture, Mutilation, and Adornment* (New York: State University of New York Press).
Masson, J. (1990) *Against Therapy* (London: Fontana).
Mead, G.H. (1967) *Mind, Self, and Society* (Chicago, IL: University of Chicago Press).
Mennell, S. (1990) 'Decivilizing process', *International Sociology* 5: 205–23.
Mennell, S. (1992) *Norbert Elias: An Introduction* (Oxford: Blackwell).
Menninger, K. (1938) *Man Against Himself* (New York: Harcourt Brace World).
Menninger, K. (1967) *The Vital Balance* (London: Penguin).
Merleau-Ponty, M. (1962) *Phenomenology of Perception* (London: Routledge and Kegan Paul).
Merleau-Ponty, M. (1964) *Signs* (Evanston, IL: Northwestern University Press)
Merskey, H. (1979) *The Analysis of Hysteria* (London: Bailliere Tindall).
Micale, M. (1994) *Approaching Hysteria* (Princeton, NJ: Princeton University Press).
Middleton, K. and Garvie, S. (2008) *Self Harm: The Path to Recovery* (Oxford: Lion).
Miller, D. (2005) *Women Who Hurt Themselves* (New York: Basic Books).
Miller, R. and Bashkin, E.A. (1974) 'Depersonalization and self-mutilation', *Psychoanalytic Quarterly* 43: 638–49.
Miller, T. (1993) *The Well-Tempered Self* (Baltimore, MD: Johns Hopkins University Press).
Miller, W.I. (1997) *The Anatomy of Disgust* (Cambridge, MA: Harvard University Press).
Mitchell, J. (2001) *Mad Men and Medusas* (London: Basic Books).
Moloney, P. (2013) *The Therapy Industry* (London: Pluto Press).
Monk, R. (2005) *How to Read Wittgenstein* (London: Granta).
Morgan, H.G. (1979) *Death Wishes?* (New York: Wiley).
Morgan, H.G. Burns-Cox, C.J., Pocock, H. and S. Pottle (1975) 'Deliberate self-harm', *British Journal of Psychiatry* 127: 564–74.
Morton, A. (1998) *Diana: Her True Story*, revised ed. (London: Michael O'Mara Books).
Moskowitz, E.S. (2001) *In Therapy We Trust* (Baltimore, MD: Johns Hopkins University Press).
Muehlenkamp, J. (2005) 'Self-injurious behaviour as a separate clinical syndrome', *American Journal of Orthopsychiatry* 75, 324–33.
Muehlenkamp, J.J. and Gutierrez, P.M. (2004) 'An investigation of differences between self-injurious behaviour and suicide attempts in a sample of adolescents', *Suicide and Life-Threatening Behaviour* 34: 12–24.

Mulhall, S. (2008) *Wittgenstein's Private Language* (Oxford: Oxford University Press).
Myers, B. (2011) *Richard: A Novel* (London: Picador).
Nada-Raja, S., Morrison, D. and Skegg, K. (2003) 'A population-based study of help-seeking for self-harm in young adults', *The Australian and New Zealand Journal of Psychiatry* 37: 600–5.
Nelkin, D. and Lindee, M.S. (1995) *The DNA Mystique* (Galway: MW Books).
NICE (2004) *Self-harm: The Short term Physical and Psychological Management and Secondary Prevention of Self-harm in Primary and Secondary Care* (Leicester: The British Psychological Society).
Nichter, M. (1981) 'Idioms of distress: Alternative in the expression of psychosocial distress: A case study from South India', *Culture Medicine and Psychiatry* 5: 379–408.
Nietzsche, F. (1993 [1872]) *The Birth of Tragedy* (S. Whiteside, transl.) (London: Penguin).
Nock, M.K. and Prinstein, M.J. (2005) 'Contextual features and behavioural functions of self-mutilation among adolescents', *Journal of Abnormal Psychology* 114: 140–6.
Offer, D. and Barglow, P (1960) 'Adolescent and young adult self-mutilation incidents in a general psychiatric hospital', *Archives of General Psychiatry* 3: 194–204.
O'Neill, J. (1972) *Sociology as a Skin Trade* (London: Heinemann Educational).
Pao, P.N. (1969) 'The syndrome of delicate self-cutting', *British Journal of Medical Psychology* 42: 195–206.
Parker, I., Georgaca, E., Harper, D., McLaughlin, T. and Stockwell-Smith, M. (1995) *Deconstructing Psychopathology* (London: Sage).
Parkinson, F. (1993) *Post-Trauma Stress* (London: Sheldon).
Parry-Jones, B. and Parry-Jones, W.L. (1993) 'Self-mutilation in four historical cases of bulimia', *British Journal of Psychiatry* 163: 394–402.
Patten, B. (1971) *The Irrelevant Song* (London: Allen and Unwin).
Pattison, E.M. and Kahan, J. (1983) 'The deliberate self-harm syndrome', *American Journal of Psychiatry* 140: 867–72.
Pembroke, L.R. (ed.) (1996) *Self-harm: Perspectives from Personal Experience* (London: Chipmunka Publishing).
Perelman, M. (2005) *Manufacturing Discontent* (London: Pluto Press).
Pierce, D.W. (1977) 'Suicidal intent in self-injury', *The British Journal of Psychiatry* 130: 377–85.
Pilgrim, D. (2007) *Real Life Issues: Self-harm* (Richmond: Trotman).
Pitts, V. (2003) *In the Flesh* (Basingstoke: Palgrave Macmillan).
Plante, L.G. (2007) *Bleeding to Ease the Pain* (London: Praeger).
Plath, S. (2005) *The Bell Jar* (London: Faber and Faber).
Ponterotto, J.G. (2006) 'Brief note on the origins, evolution, and meaning of the qualitative research concept "Thick Description"', *The Qualitative Report* 11, 538–49.
Rapley, M., Moncrieff, J. and Dillon, J. (eds) (2011) *De-Medicalizing Misery: Psychiatry, Psychology, and the Human Condition* (Basingstoke: Palgrave Macmillan).
Rawstorne, T. (2008) 'Why no child is safe from the sinister cult of emo', available at: http://www.dailymail.co.uk/femail/article-566481/Why-child-safe-sinister-cult-emo.html (accessed 1 June 2015).

Reis, E. (ed) (2001) *American Sexual Histories* (Oxford: Blackwell).
Rhodes, L.A. (1996) 'Studying biomedicine as a cultural system', in C.F. Sargent and T.M. Johnson (eds) *Medical Anthropology: Contemporary Theory and Method*, pp. 165–82 (London: Praeger).
Rice, J.S. (1996) *A Disease of One's Own* (New Brunswick: Transaction Publishers).
Rich, A. (1995) *On Lies, Secrets and Silence: Selected Prose, 1966–1978* (London: W.W. Norton).
Ricoeur, P. (2004) *The Conflict of Interpretations* (W. Domingo, transl. and D. Ihde, ed.) (London: Continuum).
Rieff, P. (1991) *The Feeling Intellect* (Chicago, IL: University of Chicago Press).
Riviere, J. (1958) 'A character trait of Freud's', in J. Sutherland (ed.) *Psychoanalysis and Contemporary Thought* (London, Hogarth Press).
Robson, A. (2007) *Secret Scars: One Woman's Story of Overcoming Self-harm* (Milton Keynes: Authentic Media).
Rose, N. (1985) *The Psychological Complex: Psychology, Politics and Society in Engalnd 1869–1939* (London: Routledge and Kegan Paul).
Rose, N. (1991) *Governing the Soul* (London: Routledge).
Rose, N. (1998) *Inventing Our Selves* (Cambridge: Cambridge University Press).
Rose, N. (2007) *The Politics of Life Itself* (Princeton, NJ: Princeton University Press).
Rose, S., Lewontin, R.C. and Kamin, L.J. (1990) *Not in Our Genes* (London: Penguin Books).
Ross, R.R. and McKay, H.B. (1979) *Self-Mutilation* (Lexington, KY: Lexington Books).
Rubin, J. (1970) *Do It! Scenarios of the Revolution* (London: Simon and Schuster).
Russell, B. (2009) *Human Knowledge: Its Scope and Limits* (London: Routledge).
Rycroft, C. (1995) *Critical Dictionary of Psychoanalysis*, 2nd ed. (London: Penguin).
Ryle, G. (1971) *Collected Papers: Volume II Collected Essays, 1929–1968* (London: Hutchinson).
Ryle, G. (2000 [1949]) *The Concept of Mind* (London Penguin).
Salecl, R. (2004) *On Anxiety* (London: Routledge).
Sass, I. (1987) 'Schreber's Panopticism', *Social Research* 54: 101–48.
Scheff, T.J. (2007) *Being Mentally Ill*, 3rd ed. (New Brunswick: Aldine Transaction).
Scheper-Hughes, N. (1989) 'Bodies under siege: self-mutilation in culture and psychiatry by Armando Favazza', *Medical Anthropology Quarterly* 3: 312–15.
Schmidt, E., O'Neal, P. and Robbins, E. (1954) 'Evaluation of suicidal attempts as a guide to therapy', *Journal of the American Medical Association* 155: 549–57.
Scitovsky, T. (1976) *The Joyless Economy* (New York: Oxford University Press).
Scull, A. (2009) *Hysteria: The Biography* (Oxford: Oxford University Press).
Segal, J.B. (1976) 'Popular religion in ancient Israel', *Journal of Jewish Studies* 17: 1–22.
Seigal, J. (2005) *The Idea of the Self: Thought and Experience in Western Europe Since the Seventeenth Century* (Cambridge: Cambridge University Press).
Sennett, R. (2006) *The Culture of the New Capitalism* (New Haven, CT: Yale University Press).
Shakespeare, W. (1992 [1603]) *Hamlet* (Ware: Wordsworth).
Sharfstein, S. (2006) 'New task force will address early childhood violence', *Psychiatric News* 41: 3.
Shilling, C. (2003) *The Body and Social Theory*, 2nd ed. (London: Sage).
Shorter, E. (1992) *From Paralysis to Fatigue* (New York: The Free Press).

Shorter, E. (1997) *A History of Psychiatry* (New York: John Wiley).
Showalter, E. (1987) *The Female Malady* (London: Virago).
Showalter, E. (1991) *Hystories* (London: Picador).
Shutz, A. (1967) *The Phenomenology of the Social World* (Evanston, IL: Northwestern University Press).
Simeon, D., Stanley, B., Frances, A., Mann, L.J., Winchel, R. and Stanley, M. (1992) 'Self-mutilation in personality disorders: Psychological and biological correlates', *American Journal of Psychiatry* 149: 221–7.
Simon, L. and Kelly, T. (2007) *Everybody Hurts* (New York: HarperCollins).
Simonds, W. (1992) *Women and Self-help Culture* (New Brunswick: Rutgers University Press).
Simpson, M.A. (1976) 'Self-mutilation and suicide', in E.S. Schneidman (ed.) *Suicidology: Contemporary Developments* (New York: Grune and Stratton).
Slaby, A.E. (1989) *Aftershock* (Westminster, MD: Random House).
Slater, D. (1997) *Consumer Culture and Modernity* (Cambridge: Polity).
Slavney, P. (1990) *Perspectives on 'Hysteria'* (Baltimore, MD: Johns Hopkins University Press).
Smith, G., Cox, D. and Saradjian, J. (1999) *Women and Self-harm: Understanding, Coping, and Healing from Self-mutilation* (New York: Routledge).
Solomon, R. (2008) *True to Our Feelings* (Oxford: Oxford University Press).
Sontag, S. (2009) *Against Interpretation and Other Essays* (London: Penguin).
Spandler, H. (1996) *Who's Hurting Who?* (Manchester: 42nd Street).
Spinelli, E. (1994) *Demystifying Therapy* (Ross-on-Wye: PCCS Books).
Stainton Rogers, W. (1991) *Explaining Health and Illness* (Hemel Hempstead: Harvester Wheatsheaf).
Stengel, E. (1964) *Suicide and Attempted Suicide* (Baltimore, MD: Penguin Books).
Strathern, M. (1996) 'Enabling identity? Biology, choice and the new reproductive technologies', in S. Hall and P. Du Gay (eds) *Questions of Cultural Identity*, pp. 37–52 (London: Sage).
Strong, M. (1998) *A Bright Red Scream* (Virago Press: London).
Sullivan, N. (2002) 'Fleshly (dis)figuration, or how to make the body matter', *International Journal of Critical Psychology* 5: 12–29.
Sutton, J. (2005) *Healing the Hurt Within: Understand Self-injury and Self-harm, and Heal the Emotional Wounds* (Oxford: How to Books).
Suyemoto, K.L. (1998) 'The functions of self-mutilation', *Clinical Psychology Review* 18: 531–54.
Szasz, T. (1974) *The Myth of Mental Illness* (New York: Harper & Row).
Tallis, R. (2011) *Aping Mankind: Neuromania, Darwinitis, and the Misrepresentation of Humanity* (Durham: Acumen Publishing).
Tantam, D. and Huband, N. (2009) *Understanding Repeated Self-injury* (Basingstoke: Palgrave Macmillan).
Taussig, M.T. (1980) 'Reification and the consciousness of the patient', *Social Science and Medicine* 14B: 3–13.
Taylor, C. (1991) *The Ethics of Authenticity* (Cambridge, MA: Harvard University Press).
Taylor, C. (1992) *Sources of the Self* (Cambridge: Cambridge University Press).
Tew, J. (ed.) (2005) *Social Perspectives in Mental Health* (London: Jessica Kingsley Publishers).

Timimi, S. (2002) *Pathological Child Psychiatry and the Medicalization of Childhood* (London: Routledge).
Trilling, L. (1974) *Sincerity and Authenticity* Harvard: Harvard University Press.
Turner, B. (2008) *The Body and Society*, 3rd ed. (London: Sage).
Turner, V.J. (2002) *Secret Scars* (London: Hazelden).
Twenge, J.M. (2006) *Generation Me* (New York: Atria).
Twenge, J.M. and Campbell, W.K. (2010) *The Narcissism Epidemic* (New York: Atria).
Ussher, J. (1991) *Women's Madness: Misogyny or Mental Illness* (Hemel Hempstead: Harvester Wheatsheaf).
Verhaeghe, P. (2014) *What About Me?* (J. Hedley-Prole, transl.) (London: Scribe).
Wagner, P. (1994) *A Sociology of Modernity* (London: Routledge).
Walkerdine, V. (1990) *Schoolgirl Fictions* (London: Verso).
Walsh, B.W. and Rosen, P. (1988) *Self-Mutilation: Theory, Research, and Treatment* (New York: Guilford).
Warner, R. (1985) *Recovery from Schizophrenia* (New York: Routledge and Kegan Paul).
Watters, E. (2011) *Crazy Like Us* (London: Constable and Robinson).
Weber, M. (1962) *Basic Concepts in Sociology* (London: Peter Owen).
Weber, M. (2011 [1905]) *The Protestant Ethic and the Spirit of Capitalism* (S. Kalberg, transl.) (Oxford: Oxford University Press).
Wegscheider, L. (1999) *Women Living With Self-injury* (Philadelphia, PA: Temple University Press).
Weil, S. (1977) *The Simone Weil Reader* (G.A. Panichas, ed.) (New York: David McKay).
Weiss, J. (1986) *Weber and the Marxist World* (London: Routledge & Kegan Paul).
Weissman, M.M. (1975) 'Wrist cutting: relationship between clinical observations and epidemiological findings', *Archives of General Psychiatry* 32: 1166–71.
Westling, S., Ahren, B., Sunnqvist, C. and L. Traksman-Bendz (2009) 'Altered glucose tolerance in women with deliberate self-harm', *Psychoneuroendocrinology* 34, 878–83.
White, E. (2009) *Rimbaud: The Double Life of a Rebel* (London: Atlantic Books).
Whitlock, J., Lader, W. and Conterio, K. (2007) 'The internet and self-injury: What psychotherapists should know', *Journal of Clinical Psychology: In session* 63: 1135–43.
Wilkins, A.C. (2008) *Wannabes, Goths, and Christians* (Chicago, IL: University of Chicago Press).
Wilkinson, R. (2005) *The Impact of Inequality* (London: Routledge).
Wilkinson, R. and Pickett, K. (2010) *The Spirit Level* (London: Penguin).
Williams, M.E. (ed) (2008) *Self-Mutilation: Opposing Viewpoints* (New York: Greenhaven Press).
Williams, R.H. (1982) *Dream Worlds* (Berkeley, CA: University of California).
Winkler, M.G. and Cole, L.B. (eds) (1994) *The Good Body* (New Haven, CT: Yale University Press).
Wittgenstein, L. (1958) *Philosophical Investigations* (G.E.M. Anscombe, transl.) (Oxford: Blackwell).
Wittgenstein, L. (1980) *Culture and Value: A Selection from the Posthumous Remains* (G.H. von Wright and H. Hyman, eds; P. Winch, transl.) (Oxford: Blackwell).
Wolff, J. (1990) *Feminine Sentences* (Cambridge: Polity).

Wollheim, R. (1971) *Freud* (London: Fontana).
World Health Organization (1973) *International Pilot Study of Schizophrenia* (Geneva: World Health Organization).
World Health Organization (1979) *Schizophrenia: An International Follow-up Study* (New York: Wiley).
Wouters, C. (2004) *Sex and Manners* (London: Sage).
Young, A. (1997) *The Harmony of Illusions* (Princeton, NJ: Princeton University Press).
Young, R., Sweeting, H. and West, P. (2006) 'Prevalence of deliberate self-harm and attempted suicide within contemporary Goth youth subculture: Longitudinal cohort study', *British Medical Journal* 332: 1058.
Younge, G. (2011) *Who are We? And Should it Matter in the 21st Century* (London: Penguin).
Zachar, P. (2000) 'Psychiatric disorders are not natural kinds', *Philosophy, Psychiatry, Psychology* 7, 167–82.
Žižek, S. (2000) *The Ticklish Subject* (London: Verso).
Žižek, S. (2007) *Enjoy Your Symptom! Jacques Lacan in Hollywood and Out* (London: Routledge).

Films

The Exorcist (1973) William Friedkin (dir.), William Peter Blatty (writer) (Burbank, CA: Warner Brothers Pictures).
Fear of God: 25 Years of The Exorcist (1998) Mark Kermode (writer and presenter) (London: BBC).
Female Perversions (1996) Susan Streitfeld (dir.), Louise J. Kaplan (writer, book), Julie Hebert (writer, screenplay) (Beverley Hills, CA: Lakeshore Entertainment).

Index

Adler, P. and Adler, P., 1, 2, 3, 13, 56, 61
affect regulation model, *see also* expressive imperative, 41, 47, 90
Ahmed, S., 166
Alderman, T., 63, 86, 130
Allie, 89–90, 91, 99, 106–7, 152, 160, 220
Alyson, 90, 162, 164, 168
Analysis of Hysteria, The (book), 35
Anderson, P., 148
Andrews, J.B., 29
Ann, 176, 181,
Anomalies and Curiosities of Medicine (book), 29
anorexia nervosa, 18, 26, 35, 60, 83, 145, 190
archaeology (Foucault's), 82–3
ascetic hedonism, 179, 189
Auden, W.H., 104
authenticity, 9, 15, 16, 53, 56, 57, 146, 147–56, 181, 182, 185, 189, 197, 200, 209, 210, 212–13
autism, 28
axis of continuity (definition), 82–4

Bacon, Francis, 143,
Barthes, R., 88, 154, 214, 217
Bartky, S., 175, 177, 179, 190, 211
Bauman, Z., 110, 178, 182, 183, 188
belaboured self, the, 16, 185, 187–9, 197, 198, 199, 205, 207, 213
Bellah, R. *et al.*, 76, 81, 107, 115
bipolar disorder, 29
bloodletting, 8
Bloodletting (book), 183
Bodies Under Siege (book), 21–6, 39
borderline personality disorder, 29, 35
Bordo, S., 11, 14, 18, 20, 54, 82–3, 140, 177, 190, 192, 194, 195, 198, 211, 216
Boswell, J., 28

'Bright Red Scream, A' (magazine article), 59
Bruner, J., 46, 63, 70, 73, 79, 86
bulimia, 28
Burke, K., 50, 53, 54
Butchart, A., 180

Calhoun, C., 183, 197
Callero, P., 73
Carla, 126, 131–2, 140, 152
Caroline, 139
Carr, E.H., 74
Carroll, L., 71
Caruth, C., 127, 132
Cash, Johnny, 57
Celebrities (who self-harm)
   Cobain, Kurt, 67
   Edwards, Richey, 52–5, 58, 61, 64–8, 70, 77–8, 81, 89, 126, 127, 150, 185, 213, 216
   Love, Courtney, 58, 216
   Manson, Marilyn, 57, 216
   Pop, Iggy, 55, 57, 61
   Princess Diana, 1, 59, 216
   Reznor, Trent, 57, 126
   Ricci, Christina, 58, 62, 64
   Vicious, Sid, 55
Changing, W., 29–31, 33
Charcot, J-M., 34
Chernin, K., 145, 205
Cioran, E.M., 120–1
civilising process, 111–13, 114, 159, 172, 176
Civilizing Process, The (book), 112–13
Cixous, H., 133
Clegg, S., 175
Clendenin, W.W. and Murphy, G.E., 37, 38
Cohen, J., 101
Coles, R., 120, 121
consumer culture, 16, 178–9, 191, 194–202, 210–11, 212
Conterio, K. *et al.*, 89–90, 103, 129

control, *see* self-control
Cornell Research Program on
  Self-injurious Behaviour, 92, 95
Craib, I., 94, 120,
Critical Essays (book), 214
Crossley, N., 49, 111, 173, 177, 178
cultural dope, 177, 196–7
cultural sociology, 11–12
Cutting (book), 63, 86, 118, 119

Dabrowski, C., 26–7, 28
Dana, 141, 161–2, 164–5, 167, 168, 170, 175, 211
Dante, 53, 54, 66, 67, 77, 78, 214
Dawn, 122–5, 126, 127, 129, 130, 132, 133, 134, 144, 151, 156, 159, 169
de Tocqueville, A., 198–9, 200
death instinct, 3, 27, 119
Deborah, 97, 98, 131, 151, 167–8
decivilising process, 177–9
definition of self-harm, 9, 40–2
deliberate self-harm syndrome, 37–8, 39
delicate wrist-cutting syndrome, 35–7
Democracy in America (book), 199
Derrida, J., 11, 18, 20, 42, 76, 86, 141–2
Descartes, Rene, 143, 145
detraditionalisation, 110
Deuteronomy (book), 47
Diagnostic and Statistical Manual of Mental Disorders 5 (book), 3, 43, 127, 219
Dineen, T., 81, 135, 137, 200
disciplinary regime/society, 16, 111, 172–82, 185, 190–1, 192, 196–8, 210, 211
Discipline and Punish (book), 172–5
discourse (definition), 44–6
dissociation, 17, 84, 92, 128–30, 144, 152
dissociative identity disorder, 35
diversity of self-harm, 8
Donna, 146, 214
Dora, 133–8, 144, 153–6
Dostoyevsky, F., 173
Douglas, M., 79
Downing, L., 82, 174, 180
Durkheim, E., 15, 110, 111

economy of desire, 16, 195–202, 216
Egan, J., 60
Elias, N., 18, 101, 110, 111–14, 172, 173, 176, 177–8, 219, 220
Eliot, T.S., 66–7, 77–8
Elliott, A. and Lemert, C., 148, 187, 188–9
Elliott, F., 130, 137
Emerson, L.E., 31–3
Emotional Intelligence (book), 94
épistème, 83
examination, 180–2
expressive imperative, 15, 89–101
expressive individualism, *see* romantic–expressive individualism

Favazza, A., 1, 2, 21–6, 28, 39, 43, 48, 60, 87–8, 131, 142, 219
Fiction
  In the Penal Colony (short story), 158–9, 162, 216
  Hamlet (play), 184–5, 216
  Minister's Black Veil, The, (short story), 101–3, 108, 124, 174, 201, 216
Films
  Exorcist, The, 204–6, 209
  Fear of God (documentary), 204
  Female Perversions, 60, 206–10, 216
  Secretary, 60
  Thirteen, 60
Fiona, 4–8, 10, 11, 55, 88, 126, 214
Foucault, M., 16, 43, 44–5, 82–3, 86, 91, 100, 110, 111, 114, 115, 172–81, 190, 196, 220
'4REAL' photograph (Richey Edwards), 1, 52–5, 64, 67, 78, 81, 89
Fragment of an Analysis of a Case of Hysteria (case history), 132–8, 154–6, 216
Frances, A., 2, 162
Freud, S., 53, 103–6, 112, 125, 132–8, 144, 145, 154–6, 216
Freud, S. and Breuer, J., 34, 182
Friedkin, William, 204–5
Friedman, L.M., 110, 111
Fromm, E., 194

Index 239

Frost, L., 36, 41, 179, 190, 195, 197, 211, 212
function of self-harm, 6–7, 9
Furedi, F., 67, 81, 94, 97, 115, 120, 137, 198, 200, 201

Gallop, J., 134
Gardner, F., 2, 49, 53, 129, 162
Gatens, M., 203
Geertz, C., 3, 5, 18, 23, 43, 73, 74, 79, 83, 86, 87, 109, 118, 219
genealogy (Foucault's), 83
Gergen, K., 56, 107, 115, 116
Giddens, A., 110, 148, 185
Girl, Interrupted (book), 36–7, 128, 140, 186, 216
Goffman, E., 73, 158, 160, 174
Goleman, D., 94, 118
Gospel of Mark (book), 17, 18, 47, 204
Gould, G.M. and Pyle, W.I., 29
governmentality, 196
Graff, H. and Mallin, R., 35, 37
Greenblatt, S., 183–4
Guardian (newspaper), letter to, 193, 194, 201, 202, 221
Guignon, C., 62, 91, 124, 144, 149

Hacking, I., 11, 14, 49, 78, 82, 144
Harré, R. and Tissaw, M., 74, 80
Harrison, D., 87
Harrison, D. and Sharman, J., 92, 98, 99, 119
Harrison, K., 60
Hawthorne, N., 101–3, 108, 124, 174, 216
Healing the Hurt Within (book), 1, 41, 42, 48, 63–4, 130, 135, 171
Health Behaviour in School-aged Children report, 1
Heather, 139
Heckler, S., 219
Helping Teens Who Cut (book), 63, 92, 95, 97, 98, 99, 118
Henry, J., 194, 195
Herman, E., 115, 200
Herman, J.L., 127, 128, 138, 145
Hewitt, K., 49, 53, 55, 128, 145, 157
Heywood, L., 98
Hill, E., 129

history, (of self-harm), 26–39, 55–61
histrionic personality disorder, 35
Hollander, M., 63, 92, 95, 97, 98, 99, 118
homo clausus, 111–18, 147, 149, 153, 159, 169, 172, 174, 189, 195, 203, 204, 209
homo psychologicus, 113–18, 121
Hook, D., 45, 91, 114, 115, 118, 120, 175, 176, 180, 181, 182
Husserl, E., 68
Hutton, P., 200
hysteria, 18, 33–5, 132–4, 145

Illich, I., 176
informalisation process, 177–9
Inglis, F., 6, 219

Jacobs, M., 104
Jamison, L., 12, 35
Janet, P., 27
Jervis, J., 111, 117, 173, 182, 183, 197, 201, 206, 207
John, 166
Johnson, Dr Samuel, 28
Jovanovic, R., 53, 58, 66–7, 77
Julie, 164, 165, 175

Kafka, F., 20, 158–9, 162, 174, 216
Kaminer, W., 115, 120
Kaplan, L., 206
Karen, 91, 93–4
Katherine, 93
Kaysen, S., 36–7, 120, 128, 140, 146, 186, 211, 212
Kermode, M., 204–5
Kilby, J., 9, 41, 66, 88
Kleinman, A., 43, 44, 46, 49
Kvale, S., 109, 114

Lamacq, S., 52, 65
Lasch, C., 185–6, 189, 194, 198
Laughter, Tristin, 57
Leatham, V., 183
Lemert, C., 75
Levenkron, S., 63, 86, 118, 119
life instinct, 3, 27, 119, 142, 170
Lindholm, C., 124, 148, 149, 197

Littlewood, R., 5, 11, 17, 19, 40, 43, 44, 54, 160, 194
Locke, John, 112
Lorey, I., 189
Lovers, The (painting), 122, 124–5, 216
Lupton, D., 43, 44, 90, 94, 95, 97, 98, 105, 106, 144, 149, 166, 204
Lyness, D., 119

McGee, M., 16, 110, 117, 182, 186–9, 197, 200–1
McKenna, T., 67, 220
McLuhan, M., 53
Magritte, R., 122, 124–5, 151, 216
Man Against Himself (book), 17, 26, 27–8
Manic Street Preachers, 52–3, 58, 65
Martin, P., 204
Marx, K., 110
Masson, J., 132, 133, 156
Mead, G.H., 74, 160
Menninger, K., 3, 17, 26, 27–8, 29, 35, 43, 49, 119, 142, 170
Merleau-Ponty, M., 76
Merskey, H., 35
Middleton, K. and Garvie, S., 48, 93, 95
Miller, D., 13, 63, 130, 135–6, 171
Miller, F. and Bashkin, E.A., 145
Miller, Helen, 29–31, 32, 33
Miller, W.I., 112
Miss A, 31–3
modernist self, *see* modernist–utilitarian individualism
modernist–utilitarian individualism, 76, 107, 109, 115–18, 142, 150, 184, 210, 212–13, 215
Monk, R., 80
Morgan, H.G., 37, 38, 39
Morton, A., 59, 219
Moskowitz, E., 81, 91, 94, 120, 137, 182, 200
Muehlenkamp, J., 41, 48
Music (self-harm in), 52–8, 67, 213, 216
  emo, emocore, emotional core, 55–8, 126, 184, 213
  goth, 56–8, 126
Hurt (song), 57
punk, 55–8, 126
Myers, B., 184–5

narcissistic self/society, 185–6, 194, 198, 203
National Health Service (NHS), 7
National Institute for Health and Care Excellence (NICE), 7
needle girls, 29, 30, 33
neoliberalism, 187–8, 193, 195, 201, 202
Nietzsche, F., 116

obsessive-compulsive disorder, 28
O'Neill, J., 65

Patten, B., 65, 146,
Pattison, E.M. and Kahan, J., 39
Pembroke, L., 87, 127
Perelman, M., 198
pharmakon, 141–2, 144, 152, 157, 209
Pierce, D.W., 2, 141
Pilgrim, D., 86, 120
Plante, L., 18, 21, 22, 24, 25, 69
Plath, Sylvia, 151, 211, 212
Poems
  Divine Comedy, The, 53, 78
  Inferno, The, *see* Divine Comedy
  Meat, 65
  See Me, 87
  Silent Scream, The, 63–4
  Waste Land, The, 66, 77–8, 126, 216
post-trauma stress, *see* traumatic estrangement
post-traumatic stress disorder, *see* traumatic estrangement
precariousness, 187–9
prison, 3–5, 17, 172–4
private language argument, 69–75
project, self as, 182–92, 210, 213
psychodynamic self, the, 101–8, 122, 189
Psychological Bases of Self-mutilation (monograph), 26–7
psy-complex, 45–6, 81, 113–18, 120, 150, 175–6, 180–2, 189, 200–1, 211–13
punctum, 88, 154

'real', the, 7, 19, 48–9, 57, 62, 65, 68–9, 127–30, 133–6, 143–6, 149–51, 156, 157, 159, 160, 161, 203, 204–5, 208–9, 213, 215
Rich, A., 66
Ricoeur, P., 18, 76, 86
Rieff, P., 111
Rimbaud, A., 73
Riviere, J., 103
Robson, A., 139–40, 166–7, 169–70
romantic–expressive self, 76, 107, 109, 115–18, 142, 150, 184, 210, 212–13, 215
romantic self, *see* romantic–expressive individualism
Rose, N., 45, 81, 109, 114, 115, 137, 175, 185, 189, 196, 210
Ross, R.R. and McKay, H.B., 38, 39
Rubin, S., 60
Rubin, J., 65
Russell, B., 70
Ryle, G., 23, 62, 79

Sadie, 93, 151
Salecl, R., 134, 135, 153
Sally, 85
Salpêtrière psychiatric hospital, 34
Sass, L., 200
Scarred Soul, The (book), 86, 130
'Scars are Stories' (magazine article), 60
Scitovsky, T., 198
Scull, A., 33, 34
second-wave feminism, 117–18, 211, 213
Secret Scars, (book, Robson), 139–40, 166–7, 169–70
Secret Scars, (book, Turner), 130
self-control, 15, 138–46
Self-harm (book, Gardner), 2, 49, 53, 129
Self-harm (book, Middleton and Garvie), 48, 93, 95
Self-harm (book, Pemberton), 87, 127
self-hatred, *see* self-persecution
Self-mutilation (book), 39, 92
self-mutilation, 20–6, 27, 28, 29
self-persecution, 15, 161–71, 183, 203
self-punishment, *see* self-persecution

Sennett, R., 188
sexual violence, 122–3, 130, 131–2, 134, 140
Shakespeare, W., 184
Sharfstein, S., 137
Showalter, E., 13, 18, 33, 34, 36, 49, 54, 117, 144, 204, 211
Shuar, 219
Sian, 63–4, 68, 126
Simmel, G., 148
Simpson, M.A., 39
skin excoriation, 8, 28
Slaby, A., 137
social ecology, 11, 14, 24, 78–82, 172, 201, 215
somatic society, 113
Sontag, S., 3
Spandler, H., 3, 163–4
Spinelli, E., 104
Stacks, M., 140
Stengel, E., 35
Stevenson, A., 211
stigma, 158–61, 191
Streitfeld, S., 206
Strong, M., 1, 10, 21, 30, 39, 59, 99, 131
Studies in Hysteria (book), 34
suicide, 7, 9, 12, 27, 35, 37–9, 53, 68, 129, 204, 219
Sullivan, N., 163
Sun dance ritual, 22
Susan, 91, 96, 98, 126, 141–2, 159, 205
Sutton, J., 1, 41, 42, 48, 63–4, 130, 135, 171
Sweet, C., 163
Szasz, T., 137

Tallis, R., 19, 63
Tantam, D. and Huband, N., 2, 3, 20, 48
Taussig, M.T., 43
Taylor, C., 91, 101, 108, 110, 143, 144, 147, 182, 187, 198
Tender Cut, The (book), 3
Television Programs
  Buffy the Vampire Slayer, 60
  Panorama, 59, 219, 220
  Six Feet Under, 60

therapy culture, 81, 118–20, 153, 180–2, 201, 210–11, 212
thick description, 3, 5, 11, 23, 79
thin description, 23–4, 219
Tourette syndrome, 28, 29
trauma, *see* traumatic estrangement
trauma reenactment syndrome, 135–6
traumatic estrangement, 15, 126–38, 150, 204, 210
trichotillomania, 8, 28
Trilling, L., 101, 147, 182
Turner, B., 21, 24, 113

uncanny, the, 53, 125,
Understanding Repeated Self-injury (book), 3
'Unkindest Cut', *The* (magazine article), 60
Ussher, J., 13, 33, 34, 117, 203, 204, 206, 208

utilitarian individualism, *see* modernist–utilitarian individualism

Verhaeghe, P., 73
verstehen, 50–1

Walkerdine, V., 202
Walsh, B.W. and Rosen, P., 39, 88
Watters, E., 11, 55
Weber, M., 50–1, 79, 148
Weiss, J., 50–1
Who's Hurting Who? (book), 3
Wittgenstein, L., 9, 48, 69–75, 76, 80, 86, 220
Wollheim, R., 106
Women Who Hurt Themselves (book), 13, 63, 130, 135–6, 171
wounded womanhood, 12, 35

Printed and bound in Great Britain by
CPI Group (UK) Ltd, Croydon, CR0 4YY